MPT-MEE Bar Points

Subject Memorization & Review

2019

Course Companion

Special thanks to: Lauren Allen, Esq., Adam Feren, Esq., Christopher Fromm, Esq., Elizabeth Horowitz, Esq., Steven Marietti, Esq., Adam Maze, Esq., Nicole Pirog, Esq., Mike Power, Esq., Tammi Rice, Esq., Shalom Sands, Esq., Lisa Young, Esq.

Published by Kaplan Publishing, a division of Kaplan, Inc.
750 Third Avenue
New York, NY 10017

10 9 8 7 6 5 4 3 2 1

ISBN: 978-1-5062-5142-4

MASTER TABLE OF CONTENTS

SIMULATED PRACTICE EXAM

Agency

Agency

Agency: fiduciary relationship between a principal and agent, whereby the agent acts on the principal's behalf and subject to the principal's control

Principal: person who manifests an intention that another act on his behalf

Agent: person who acts on behalf of principal

Subagent: person entitled to do work for the original agent in the agency relationship

General Agent: agent employed by a principal to transact all of his business of a particular kind

Special Agent: agent employed by the principal specifically for one transaction

Gratuitous Agent: agent who agrees to perform all the duties of an agent without compensation

Actual Authority: authority that the agent reasonably believes he possesses based on principal's dealings with agent

Implied Authority: authority that the agent reasonably believes he has as a result of the actions of the principal

Respondeat Superior: doctrine that imposes vicarious liability upon a principal for the torts his agent committed in the course of agency

Disclosed Principal: a principal is disclosed if, at the time of the transaction, the third party has notice that the agent is acting for a principal and has notice of the principal's identity

Undisclosed Principal: a principal is undisclosed if the third party has no knowledge of the existence or identity of a principal

Partially Disclosed Principal: a partially disclosed principal is one whose existence, but not identity, is known to the third party

- **Agency Basics**
- **Agency Relationship and Third Parties**
- **Creation of the Agency Relationship**
- **Principal and Agent**
- **Termination of the Agency Relationship**

- An agent owes a principal a duty of loyalty, including a duty not to compete with the principal, not to usurp opportunities, no self-dealing, and no secret profits. When an agent competes with the principal in breach of his duty of loyalty, the principal can recover the profits made by the agent while competing against the principal or enforce a constructive trust on those profits.

- Apparent authority exists when a principal gives third parties a reason to believe that the agent is acting with actual authority and the third party reasonably relies upon it (i.e., the principal has held out the agent to the third parties as though he had actual authority).

- Implied actual authority is authority that the agent reasonably believes he has as a result of necessity, prior acquiescence or custom/title.

AGENCY BASICS

Definitions

- The law of agency is concerned with how the actions made on behalf of another person consequently bind that other person.

> **DEFINITION** **Agency** is a fiduciary relationship that arises when one person, the **principal**, manifests assent to another person, the **agent**, that the agent shall act on the principal's behalf and be subject to the principal's control, and the agent manifests assent or otherwise consents so to act.

- The **person** may manifest itself in many forms, including:

    (1)   an individual;

    (2)   an organization or association with the capacity to possess rights and incur obligations;

    (3)   a government, political subdivision, or entity created by the government; or

    (4)   any other entity that has the legal capacity to possess rights and incur obligations.

Nature and Characteristics of Agency

- The agency relationship allows the agent to bind the principal and act on his behalf, without the principal having to act personally. Thus, the law deems a principal to have intentionally engaged an agent to represent him in business or legal affairs.

THE FOUR CONSEQUENCES OF ENTERING AN AGENCY RELATIONSHIP

- Duties arise between the principal and agent.

- The agent has the power to bind the principal and act on his behalf without the principal having to act personally, but under the principal's control.

- Liability is imposed on the principal for the agent's actions within the scope of the agency.

- Knowledge of the agent is imputed to the principal.

Examples of Agency Relationships

- An agency relationship can take many forms, the most common of which are the master-servant (employer-employee) and employer-independent contractor.

Master and Servant (Employer and Employee)

- The master-servant relationship is an employment relationship in which the master has the right to control the details of the physical conduct of the servant in the performance of the service, not only as to the result, but also as to the means to be used to achieve the result.

- Under the doctrine of *respondeat superior*, a master is generally liable for his servant's torts committed within the scope of his employment.

Employer and Independent Contractor

- The employer-independent contractor relationship is also an employment relationship.

- However, the employer, unlike the master in the master-servant relationship, has no right to control the details of the performance of the independent contractor. The distinction lies in the right to control—the degree to which the employer could intervene in the control of the employee's manner of performance.

CREATION OF THE AGENCY RELATIONSHIP

Required Elements of the Agency Relationship

- An agency relationship is formed by the principal granting authority to the agent to act for him.

- There must be some manifestation of the principal's intention to grant authority. Such manifestations can be express or implied, verbal, or evidenced by conduct.

- Both parties must assent to the agency. An agent can neither force an unwilling principal nor be forced to be an agent against his will.

- However, a principal may be liable for unauthorized actions of his agent if the agent acts with apparent authority.

- The agent must agree to act on behalf of the principal. If the agent is compensated, it is primarily to advance the interests of the principal.

- The agent must act under the control of the principal.

Capacity

Principal

- Any person who has capacity to effect his own transactions has capacity to appoint an agent to act on his behalf.

- An incompetent may not act as a principal.

- A minor generally cannot act as a principal except when contracting for necessaries.

- A corporation may act as a principal only as to matters within its corporate powers.

Agent

- Generally, anyone with minimum mental capacity may act as an agent.

- Both minors and incompetents may act as agents.

- The agent will be endowed with the same capacity as the principal.

- One may not be an agent for two adverse parties to a transaction unless both parties are fully advised and give their consent. The burden is upon the agent to show full disclosure and consent.

Proof of Agency

- Existence of an agency relationship may be established by direct or circumstantial evidence. Relevant factors include:

  (1) the situation of each party; and

  (2) their words and actions.

- The existence of an agency relationship is ordinarily a question of fact for the jury, and the burden of proof rests with the party asserting the relationship. It is to be determined from all the evidence, direct or circumstantial, and must be proved by a fair preponderance of the evidence.

Presumption of Agency in Motor Vehicle Operation

- At common law, the owner of a motor vehicle is not presumed liable for the negligent use of the vehicle by another.

- A number of states, however, have enacted statutes which create a presumption that the driver of a motor vehicle is operating as the agent of the owner. In such a case, the owner of the automobile is liable for the negligence of any person operating the vehicle with the express or implied permission of the owner. If the presumption of agency is rebutted, the owner may be held directly liable for his own negligence in entrusting the car to an unfit person.

Types of Principals

Disclosed, Undisclosed, and Partially Disclosed Principals

DEFINITION A principal is **disclosed** if, at the time of the transaction, the third party has notice that the agent is acting for a principal and has notice of the principal's identity.

DEFINITION If the third party has no knowledge of the existence or identity of a principal, the principal is **undisclosed**.

DEFINITION A **partially disclosed** principal is one whose existence, but not identity, is known to the third party.

TYPES OF PRINCIPALS		
Type of Principal	Does Third Party Know P Exists?	Does Third Party Know P's Identity?
Disclosed	Yes	Yes
Partially Disclosed	Yes	No
Undisclosed	No	No

- An agent for a fully disclosed principal does not ordinarily incur personal liability.

- An agent who enters into a contract for an undisclosed or partially disclosed principal is personally liable on the contract.

Types of Agents

General and Special Agents

- The authority conferred by a principal on his agent may be general in nature (a **general agency**), or limited in scope (a **special agency**).

- In either case, the agent possesses the authority to conduct transactions that are incidental to the main business at hand—acts that are reasonably necessary to accomplish it.

DEFINITION A **general agent** is employed by a principal to transact all of his business of a particular kind.

- The authority of a general agent to perform all things usual in the line of business in which he is employed cannot be limited by any private order or direction (secret instructions) not known to the party dealing with him.

DEFINITION A **special agent** is employed by the principal specifically for one transaction.

- A special agent has no authority to bind his principal beyond the terms of the specific authority conferred upon him by the agreement for employment.

Types of Special Agents

- A **real estate agent** is a special agent who may be either an agent or a broker licensed by the state to conduct sales of real property. A listing broker merely has authority to promote property, while a selling agent possesses apparent authority to bind a seller.

- A **salesperson** is an agent to sell chattels and warrant goods under the Uniform Commercial Code, although he usually may not modify terms of a sale.

- An **auctioneer** is a special sales agent with authority to sell goods within the auction's terms, usually to the highest bidder. The auctioneer is the agent of the seller, and as a result, warrants title to the goods.

- An **insurance agent** is a representative of an insurer (i.e., insurance company), which is liable for the acts of its agents acting within the scope of their authority.

Subagents

DEFINITION **Subagents** are persons entitled to do work for the original agent in the relationship and, as a consequence, a new agency relationship is created with the original agent becoming the principal to the subagent.

- Where the principal has authorized the agent to appoint subagents, the subagent has the same responsibilities to the principal as the original agent does. Any breaches of duty by the subagent will be imputed to the agent.

- If the subagent has been appointed without the principal's authority, no agency relationship exists between the principal and the subagent.

Gratuitous Agents

- A **gratuitous agent** agrees to perform all the duties of an agent without compensation.

PRINCIPAL AND AGENT

Duties of Principal to Agent

RULE Duties begin when the agency relationship is created and end when the agency relationship is terminated.

- Absent an agreement to the contrary, the principal is obligated to his agent to:

   (1) compensate the agent for services rendered, either for an agreed-upon amount or for the reasonable value of those services;

   (2) reimburse the agent for reasonable expenses incurred by the agent in the scope of his agency;

   (3) indemnify and exonerate the agent for any liability that results from his good-faith performance of his duties;

   (4) cooperate with the agent in the performance of his duties; and

   (5) exercise due care toward the agent.

Agent's Remedies for Principal's Breach

- The agent may seek the usual remedies available for breach of an agency contract.

- The agent retains a lien on any property of the principal of which he has lawful possession.

- The agent may set off any money owed to him by the principal against monies collected on behalf of the principal.

- The principal may use any of the following defenses in the event of his breach:

   (1) the Statute of Frauds;

   (2) illegality;

(3)   the agent's disobedience; or

(4)   the agent's contributory negligence (such as in defense of a tort claim).

Duties of Agent to Principal

Duty of Care

- Absent an agreement to the contrary, the agent is obligated to show a duty of care to the principal, with a duty to:

  (1)   perform the contract and render services with reasonable care;

  (2)   act only within the scope of his actual authority;

  (3)   act with the care, competence, and diligence normally exercised by agents in similar circumstances, and if the agent is possessed of a higher level of skill, to exercise that level of skill; and

  (4)   indemnify the principal against loss caused by the agent's wrongful behavior or failure to act with reasonable care.

Duty of Loyalty

- The agent also has a duty of loyalty to the principal, arising from the fiduciary character of the relationship, with a duty to:

  (1)   not engage in self-dealing;

  (2)   not usurp a business opportunity of the principal;

  (3)   protect confidential information; and

  (4)   not to compete against the principal.

- **Self-Dealing:** An agent must prefer the interests of the principal to his own or others in acting for the principal. An agent who acts for his own benefit instead of that of the principal is said to be self-dealing.

- **Usurpation of Business Opportunity:** An agent may not usurp a business opportunity belonging to the principal. A **business opportunity** is one that is so closely related to the principal's business that it could be deemed incidental to that business. An employee may take personal advantage of a business opportunity only if the employer knows and consents.

- **Duty of Confidentiality:** An agent may not use confidential information obtained from the principal to the detriment of the principal, even if the information is not obtained through his agency.

> EXCEPTION   However, an ex-employee may use skills learned on the job in later employment and may solicit former customers so long as he does not reveal confidential information in violation of any contract restrictions.

- **Duty Not to Compete:** An employee may, while still employed, prepare to enter into competition once his employment ends by setting up his own business, so long as he does not take away from his employer's business by soliciting customers or key employees.

- **Noncompete Agreements:** Agreements restricting an employee from competition must rest upon a protectable interest and be reasonable in time, geographic area, and subject matter scope to be enforceable. Courts may adjust an overreaching agreement to sever the non-enforceable provisions from the enforceable ones or reduce the area or time covered by the agreement.

Duty of Obedience

- An agent has a duty to obey all reasonable directions from his principal, outside of illegal or unethical orders. What constitutes reasonableness depends on the nature of the work, the contractual understanding between the parties, and the customary procedures in that trade.

Duty to Account

- An agent has a duty to account for money or property received for the principal and to keep the principal's assets separate from his own assets.

Duty of Candor

- An agent must fully disclose to the principal any facts relevant to the agent's duties that he reasonably believes the principal might want to know.

Dual Agency Rule

- When an agent acts for more than one principal in negotiations between multiple principals, the transaction is voidable by either principal, unless both principals are fully informed of the representation and give their consent.

Principal's Remedies for an Agent's Breach of Fiduciary Duties

- A compensated agent may be held liable for damages to the principal that result from the agent's breach of his fiduciary duties. Generally, an uncompensated agent cannot be held liable.

- Any transaction resulting from a breach of the agent's fiduciary duty is voidable by the principal.

- Where the agent breaches his duty of loyalty to the principal, the appropriate remedy is disgorgement of any profits the agent made from his disloyalty, and, if others have also benefited from the breach, liability of the agent for the profits of third parties, even if the agent did not receive any part of the profits. The principal need not have suffered a loss in order to recover.

- Punitive damages may be awarded to the principal if the agent acts with malice or in bad faith.

- If the agent has intentionally breached his fiduciary duty, the principal may withhold compensation.

Agent's Duties and Obligations to Third Parties

- Liability to a third party on a contract signed by the agent depends on whether the principal was fully disclosed.

- If a third party knows of the principal's existence and identity at the time of the transaction (i.e., the principal is disclosed), the agent will not incur personal liability unless he takes additional actions to assume personal liability.

- To guarantee that he does not assume personal liability, the agent should sign any documents with his name and the principal's name, as well as with a notation that he is acting as an agent.

- If the principal is partially disclosed or left unidentified at the time of the transaction, the agent is presumed to be a party to the contract.

- If the existence of a principal directing the agent's actions is unknown, the agent will be assumed to be contracting on his own behalf.

- Disclosure of the principal after the execution of the contract will not relieve the agent of liability.

RULE ▶ Where an agent lacks authority to bind a principal to a contract, the agent breaches the warranty of authority and is liable to a third party for any damages suffered. The principal may indemnify the agent for all damages caused by the agent's breach of the warranty of authority.

Election to Sue Principal or Agent

- Upon learning of the identity and existence of an undisclosed principal, the third party may elect to sue either the principal or the agent.

- To be binding, the election to sue must be made with knowledge of the fact of the previously undisclosed principal.

- Suit brought against an agent prior to learning the identity of the principal does not act as a waiver of the third party's rights against the principal (i.e., there is no "election" in such a situation).

Enforcing Contracts

- If the principal is disclosed, only the principal and not the agent may enforce the contract and hold a third party liable.

- Generally, if the principal is partially disclosed or undisclosed, either the principal or the agent may enforce the contract and hold a third party liable.

- However, if the agent has fraudulently concealed the principal's identity, the principal may not enforce the contract, and the third party is granted a right of recession.

- A majority of states hold that the agent must have affirmatively misrepresented the principal's identity in order to deny the principal's right to enforce the contract.

POWER OF AGENT TO BIND PRINCIPAL

Authority of the Agent

RULE The general rule is that an agent, acting within the scope of his authority, may bind his principal in contract.

Actual Authority

DEFINITION **Actual authority** is created by the manifestation of the principal to the agent of the principal's request that the agent act for the benefit of the principal in a particular way, and that the principal agrees to be bound by the actions of the agent. Actual authority may be either express or implied.

- The consent for actual authority may be written, oral, or through any other method of communication.

- An agent has actual authority to take actions designated or implied in the principal's manifestations and acts that are necessary or incidental to achieving the principal's objectives, as the agent reasonably understands them when the agent determines how to act.

- **Express authority** arises when the principal directly requests the agent to act on the principal's behalf in a specific matter.

- Inherent in a grant of express authority is the principal's consent to any actions that are incidental to the agent's carrying out of his primary grant of authority.

- The **equal dignity rule**, followed in many states, holds that if a contract must be in writing, the grant of authority to an agent to enter into such contract on behalf of the principal must also be in writing.

- **Implied authority** includes the authority to do:

  (1) anything necessary to accomplish the principal's express request of his agent; or

  (2) those things the agent believes the principal wishes him to do based on his reasonable understanding of the principal's expressed request.

Apparent Authority

DEFINITION **Apparent authority** arises based on the principal's representations made not directly to the agent, but to a third party. Because of the behavior of the principal, the third party is led to believe the agent is acting with the principal's authority.

- Under the doctrine of apparent authority, a principal is accountable for the results of third-party beliefs about an actor's authority to act as an agent when the belief is reasonable and is traceable to a manifestation of the principal.

- The third party must reasonably rely to his detriment upon the authority of the purported agent in order to bring suit against the principal.

- A principal may be liable to a third party for knowingly or negligently allowing a purported agent to assume authority or to overextend his legitimate authority. The overreaching agent will still be held liable to the principal for his unauthorized actions.

RULE ▶ Only the principal has the ability through his actions to create apparent authority of an agent with respect to third parties; the agent cannot create his own apparent authority with respect to third parties.

- Apparent authority requires some overt action by the principal. A principal's holding out may be accomplished by words, conduct, or a failure to act (e.g., by failure to notify customers of the termination of an actual agency).

Estoppel to Deny Existence of Agency Relationship

- A principal may properly deny the existence of an agency relationship, including apparent authority, if there is a lack of a manifestation by the principal that the purported agent holds authority to complete the transaction in question.

- A third party may fight an estoppel claim by showing justifiable inducement under the circumstances because:

    (1) the principal intentionally or carelessly caused such belief; or

    (2) having notice of such belief and that it may induce others to change their positions, the principal did not take reasonable steps to notify them of the facts.

Ratification

In General

- Ratification allows a principal to grant retroactive authority for his agent's earlier unauthorized actions.

- The ratified act must be one that the principal could have authorized at the time of the act, meaning the principal must have been in existence.

- Ratification will only grant authority; it does not legitimize an otherwise illegitimate transaction, nor will it grant authority to a nondelegable act.

REQUIREMENTS FOR RATIFICATION	
Elements of Ratification	1. Manifesting assent that the act shall affect the person's legal relations; or 2. Conduct that is justifiable only on the assumption that the person so consents.
Requirements for Effective Ratification	1. The act the principal is seeking to ratify must have been otherwise valid at the time it was performed; 2. The principal must have been in existence when the act was performed, and must be legally competent when he attempts to ratify; 3. The act must have been performed on behalf of the principal; 4. The ratification must have the same formalities that would have been required to give authorization initially and, by extension, any formalities that the original act itself would have required; and 5. At ratification, the principal must know of all material facts concerning the transaction.

Limitations on Ratification

- A principal may not partly ratify an act; ratification of any part of the act or contract is deemed to constitute ratification of the whole.

- A ratification will not be effective if, prior to ratification, the ratification would have an adverse effect on third parties in the following circumstances:

    (1) manifestation of intention to withdraw from the transaction by the third party;

    (2) a material change in the circumstances that would make it inequitable to bind the third party, unless the third party chooses to be bound; and

    (3) a specific time that determines whether a third party is deprived of a right or subjected to a liability.

Retroactive Effect of Ratification

- Generally, a ratified transaction is given retroactive effect. Once an act has been ratified, it has the effect as if it were originally done by the agent with actual authority.

Delegation

- In general, if the authority given involves the agent using his own judgment, he cannot delegate his responsibilities absent an emergency or explicit agreement of the principal.

- An example of a responsibility that an agent may not delegate is a duty to perform personal services on behalf of the principal for another. Delegation of such a duty would be a material change in understanding when a principal has hired a particular person to perform a particular act.

VICARIOUS LIABILITY OF PRINCIPAL FOR ACTS OF OTHERS

Distinguishing an Employee from an Independent Contractor

Master and Servant or Employer and Employee

DEFINITION   A **master**, commonly known as an **employer**, is a principal who employs an agent to perform service in his affairs, and who controls, or has the right to control, the physical conduct of the agent in the performance of the service.

DEFINITION   A **servant**, commonly known as an **employee**, is an agent employed by a principal to perform service in his affairs, and whose physical conduct in the performance of the service is controlled, or is subject to the right of control, by the master.

Independent Contractor

DEFINITION   An **independent contractor** is a person who contracts with another to do something for him, but who is not controlled by the other nor subject to the other's right to control with respect to his physical conduct in the performance of the undertaking.

- The following nine factors are used to determine, for agency purposes only, whether an agent is a servant (employee) or an independent contractor:

    (1) the amount of control the principal exerts over how the agent performs his work;

    (2) whether the agent is engaged in a distinct occupation or business;

    (3) whether the type of work the agent is doing is customarily done under the supervision of the principal;

    (4) the skill required in the agent's occupation;

(5)   who supplies the tools required for the agent's work and the place of performance;

(6)   the length of time the agent is engaged by the principal;

(7)   whether the agent is paid by the job or by the hour;

(8)   whether the principal and agent intend to create an employment relationship; and

(9)   whether the principal is in business.

Tort Liability

Respondeat Superior

DEFINITION   ***Respondeat superior*** is the doctrine that imposes vicarious liability upon a principal for the torts his agent committed in the course of agency.

- The liability of the employer is in addition to, not instead of, the employee's liability. In most cases, the employer and employee are jointly and severally liable.

- *Respondeat superior* is a strict liability doctrine, in that the principal has no defenses.

- The employer is liable for harm caused by an employee while he was acting within the scope of his employment.

Scope of Employment

RULE   An employee acts within the scope of employment when performing tasks assigned by the employer or engaging in a course of conduct subject to the employer's control.

EXCEPTION   An employee's act is not within the scope of employment when it occurs within an independent course of conduct not intended by the employee to serve any purpose of the employer (i.e., it is done for the employee's purposes only).

- Torts committed by the employee on the way to or from work are generally considered outside the scope of employment, unless the employer places an employee's travel to and from work within the scope of employment by providing the employee with a vehicle and exerting control over how the employee uses the vehicle so that the employee may more readily respond to the needs of the employer's enterprise.

- **Frolic and Detour:** An employer will not be liable if the employee has substantially deviated from the authorized route (a **frolic**), but will be liable if the deviation is slight (a **detour**). However, an employee can return to the scope of employment after a frolic occurs. The extent of the deviation is a question of fact. In general, courts consider:

  (1)   the advancement of the employer's interests;

  (2)   whether the accident occurred before or after the employer's objective was served;

  (3)   the scope of the deviation in terms of time and distance; and

  (4)   whether the deviation was in keeping with the type of employment.

- **Employee Driving His Own Automobile:** An employer-employee relationship may still be found even if the negligent employee was using his own automobile and choosing his own route and speed at the time of the accident.

Liability for Negligently Selecting an Agent

- A principal is liable to a third party for harm caused by the principal's negligence in selecting, training, retaining, supervising, or otherwise controlling the agent.

Intentional Torts

RULE ▶ Employers will generally not be held liable for the intentional tort of an employee unless the tort occurred during an attempt to serve the interest of the employer.

EXCEPTION ▶ An employer may be held liable for his employee's intentional torts if the act was done in the course of doing the employer's work, and for the purposes of accomplishing it.

- A controlling factor is whether an employer-employee relationship existed with respect to the particular transaction from which the tort arose.

- The trend is to extend an employer's liability for an employee's intentional torts to situations where the type of employment provides a peculiar opportunity and incentive for the commission of an intentional tort. Thus, where argument is likely to be part of the employee's duties, and such conduct is wholly or partially in furtherance of the employer's business (e.g., as a bouncer or bill collector), liability will be imposed on the employer for those intentional torts that arise from the argument.

- **Common Carriers:** An employer is even more likely to be held liable for the intentional torts of his employee in common carrier cases.

Vicarious Liability of Principal When Agent Is Not Liable

- Generally a principal cannot be held vicariously liable for the acts of his agent if:

  (1) a court finds the agent not liable for the tort;

  (2) the agent is immune from liability under common law or by statute; or

  (3) the plaintiff agrees to a settlement with the agent.

Other Agents

Independent Contractors

- Generally, a principal is not responsible for the tortious conduct of an independent contractor.

- The following are exceptions to the rule that principals are not liable for torts of independent contractors:

  (1) inherently dangerous activities;

  (2) nondelegable duties; and

  (3) the negligent selection of a contractor.

- **Inherently Dangerous Activities:** Work is inherently dangerous where the nature and circumstances of the work to be performed are such that injury to others will probably result unless precautions are taken.

- **Nondelegable Duty:** Certain relationships impose a duty of care that cannot be discharged even by the employment of a carefully selected independent contractor.

- **Dangerous Disrepair:** Where the employer's premises are in a state of dangerous disrepair and an independent contractor is employed to correct the situation, the risk of harm due to the disrepair cannot be delegated to an independent contractor by the owners of the premises.

NOTE ▶ There is a middle ground whereby the actor is a non-employee agent, but some control is exerted over the actor. If the tort occurs within the scope of that limited control, the principal will be liable.

Police Officers

- Police officers are often employed by a private person to perform such services as directing traffic or maintaining order.

- Tort liability depends on the extent to which the private person has the right to control the activities of the officer. If the tort arises from an activity for which the officer has been given instructions by the employer, then the employer may be liable.

Borrowed Employee

- A person who is generally the employee of one employer may become the **borrowed employee** of another. If the employer who loaned the employee does not continue to exercise control over the employee, he will not be liable even though he continues to pay the employee.

- The right to control is the key test. Important factors in determining whether control has been completely transferred to the new employer include:

    (1)   the manner of hiring;

    (2)   the mode of payment;

    (3)   the right to discharge; and

    (4)   the manner of direction of services.

- There is a rebuttable presumption that the original employer maintains the right to control the employee, but if the borrowed employee commits the tort at the bidding of the borrower, vicarious liability attaches to the borrower.

- If the original employer and the borrowing employer jointly control the activities of the employee, they may both be held liable for his tortious acts.

IMPUTED KNOWLEDGE

 RULE   The knowledge of an agent is imputed to his principal. For knowledge to be imputed, the agent must have a duty to speak to his principal about the specific item of knowledge.

EXCEPTION   Generally, knowledge is not imputed to the principal where the agent is acting adversely to the principal and for his own or another's benefit or where the agent colludes with a third party in order to defraud the principal.

TERMINATION OF THE AGENCY RELATIONSHIP

Termination by the Parties

 RULE   Regardless of any remedies available for breach of contract, both the principal and the agent have the power to terminate the agency relationship at any time.

- The ability to terminate an agency at will does not preclude either party from institution of a breach of contract action.

- Death or incapacity of the principal or the agent will automatically terminate the agency.

- However, if the agency relationship was created via a durable power of attorney, the death of the principal will only serve to revoke the agent's authority when the agent receives actual knowledge of the principal's death.

- For termination to be effective, the principal must notify the agent of termination, unless:

    (1)   the agency naturally expires upon completion of an action; or

    (2)   the agency is set to expire at a particular time.

- The agency will end if, by an objective standard of reasonableness, the agent should have understood his authority to be terminated by the principal's actions.

- To terminate the agent's apparent authority, the principal must notify all third parties with whom the agent has dealt who might expect the agent to still be acting for the principal.

EXCEPTION An agency is not terminable at the will of either party if the agency is coupled with an interest or the agent has a power given for security.

- An **agency coupled with an interest** exists when the agent has an interest in the subject matter of the agency.

- A **power given for security** exists when the agency was created for the purpose of the payment of a debt owed by the principal to the agent.

Conflict of Laws

Conflict of Laws

DEFINITIONS

Domicile: the place where a person has a settled connection for certain legal purposes, either because his home is there or because that place is assigned to him by the law

Vested Rights Approach: choice-of-law theory advocated by the First Restatement, where the forum state must apply the law of the state in which the rights of the parties vest—i.e., where the act or relationship giving rise to the cause of action occurred or was created

Most Significant Relationship Approach: choice-of-law theory followed by the Second Restatement, which directs a court to look to all the circumstances surrounding a cause of action and to determine which state has the most significant relationship to each issue raised

Depeçage: process of applying the law of different states to decide different issues

Lex Loci Delicti: traditional rule in tort actions that applies the law of the place where the tort was committed

Dram Shop Act: statutes that impose liability on tavern keepers for injuries caused to an individual by an intoxicated person

Renvoi: conflict of law doctrine to be applied whenever a forum court is directed to consider the law of another state

Forum Non Conveniens: doctrine that establishes that a state will not exercise jurisdiction where it is a significantly inconvenient forum for the action, provided that a more appropriate forum is available to the plaintiff

The Full Faith and Credit Clause: precludes a state from discriminating against claims arising under the law of a sister state, which means that if a state allows a substantive claim, such as a claim for wrongful death, under its own law, it cannot bar a claim for wrongful death arising under the law of a sister state

KEY TOPICS

- **Application to Specific Areas**
- **Choice-of-Law Theories**
- **Defenses against Application of Foreign Law**
- **Federal-State Conflicts**
- **Sister-State and Foreign Judgments**

IMPORTANT RULES OF LAW

- The validity of a marriage is generally governed by the law of the state where the ceremony took place, unless another state has the most significant relationship with the marriage (such as the domicile of the parties) and the marriage violates a strong public policy (not merely a law) of the other state.

- When determining which state law governs in contracts cases, in the absence of a choice of law provision, courts will generally use the most significant relationship approach, meaning that a court will examine which forum has the most meaningful relationships to the issues and parties involved in the case.

- In diversity cases, the federal district court is required to apply the choice of law rules of the state in which the court sits.

INTRODUCTION

Conflicts of Law

- A problem in Conflicts of Law is usually presented on a bar examination in conjunction with the substantive law of torts, contracts, family law, or wills. If a bar examination question contains any fact or reference associated with two different states be prepared to discuss the possible applicability of foreign law.

Choice of Law

- Traditionally, under the theory of **vested rights**, courts applied a rigid rule requiring application of the law of the place where the cause of action arises to all substantive aspects of the case and the law of the forum (*lex fora*) to all procedural questions.

- These rules have been under attack in recent years, however, and the modern trend is in favor of the significant contacts or governmental interests approaches. These approaches generally suggest that the law of the state having the most significant relationship with the cause of action should be applied.

DOMICILE

In General

DEFINITION | **Domicile** is the place where a person has a settled connection for certain legal purposes, either because his home is there or because that place is assigned to him by the law.

RULE | Each person must have one (and only one) domicile. The acquisition of a new domicile extinguishes a former domicile.

- Before a domicile can be changed, the old domicile must be abandoned without intent to return, and a new domicile must be acquired by actual residence in another place with the intention of staying there.

- Domicile is an important legal concept in Conflicts of Law because if a person is domiciled in a particular state:

  (1) he is liable to personal jurisdiction in its courts, whether or not he can be found and personally served;

  (2) matters relating to his personal status, such as the validity of his marriage, adoption, or legitimacy, may be determined by the laws of that state;

  (3) the transfer of his personal property upon death, and the validity of his will, with respect to such property or its distribution in the event of intestacy, is determined by the laws of the domiciliary state;

  (4) domicile is considered to be an important contact if a court applies a contacts approach to choice of law; and

  (5) he is likely liable for state inheritance, income, and personal property taxes.

Domicile of Choice

Requirements to Change Domicile

- Any person who is legally competent can choose or change his domicile.

- Two elements must coincide to effect a change of domicile:

  (1) physical presence in the place where domicile is alleged to have been acquired; and

  (2) an intention to make it his home without any fixed or certain purpose to return to his former place of abode.

Physical Presence

- Actual physical presence in the new domicile is generally required, but need not be for a prolonged period, and need not be a fixed or permanent place of residence in the locality.

Intent

- An attempt to establish domicile in another state merely to make use of more favorable laws, including tax laws, will be unsuccessful if there is no intent to remain indefinitely.

- Intent is usually proved by an individual's actions and statements. Relevant factors are:

  (1)   owning real estate;

  (2)   voting;

  (3)   paying taxes to the state or a town;

  (4)   having a bank account; or

  (5)   registering an automobile in the state.

Miscellaneous Rules

- There is a presumption that a domicile continues until a new one is affirmatively established.

- A person traveling continually would retain his old domicile.

- Domicile is not changed by an extended absence from the state, as long as there is an intent to return to the original domicile.

Domicile by Operation of Law

Minors

- At birth, a child is assigned the domicile of his origin, which is the domicile of his parents and generally the place of his birth.

- The child's domicile changes whenever the parent's changes, until the child is emancipated, such as upon reaching majority or marrying, when he may establish his own domicile.

Married Persons

- At early common law, the domicile of a married woman was that of her husband; later, she was permitted to establish her own domicile if legally separated from her husband. The modern trend allows a person who lives apart from his or her spouse to acquire a separate domicile.

- Currently, the law appears to apply a family domicile interpretation.

Incompetents

- An infant who is insane has the domicile of his parents.

- A person who becomes insane after infancy retains the domicile he had prior to his insanity. He may, however, change his domicile if, although incompetent for some purposes, he has sufficient mental capacity to choose the place he regards as home.

Corporations

- A corporation is domiciled in the state of its incorporation.

WHAT LAW APPLIES

In General

- When a cause of action involves contacts with more than one state, the forum court is confronted with the problem of which state's law to apply.

WHAT IS THE PROBLEM?	HOW IS IT RESOLVED?
Which state's law is consulted to characterize the cause of action (e.g., is it a torts or contracts problem)?	The court makes this characterization according to its own law.
Which state's law governs which issues?	The forum applies its own procedural rules even if it is applying a foreign state's substantive law; the characterization of an issue as procedural or substantive is made according to the forum state's law.
How much of the foreign law is to be applied—only its internal law or its choice-of-law rules as well (the *renvoi* problem)?	The majority view rejects *renvoi*, or reference back to the foreign state's choice-of-law rules, and applies only the foreign state's internal law.

- If the forum state's statute expressly or impliedly extends to out-of-state transactions, there is no choice-of-law problem and the forum state applies its own laws.

- A federal court exercising diversity jurisdiction applies the choice-of-law rules of the state in which it sits.

CHOICE-OF-LAW APPROACHES

The Vested Rights Approach

- Under this traditional approach, advocated by the First Restatement, the forum state must apply the law of the state in which the rights of the parties vest—i.e., where the act or relationship giving rise to the cause of action occurred or was created.

- Thus, the forum first characterizes the cause of action, for example, as a tort, and then applies the substantive law of the state where the wrong occurred.

The Most Significant Relationship Approach

Introduction

- The Second Restatement directs a court to look to all the circumstances surrounding a cause of action and to determine which state has the most significant relationship to each issue raised. Thus, the forum state may apply its own law on some issues and the foreign state's law on others.

Depeçage

DEFINITION ▶ Choice of the applicable law depends upon the issue involved, and different issues in the same case may be decided by applying the law of different states. This process of applying the law of different states to decide different issues is known as ***depeçage***.

- In general, a court will assume that a case is to be governed by the laws of the forum unless a party-litigant timely invokes the law of a foreign state and establishes that such foreign law should apply.

- The important principles to be considered are:

    (1) the needs of the interstate and international systems (choice-of-law rules should further harmony between states and facilitate commerce between them);

    (2) the relevant policies of the forum;

    (3) the relevant policies of other interested states and the relative interests of those states in the determination of the particular issue;

    (4) protection of justified expectations;

    (5) the basic policies underlying the particular field of law (for example, to validate contracts whenever possible);

    (6) certainty, predictability, and uniformity of result; and

    (7) ease in the determination and application of the law to be applied.

- The governmental interests approach focuses on the policies underlying the laws of the various states involved and on their respective interests in furthering those policies. Thus, the court must examine the policies behind the substantive laws of the states involved and then determine which state has a policy interest in having its law applied.

CHOICE-OF-LAW IN SPECIFIC AREAS

Characterization

- There are two aspects of characterization:

    (1) the classification of a given factual situation under the appropriate legal categories and specific rules of law; and

    (2) the interpretation of the terms employed in the legal categories and rules of law.

Torts

In General

- Many states continue to follow the traditional rule in tort actions and apply the law of the place where the tort was committed (***lex loci delicti***). A tort is committed in the state where the injury occurred.

- However, when application of the traditional rule would produce an arbitrary or irrational result, even some of these courts may apply the Second Restatement most significant relationship test.

- Over the past few decades, courts in a number of states have expressly rejected the mechanical application of the *lex loci delicti* doctrine to multistate tort controversies in general and have substituted in its place the modern rule, under which applicable law is determined by analyzing a number of objective factors via the **most significant relationship** approach.

Wrongful Death

- The Second Restatement holds that in an action for wrongful death the local law of the state where the injury occurred determines the rights and liabilities of the parties unless with respect to the particular issue some other state has a more significant relationship to the occurrence and the parties, in which event the local law of the other state will be applied.

- Accordingly, the law selected by application of this rule determines both the defenses that may be raised on the merits and the measure of damages in a wrongful death action.

- Usually the statute of limitations in a wrongful death action is deemed to be so closely identified with the right of action that it thereby qualifies as substantive and is governed by the foreign law.

Dram Shop Act

- At common law, a tavern owner who furnished alcoholic beverages to another was not civilly liable for a third person's injuries caused by the acts of an intoxicated patron, since the proximate cause of the injuries was deemed to be the voluntary consumption by the intoxicated person, not the sale of liquor by the tavern owner.

- Many states have since enacted statutes known as **dram shop acts** that impose liability on tavern keepers for injuries caused to an individual by an intoxicated patron.

- Where the injuries occur in a state other than that in which the liquor was served, a choice-of-law problem arises. If a patron becomes intoxicated in a tavern in a state without a dram shop act and then causes injury in a state that has a dram shop act, a state court may likely not impose liability, under the traditional reasoning that the tavern keeper would have a vested right in his exemption from such liability in his own state.

Workers' Compensation

Jurisdiction

- Any state that has a legitimate interest in an injury and its consequences may apply its compensation act. State statutes usually spell out their applicability in detail, but generally a state would have a legitimate interest if it were where:

  (1) the injury occurred;

  (2) the employment is principally located;

  (3) the employer supervised the employee's activities from a place of business in the state;

  (4) the state was that of most significant relationship to the contract of employment;

  (5) the parties agreed in the contract of employment that their rights should be determined under that state's workers' compensation act; or

  (6) the state had some other reasonable relationship to the occurrence, the parties, and the employment.

- A stipulation in the employment contract that the law of a particular state shall be applied will be upheld as long as it is reasonable and not violative of the public policy of another state that has a legitimate interest.

Successive Awards

- Because more than one state may have a legitimate interest in a single injury, an employee may file and receive awards under the Workers' Compensation Acts of different states.

- A subsequent award in another state is barred only if "unmistakable language by a state legislature or judiciary" precludes recovery in another state.

- The amounts paid under a prior award are credited against the subsequent award, so a dual recovery is not had.

Contracts

Categories

- Contracts fall into three distinct categories for choice-of-law purposes:

  (1) contracts that specify the governing law;

(2)   contracts that specify no choice of law; and

(3)   contracts governed by the Uniform Commercial Code (UCC).

Contracts That Specify The Governing Law

■   Generally, the power of the parties to select jurisdiction is subject to certain definite limitations. Such stipulation is thus deemed valid and enforceable unless:

(1)   the chosen state has no substantial relationship to the parties or the transaction and there is no other reasonable basis for the parties' choice; or

(2)   it is contrary to a fundamental policy of the forum which has a materially greater interest than the chosen state and which would be the state of the applicable law in the absence of an effective choice of law by the parties.

■   The parties' power to choose the governing law is frequently subject to the additional requirement that such state have a significant relationship to the transaction or subject matter of the contract.

Contracts That Specify No Choice of Law

■   Under the traditional rule, the validity and construction of a contract are determined by the law of the place where the contract was made.

■   Where a conflict between the place of making and the place of performance exists, some courts have broadly held that contracts are to be governed by the place of performance.

■   Problems arising from the mechanical application of the traditional rule have led many states to employ a modern most significant relationship approach to conflicts concerning contracts.

■   Under this approach, adopted by the Second Restatement in 1971, the determination turns upon the law of the place that has the most significant relation, connection, or contacts with the matter in dispute. In the absence of a choice of law by the contracting parties, the concepts to be evaluated and weighed include:

(1)   the place of contracting;

(2)   the place of negotiation of the contract;

(3)   the place of performance;

(4)   the location of the subject matter of the contract; and

(5)   the domicile, residence, nationality, place of incorporation, and place of business of the parties.

Contracts Governed by the U.C.C.

■   Generally, when a transaction bears a reasonable relation to this state and also to another state or nation, the parties may agree that the law of either state or nation shall govern their rights and duties.

■   Failing such an agreement, the UCC applies to transactions bearing an "appropriate relation" to the state.

Property

Characterization

■   In property cases, two characterizations must be made. First, the problem must be characterized as to whether or not it involves a property interest (e.g., an agreement to sell land might be characterized as a contract, rather than a property, problem).

- Once it is determined that a property interest is involved, that interest must be characterized as a "movable" or "immovable" interest.

Movable vs. Immovable Interest

- If an interest is closely connected with or related to land (e.g., a leasehold or the right to rents), it is immovable; if it is not, the interest falls into the movable category.

- Characterization of the interest traditionally has been made by the forum using its own internal law. However, the Second Restatement suggests that characterization should be made according to the law of the *situs* of the property.

- The law of the *situs* governs all rights in land and other immovables. In applying the law, the forum state refers to the whole law of the *situs,* including its choice-of-law rules.

- An intangible—or **chose in action**—has no *situs*; however, if the intangible is represented by an instrument, the law of the *situs* of the instrument may be applied. If there is no instrument, the law of the place of transfer may be applied, or contracts choice of law may be applied.

Trusts

- In general, the validity of a trust of realty is determined by the law of the *situs* of the land, and the legality of a trust of personalty by the law of the settlor's domicile.

- The Second Restatement establishes a tendency to respect the will of the settlor as to the controlling law of the administration of a trust. In the absence of such a provision, the administration of a testamentary trust of personalty will be controlled by the state of the testator's domicile.

Wills and Administration of Estates

Intestate Succession

- The succession to an intestate's personalty—wherever located—is governed by the law of his domicile.

- The succession to an intestate's realty is governed by the law of the state where it is located.

Wills

- Whether one dies testate or intestate is to be determined as to personalty by the law of the decedent's domicile and as to realty by the law of the *situs* of the realty.

- However, any will executed in compliance with the law of the jurisdiction where the testator was domiciled at the time of the execution of the will or at the time of his death is validly executed and will be effectual to pass any property of the testator situated in such state.

Corporations

- The law of the state of incorporation determines the existence of a corporation and governs issues relative to its structure, such as the manner of electing directors, their authority and liability, the rights of its shareholders, the attributes of its shares, and the procedure for its dissolution.

Family Law

Validity of Marriage

- The validity of a marriage is generally governed by the law of the state where the ceremony took place, unless another state has the most significant relationship with the marriage (such as the domicile of the parties) and the marriage violates a strong public policy (not merely a law) of the other state.

Divorce Decree from Sister State

- The domicile of one of the parties to a marriage is a sufficient basis for a state to render a divorce, even if there is no personal service or domicile on the other party. Therefore, where one spouse establishes a valid new domicile in another state and secures a divorce, the state of the stay-at-home spouse must give full faith and credit to the divorce.

- However, where only one spouse participates in a divorce proceeding, the stay-at-home spouse has the right to attack the finding of domicile of the procuring spouse because there has been no contested hearing on the issue of domicile in the rendering state.

- The divorce decree is presumptively valid until attacked.

- Where both spouses participate in the divorce proceedings, jurisdiction must still be based upon the domicile of one of the parties. By participating in the out-of-state divorce, the stay-at-home spouse is barred by the doctrine of collateral estoppel from attacking the validity of the divorce, because the question of domicile has either actually been litigated or could have been litigated in the rendering state.

Divorce Decree from Foreign Nation

- A state need not recognize the validity of a foreign country divorce decree.

- Many states, however, will generally recognize such decrees on the basis of comity if both spouses were represented.

DEFENSES AGAINST APPLICATION OF FOREIGN LAW

The Substance-Procedure Distinction

In General

- Because the forum state has a great interest in how cases are presented and tried in its own courts, when presented with a choice-of-law problem, it will usually apply its own procedural rules and practices.

- Consequently, the general conflicts principle is that matters of procedure are determined according to the law of the forum and matters of substance are determined according to the forum's "choice-of-law" rules—rules which in some instances will result in the application of the substantive law of a sister state and in other instances will result in the application of the substantive law of the forum.

- Whether a matter is substantive or procedural for choice-of-law purposes is determined according to forum law.

- The forum sometimes will apply its own substantive law as well, either because it will not enforce the penal laws of another state, or because application of a particular foreign law would offend some strong public policy of the forum state.

PROCEDURAL VERSUS SUBSTANTIVE: SPECIFIC APPLICATIONS		
Subject Matter	Procedure or Substance?	Exception(s)
Statute of Limitations	Procedure	If the foreign statute of limitations is so interwoven with the statute creating the cause of action as to become one of the elements necessary to establish the right, the time fixed is a limitation on the cause of action and therefore substantive and governed by the foreign law.
Evidence	Procedure	Forum law determines the competence and credibility of witnesses. However, if an evidentiary ruling would be "outcome determinative," it would be considered substantive (e.g., if violation of a statute is mere evidence of negligence in one state, and is negligence *per se* in the other state).
Burden of Proof	Procedure	If the primary purpose of a rule as to burden of persuasion is to affect the outcome (e.g., plaintiff has the burden of proving lack of contributory negligence), the forum will apply the foreign state's rule.
Presumptions	Procedure	A conclusive presumption would be treated as substantive.
Legal Duty Owed	Substance	
Sufficiency of Facts and Evidence	Procedure	
Parol Evidence Rule	Substance	
Measure of Damages	Substance	
Statute of Frauds	Substance	

Borrowing Statute

■ Most states have enacted borrowing statutes under which one state may "borrow" a shorter statute of limitations for a cause of action arising in another state.

■ The purpose of borrowing statutes is twofold:

(1) to prevent plaintiffs from engaging in forum shopping in order to find the longest available statute of limitations; and

(2) to prevent state tolling statutes from extending the period of time for which a cause of action could be brought beyond the limitation period in any of the states involved in the controversy.

Renvoi

■ Once the court decides that it must refer to the law of another jurisdiction, the issue becomes how much foreign law applies—only the substantive law or the "whole" law, including its conflicts rule?

DEFINITION   The doctrine of *renvoi* would apply the whole law, forcing the forum state to use the foreign state's conflict-of-law rules; these rules may refer back to the forum state's rules (remission) or to those of yet a third state (transmission).

■ The Second Restatement and most states have rejected *renvoi*.

EXCEPTION   The Federal Tort Claims Act requires application of "the law of the place where the act or omission occurred," and this has been interpreted to mean the whole law, including its conflicts rules.

Limitations on Applying Foreign Law

Penal Laws

- Courts will generally not enforce the penal laws of another state.

Revenue Laws

- As a general rule, a state will refuse to enforce the revenue laws of another state.

Public Policy

- Ordinarily, a state's courts will refuse to enforce a foreign state's rule if it is contrary to a strong public policy of the forum state. Conversely, public policy has been used to circumvent a limitation in a foreign state's law.

Actions Involving Land in Another State

- Courts of the forum state will not ordinarily entertain cases in which the principal issue is title to land situated in another state because of the local expertise necessary to litigate such actions.

- However, if the court has *in personam* jurisdiction over the parties, it may exercise its equitable power to require one party to convey property to the other.

JURISDICTION OF COURTS: LIMITS ON EXERCISE OF JURISDICTION

Choice of Forum by Agreement

- Limitations on the exercise of judicial jurisdiction may be imposed by contract of the parties. Choice of forum by agreement of the parties will be given effect unless it is unfair or unreasonable.

- The parties cannot by their agreement oust a state of judicial jurisdiction.

Fraud, Force, and Privilege

- A state will not exercise judicial jurisdiction:

  (1)   over a defendant or his property where such jurisdiction has been obtained by fraud or unlawful force;

  (2)   when required to refrain by the needs of judicial administration; or

  (3)   when prohibited by international law or by treaty.

Forum Non Conveniens

DEFINITION The doctrine of ***forum non conveniens*** establishes that a state will not exercise jurisdiction where it is a significantly inconvenient forum for the action, provided that a more appropriate forum is available to the plaintiff.

- It is within the discretion of the trial judge to determine the applicability of the rule as founded upon the following two most important factors:

  (1)   that the plaintiff's choice of forum should not be disturbed except for weighty reasons; and

  (2)   that the action will not be dismissed unless a suitable alternative forum is available to the plaintiff.

- Other significant considerations are:

  (1)   the relative ease of access to sources of proof;

  (2)   availability of compulsory process for attendance of unwilling witnesses and the cost of obtaining attendance of willing witnesses;

(3) possibility of a view of the premises, if appropriate;

(4) enforceability of a judgment;

(5) judicial administrative difficulties; and

(6) all other practical problems.

- Usually, if a court finds itself an inappropriate forum, it will stay the action until suit is brought in another forum, or dismiss it conditionally, requiring that the defendant stipulate to accept process and not plead the statute of limitations in another state.

CONSTITUTIONAL LIMITS ON CHOICE OF LAW

Due Process

- According to the United States Supreme Court's current doctrine, "[f]or a State's substantive law to be selected in a constitutionally permissible manner, that State must have a significant contact or significant aggregation of contacts, creating state interests, such that choice of its law is neither arbitrary nor fundamentally unfair."

Full Faith and Credit

- The Full Faith and Credit Clause precludes a state from discriminating against claims arising under the law of a sister state.

- This means that if a state allows a substantive claim, such as a claim for wrongful death, under its own law, it cannot bar a claim for wrongful death arising under the law of a sister state.

- A state is not required to accord special treatment to claims arising under the law of a sister state. It can apply neutral rules to these claims such as its own statute of limitations to determine the timeliness of the claim and rules relating to the dismissal of a case on grounds of *forum non conveniens*.

RECOGNITION AND ENFORCEMENT OF SISTER STATE AND FOREIGN JUDGMENTS

Full Faith and Credit

- The Full Faith and Credit Clause, and its implementing legislation, embody a national policy of maximum recognition of sister state judgments (including federal court judgments) by sister state courts.

- A state court must recognize a final judgment on the merits issued by a sister state court, and cannot refuse recognition of the judgment on the grounds that:

(1) it is contrary to the public policy of the forum jurisdiction;

(2) that the judgment is wrong;

(3) that the judgment is based on a tax law; or

(4) that the forum jurisdiction has an interest in not recognizing the judgment.

- The Full Faith and Credit Clause does not require a court to recognize a judgment of a sister state court that:

(1) is not a final judgment;

(2) is not a judgment on the merits; or

(3) is not valid.

- There are three circumstances in which a forum court can refuse to recognize a final sister state judgment on the merits:

    (1) the sister state court lacked jurisdiction in the due process sense, and the issuing court's decree was entered ex parte so that the party challenging the judgment in the present forum could not litigate the jurisdictional question in the issuing court;

    (2) the judgment is subject to collateral attack in the issuing jurisdiction on grounds such as lack of subject matter jurisdiction or fraud. The present forum can permit a collateral attack on those grounds, applying the issuing jurisdiction's law to determine whether the collateral attack will be sustained; and

    (3) where enforcement of the judgment is barred by the non-discriminatory application of the forum's statute of limitations, that is, the forum must apply the same statute of limitations to the enforcement of viable foreign judgments that it applies to the enforcement of domestic judgments. If the judgment has been revised in the issuing jurisdiction, the forum must apply its statute of limitations to the revised judgments.

PREEMPTION

Four Situations Where Federal Law Preempts State Law

Express Preemption

- Congress may specifically prohibit the states from enacting a particular substantive rule of law, as Congress did when it prohibited the states from imposing vicarious liability on automobile rental companies. This statute preempted a New York law imposing such liability on automobile rental companies.

Actual Conflict Preemption

- Whenever a state law is in direct conflict with a federal law, the state law is preempted to the extent of the conflict.

Implied Conflict Preemption

- When the applicable federal law itself establishes a standard of federal preemption, the law preempts state law that is inconsistent with the federal standard of preemption. For the same reason, a state law regulating a matter in issue that is consistent with the federal statute of preemption is not preempted.

Field Preemption

- In limited cases, "the scheme of federal regulation is so pervasive as to make reasonable the inference that Congress left no room for the state to supplement it." This is called implied field preemption.

- A state law is invalid as a matter of federal supremacy if it conflicts with a federal treaty or interferes with federal power over foreign affairs.

Corporations

Corporations

Corporation: a legal entity created by complying with the statute governing incorporation, which has freely transferable shares, a continuous existence, limited liability of the shareholders, and centralized management of assets by directors and officers

Incorporator: a person who assists in creating, developing, and organizing an enterprise into a corporation

Bylaws: internal rules and regulations enacted by the corporation to govern its actions and its relation to its shareholders, directors, and officers

Novation: where the corporation adopts a preincorporation contract and all parties agree to substitution of the corporation as a party to the contract in place of the promoter

Piercing the Corporate Veil: where a court disregards the corporation's separate entity and holds shareholders or affiliated corporations liable on corporate obligations

Business Judgment Rule: a rebuttable presumption, that shields directors from liability and insulates board decisions from review, that directors are honest, well-meaning, and acting through decisions that are informed and rationally undertaken in good faith

Direct Suit: a shareholder sues on his own behalf to redress an injury to his interest as a shareholder

Derivative Suit: a shareholder sues on behalf of the corporation to redress a wrong to the corporation when it fails to enforce its right

Preemptive Rights: the rights of existing shareholders to acquire unissued shares in the corporation in proportion to their holdings of the original shares upon the board of director's decision to issue them

- **Close Corporations and Special Control Devices**
- **Fiduciary Duties & Liabilities**
- **Financing the Corporation**
- **Formation**
- **Fundamental Changes**
- **Management & Control**
- **Other Business Entities**
- **Preincorporation Transactions**

- To exercise a shareholder's right to inspect the corporation's books, the shareholder must submit a written request to the secretary of the corporation to inspect the books, stating the purpose of the inspection.

- The decision to issue dividends is done by the board of directors and would be covered by the duty of care.

- A limited liability company is a form of business entity that combines the limited liability of corporations with partnership treatment for federal income tax purposes.

- To form a corporation, one must file a certificate of incorporation with the secretary of state and pay the required fee. Once formed, the corporation must follow prescribed formalities.

INTRODUCTION

General Law

- The summary generally follows the Model Business Corporation Act ("MBCA" or "Model Act"). The MBCA, in some form, has been adopted in substance in most states.

DEFINITION A **corporation** is a legal entity created by complying with the statute governing incorporation; it exists only because it is permitted to by statute. There is no common law right to organize a corporation.

Characteristics

- The major characteristics of a corporation are:

    (1) freely transferable shares;

    (2) a continuous existence, despite the death of individual shareholders;

    (3) limited liability of the shareholders; and

    (4) centralized management of assets by directors and officers.

- Unless the articles of incorporation provide otherwise, corporations have perpetual existence.

FORMATION OF CORPORATIONS

Articles of Incorporation

Generally

- A corporation is ordinarily created by filing the articles of incorporation with the Secretary of State.

- Any individual or entity may act as incorporator.

Mandatory Provisions

- The articles of incorporation must include:

    (1) the incorporators' names and addresses;

    (2) the name of the corporation;

    (3) the name and address of the initial registered agent;

    (4) the number of shares the corporation is authorized to issue; and

    (5) if any preemptive rights are to be granted to the shareholders, the provisions applicable to those rights.

- The name must contain the word "corporation," "company," "incorporated," or "limited," or an abbreviation of one of these words.

- The articles of incorporation may also include:

    (1) the names and addresses of the individuals who will be serving as the initial directors;

    (2) any lawful provision regarding:

        (a) the purpose(s) for which the corporation is being organized;

        (b) managing the business and regulating the affairs of the corporation;

(c) defining, limiting, and regulating the powers of the corporation, its board of directors, and shareholders;

(d) a par value for authorized shares or classes of shares; or

(e) the imposition of personal liability on shareholders for debts of the corporation;

(3) any provision required, or permitted to be set forth, in the bylaws;

(4) a provision eliminating or limiting the personal liability of a director for breach of the duty of good faith; and

(5) a provision permitting or making obligatory indemnification of a director for certain liability.

Organization Meeting and Bylaws

- After incorporation, if initial directors are named in the articles of incorporation, they must hold an organizational meeting at a call of the majority of directors to complete the organization of the corporation by:

    (1) appointing officers;

    (2) adopting bylaws; and

    (3) carrying on any other business brought before the meeting.

- If initial directors are not named in the articles of incorporation, the incorporators must hold an organizational meeting at the call of a majority of incorporators to:

    (1) elect directors and complete organization; or

    (2) elect a board of directors who will then complete the organization of the corporation.

Bylaws

In General

- **Bylaws** are internal rules and regulations enacted by the corporation to govern its actions and relations to its shareholders, directors, and officers.

- The bylaws often specify:

    (1) the time and place for the annual shareholders' meeting;

    (2) the record date for determining the shareholders entitled to vote at meetings or to receive dividends;

    (3) the number of shareholders necessary to constitute a quorum;

    (4) the percentage of votes necessary to authorize corporate action; and

    (5) any restrictions on transferability of shares.

Adoption and Amendment

- The board of directors must adopt the initial bylaws. The board of directors may alter, amend, or repeal the bylaws, or to adopt new bylaws, except as otherwise provided in the articles of incorporation or in a bylaw adopted by the shareholders.

Defective Incorporation

De Jure Corporation

- A corporation organized in compliance with the statute is a **de jure corporation**.

- Failure of the organizer(s) to comply with a mandatory statutory provision will preclude *de jure* status.

- In general, corporate existence begins when the articles of incorporation become effective (generally upon being filed with the proper state agency as prescribed by statute); a certified statement of the fact of incorporation by the state is generally considered evidence of *de jure* status.

De Facto Corporation

- If statutory compliance is insufficient for *de jure* status, a **de facto corporation** may still have been formed if:

    (1) a good-faith, colorable attempt was made to comply with the incorporation statute; and

    (2) the corporate principals, in good faith, acted as if they were a corporation.

- *De facto* status insulates directors and shareholders from liability except in a direct action by the state.

- The *de facto* doctrine rarely applies today, however, because the state must approve the articles before they are filed, and a statement by the state of the fact of incorporation is conclusive evidence of incorporation.

Corporation by Estoppel

- Absent *de jure* or *de facto* status, a corporation may still exist by **estoppel**.

- If a creditor always dealt with the principals as if they were a corporation, he will be estopped from later alleging that the corporation is defective if that would unjustly harm the principals.

- In the same manner, a defendant that has held itself out to be a corporation cannot try to avoid liability by claiming the plaintiff has no cause of action because the defendant is not a legal entity.

Ultra Vires

> **RULE** The board of directors is not permitted to undertake action that is beyond the corporation's authority, as set forth in the articles of incorporation or bylaws.

- Under the ***ultra vires* doctrine**, a corporation cannot be obliged to undertake a contract or activity that is beyond the scope of its powers, as described in the articles of incorporation or bylaws.

- Under the Model Act, a corporation's power to act may only be challenged:

    (1) in a proceeding by a shareholder to enjoin the act;

    (2) in a proceeding by the corporation (directly, derivatively, or through a representative) against a current or former director, officer, employee, or agent of the corporation; and

    (3) in a proceeding by the attorney general based on the grounds that the corporation obtained its articles through fraud, or has continued to exceed or abuse the authority conferred upon it by law.

- The *ultra vires* doctrine has little applicability today since the articles of incorporation typically authorize the corporation to engage in all legal activities.

Piercing the Corporate Veil

Generally

- As a general rule, a corporation will be looked upon as a separate legal entity; however, a court may disregard its separate entity and hold shareholders or affiliated corporations liable on corporate obligations. This is known as **piercing the corporate veil**.

- There are three main factors that courts analyze when facing this issue:

    (1) alter ego;

    (2)   inadequate capitalization; and

    (3)   failure to comply with corporate formalities.

Alter Ego

- To pierce the corporate veil, a plaintiff must demonstrate that:

    (1)   there is control so complete that the corporation has no separate will or existence of its own, and in fact the shareholder was the alter ego of the corporation or a mere instrumentality of a parent corporation;

    (2)   the corporate form has been used fraudulently or for an improper purpose (e.g., using corporate assets for personal benefit or a commingling of funds); and

    (3)   injury or unjust loss resulted to the plaintiff from such control and wrong.

- Common ownership of the stock of two or more corporations, together with common management, such as a parent-subsidiary relationship, will not alone render one corporation liable for the acts of the other corporation or its employees. However, liability may be imposed where:

    (1)   the representatives of one corporation actively and directly participate in and apparently exercise pervasive control over the activities of the other corporation, and some fraudulent or injurious consequence of the relationship results; or

    (2)   there is an intermingling of activity of corporations engaged in a common enterprise, with substantial disregard of the separate nature of the corporate entities, or serious ambiguity about the manner and capacity in which the corporations and their representatives are acting.

- Where there is common control of a group of separate corporations engaged in a single enterprise, disregard of the separate entities may be warranted to prevent gross inequity if the corporations failed to:

    (1)   make clear which corporation was taking action in a particular situation, and the nature and extent of that action; or

    (2)   observe with care the formal barriers between the corporations, with a proper segregation of their separate businesses, records, and finances.

Inadequate Capitalization

- Although adequacy of capitalization is a factor considered by the courts, inadequate capitalization alone will not ordinarily lead to disregard of the corporate entity if the corporate formalities are carefully observed.

- Adequate capital is not precisely defined, but generally capital must be sufficient for the corporation's prospective needs and for meeting corporate debts as they become due.

Failure to Comply with Corporate Formalities

- If, through a defect in incorporation, no corporation was formed, those attempting to act as a corporation may be held personally liable.

- However, only those active in managing the corporation would be held personally liable, as individual contractors, as agents of a nonexistent principal, or for fraud.

Liability

- If the corporate veil is pierced, liability is generally imposed only upon shareholders active in management, although it is sometimes imposed on inactive shareholders as well.

PREINCORPORATION TRANSACTIONS

Promoters

DEFINITION ▶ A **promoter** is one who causes a corporation to be formed, organized, and financed.

- Typically, the promoter will:

    (1) manage the initial financing of the corporation;

    (2) arrange for a meeting of the investors;

    (3) negotiate and prepare the preincorporation agreements;

    (4) lease office and factory space; and

    (5) contract for the initial needs of the business.

Promoters' Relationship to the Corporation

In General

- Promoters stand in a fiduciary relationship to the corporation, its subscribers for stock, and those who are expected will afterwards buy stock from the corporation. They are under a duty to avoid self-dealing (duty of loyalty) concerning any assets they sell to the corporation.

Duty of Disclosure

- Promoters are under a duty to disclose fully all material facts concerning any assets they sell to the corporation, including whether the promoters are making a profit on the sale.

- If the cost and manner of acquisition of the assets by the promoter were fully disclosed to an independent board of directors, and the board approved the transaction, the promoter has not breached his fiduciary duty of loyalty and he may keep any profit from the sale.

- If the only shareholders of the corporation are the promoters and no further issuance of stock is contemplated, failure to disclose their financial interest is not a violation of the fiduciary duty to the corporation, even if the shares are later sold to the public without disclosure.

- If the original promotional scheme contemplates sale of stock to other investors, the corporation has an action for breach of fiduciary duty against a promoter who fails to fully disclose material facts about property transferred in an interested transaction. However, the promoter will not be liable to the corporation if he made full disclosure to:

    (1) all the original subscribers for shares and obtained their approval; or

    (2) the shareholders of the established corporation and they ratified the transaction.

Promoters' Liability for Breach of Fiduciary Duty

- In an action for breach of the promoters' fiduciary duty of loyalty, the corporation may either:

    (1) avoid the transaction; or

    (2) hold the promoters liable for the secret profits.

Promoters' Relationship with Other Promoters

- If there is more than one promoter of a corporation, the promoters are, in effect, joint venturers and owe each other a fiduciary duty.

- As fiduciaries, they cannot make a secret profit on assets that they transfer to the promoters as a group, and must fully disclose to each other information concerning the formation of the corporation.

- There is a mutual agency among the promoters, so that each can bind the others on contracts within the scope of the promotion.

Preincorporation Contracts

In General

- Generally, promoters are liable for the contracts entered into on behalf of the corporation not yet formed, but where the contract specifically disclaims personal liability of the promoter, the obligee will not be able to successfully maintain an action against the promoter.

- To determine whether the obligee intended to hold the promoter personally liable or to look exclusively to the future corporation, courts examine the circumstances carefully to determine the intent of the parties, including whether the third party had knowledge that the corporation would come into existence and adopt the contract.

Liability of the Promoter

- As a general rule, the promoter is personally liable on any contract he enters into on behalf of the yet nonexistent corporation, unless the circumstances demonstrate that the other party looked only to the corporation for performance.

- Personal liability will continue even after the corporation is formed, unless there is:

    (1) a valid novation; or

    (2) an agreement to release liability.

DEFINITION ▶ A **novation** occurs if the corporation adopts the contract and all of the parties agree that the promoter will be discharged from the contract and the corporation substituted in the promoter's place. Even if the promoter is personally liable on the contract, a novation will release him from that liability. A novation is usually express by way of a board resolution, but might be implied from the actions of the parties.

- If the promoter signs as an agent, he is generally personally liable because he cannot be an agent for a nonexistent principal. A promoter may be personally liable for obligations created by another promoter under normal agency principles, as when the promoters are joint venturers, or when adoption occurs.

- Even if the promoter is held liable on the contract, he may be entitled to reimbursement by the corporation if he undertook the contract in good faith, at least to the extent that the corporation benefited from the contract.

Liability of the Corporation

- As a general rule, a corporation is not liable on any preincorporation agreements its promoters entered into on its behalf, unless it assumes liability by its own act after it comes into existence.

- The new corporation may assume liability if:

    (1) the contract was made for the corporation's benefit;

    (2) concerned a matter on which the corporation could legally contract; and

    (3) full disclosure was made to an independent board.

Novation or Adoption

- If all the parties agree to substitute the liability of the corporation for that of the promoter, there is a novation and the promoter is discharged. If the corporation **adopts** the contract of the promoter, the promoter may remain liable on the contract with the third party, but will be entitled to indemnification from the newly created corporation.

- Adoption can be express or implied.

  (1) **Express adoption** occurs where the contract is explicitly approved or adopted by the board of directors.

  (2) **Implied adoption** occurs where the corporation accepts or acknowledges the benefits of the contract in some manner.

Acceptance of Benefits

- A corporation may become bound to fulfill a contract made in its name and on its behalf in anticipation of its existence by afterwards accepting the benefits of the contract, at least to the extent of the fair value of the goods or services received.

Liability of a Third Party

- A third party who enters into a contract with a promoter is liable from the contract's inception.

Subscriptions for Shares

- A person may become a shareholder of a corporation by agreeing to purchase shares pursuant to a subscription for shares either before or after incorporation. This is called a **stock subscription agreement**.

- A subscription for shares entered before incorporation is irrevocable for six months unless agreed by all subscribers.

- Payment terms of preincorporation subscriptions for shares are set out in the subscription agreement, or are determined by the board of directors in the absence of provisions in the agreement.

FINANCING THE CORPORATION

Sources of Finance

Debt Securities

DEFINITION   **Debt securities** represent money loaned to the corporation, and a person holding debt securities is a creditor of the corporation.

- The creditor's rights are fixed by the instrument creating the debt; usually he is entitled to repayment of his principal at a specified time, with a return on the principal in the form of interest.

- Holders of debt securities have priority over equity security holders upon liquidation of the corporation, but they do not ordinarily have the right to vote.

- The three major kinds of debt securities are:

  (1) **debentures**, which are unsecured obligations of the corporation (holders of these debt securities are general creditors);

(2) **bonds**, which usually are secured by a mortgage or a security interest in specific assets of the corporation (thus, holders are secured creditors); and

(3) **notes**, which are short-term debt securities with durations of less than five years.

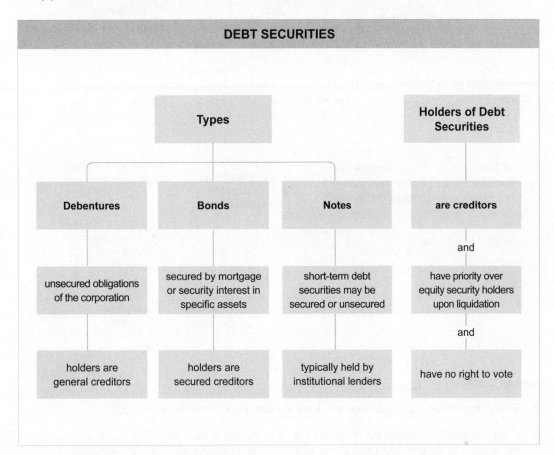

Equity Securities

Equity securities represent the capital of the corporation that is at risk in the business.

■ Equity security holders have no right to repayment of the amount invested, or to a return on the investment. Upon liquidation, however, once the creditors are satisfied, all the remaining corporate assets belong to the shareholders (the **right to the residual**).

■ Shareholders usually have:

(1) **dividend rights**—the right to a dividend, if any are declared, at the board's discretion;

(2) **liquidation rights**—the right to a share of the corporate assets at the end of the corporation's existence; and

(3) **voting rights**—the right to a voice in the management of the corporation.

■ All shares have equal voting rights unless otherwise provided in the articles of incorporation. The articles may create several classes of shares and delineate the different rights of each.

■ The Model Act does away with the traditional designations of common and preferred stock.

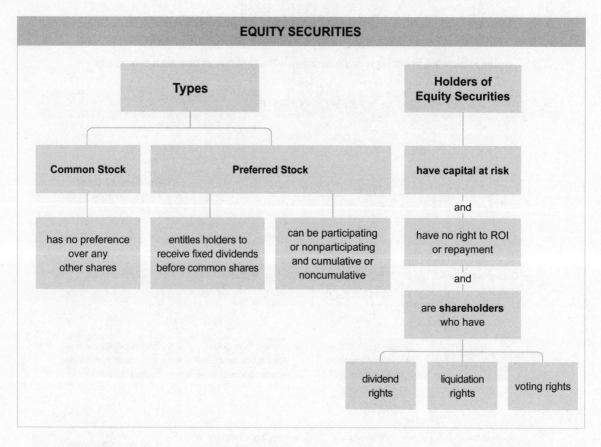

Common Stock

- Every corporation must authorize and issue at least one class of common stock.

- Common stock represents the residual ownership interest in the corporation; upon liquidation, the holders of the common stock divide all the assets remaining after satisfaction of creditors and payment to the preferred shareholders of their liquidation preference.

- Holders have no right to a dividend unless declared by the directors after payment of preferred stock dividends.

Preferred Stock

- Any corporation may authorize one or more classes of preferred stock, if allowed in the articles of incorporation.

- Preferred shareholders are generally entitled to receive fixed dividends before any dividends are paid to common shareholders.

- Although preferred stock may have a variety of privileges and limitations, the following characteristics are common:

  (1) it is usually nonvoting stock, but voting rights may accrue if the dividend is not paid, or if an attempt is made to alter its rights by amending the articles of incorporation;

  (2) it is usually nonparticipating—i.e., they receive no more than their stipulated dividend;

  (3) it is usually cumulative or noncumulative dividends, depending on the provisions in the articles of incorporation;

(4)   it is usually preferred and limited as to liquidation rights; and

(5)   it is usually redeemable at a stated price at the option of the corporation, or the articles may provide that it is redeemable at the option of the shareholder.

Shares in Series

■   The articles of incorporation may provide that any preferred or special class is to be divided into series, which allows variations in the rights and preferences of the different series within a class.

Fractional Shares and Scrip

■   A corporation may issue **fractional shares**; usually this is not done in the initial capitalization, but is in connection with stock dividends, reverse stock splits, or corporate reorganizations. The holder is entitled to voting rights, dividends, and other distributions in proportion to his fractional holdings.

■   **Scrip** is a certificate exchangeable for stock or cash, and it is usually transferable. Its holder is not entitled to any rights as a shareholder, and if scrip is not exchanged by a specified date, it usually becomes void.

Hybrid Securities

■   Occasionally, **hybrid securities**, combining features of debt and equity securities, are issued. However, hybrid securities raise difficulties as to how they should be treated for tax purposes.

Balancing Debt and Equity

■   Extensive debt financing is attractive to corporations for several reasons:

(1)   For tax purposes, the interest paid on debt is deductible by the corporation. Interest payments avoid double taxation of dividends (once as corporate profits, and once as income to the dividend recipient).

(2)   If the corporation becomes insolvent, a holder of debt securities participates with the other creditors in the assets, whereas an equity holder receives a distribution only after all the creditors are satisfied.

Securities Issuance

Share Issuance

■   The corporation must issue at least one share of stock representing ownership interests in the corporation. This is typically done at the first meeting of the board of directors. The corporation need not issue as many shares as are authorized. Once issued, shares are outstanding, until they are redeemed, which become treasury shares.

Authorization of Additional Shares

■   If the corporation has used all of its authorized shares in its articles of incorporation and needs to sell more, the articles must be amended to authorize more shares.

■   The authorization of additional shares requires the approval of the board of directors and the shareholders by a majority vote.

Consideration for Shares

■   There is no longer any provision relating to par value under the Model Act, and therefore, no minimum price at which specific shares must be issued. Unless there is fraud, the judgment of the board of directors or the shareholders is conclusive as to the value of consideration received for shares.

- Under the Model Act, valid consideration for shares may be:

    (1) money or obligations (promissory notes);

    (2) property, tangible or intangible, actually received by the corporation; or

    (3) services actually performed for the corporation or contracts for future services.

Share Certificates

- The shares of a corporation may be represented by **certificates**. Shares not represented by a certificate are **uncertificated**.

- All certificates must state the number of shares, and the class and series, if any, that the certificate represents. The certificate must be signed by the president or a vice president, and by the treasurer or an assistant treasurer.

- In most states, any restriction on the transferability of stock, whether imposed by the articles of incorporation, the bylaws, or any agreement to which the corporation is a party, must be noted conspicuously on the share certificate or it will be ineffective, except against a person with actual knowledge of it at the time he acquired the shares.

Shareholders' Preemptive Rights

In General

DEFINITION ▶ **Preemptive rights** are the rights of existing shareholders to acquire unissued or treasury shares in the corporation, or options or rights in proportion to their holdings of the original shares, when the corporation seeks to issue additional stock that would reduce existing shareholders' ownership percentage.

- Under the Model Act, shareholders have no preemptive rights, except to the extent provided in the articles of incorporation.

- A shareholder whose rights are violated may:

    (1) enjoin the sale and recover from the purchaser shares bought knowingly in violation of the preemptive right;

    (2) cancel issuance of additional shares to himself; or

    (3) purchase the shares on the open market and recover from the corporation the difference between the offering price and the price he paid.

- Absent preemptive rights, a shareholder's equity suit may still block issuance of stock that would unfairly dilute or transfer control on a theory of breach of fiduciary duty under some circumstances, such as a sale for less than fair market value.

Dividends and Distributions

In General

DEFINITION ▶ A **dividend** is a distribution by a corporation to its shareholders of cash or property of the corporation. A dividend differs from a distribution in redemption of stock in that a dividend is distributed with respect to the shareholder's stock, rather than in exchange for his stock.

Shareholders' Right to Dividends

- A shareholder has no inherent right to be paid a dividend.

- Generally, the board of directors has discretion to decide whether and when to declare a dividend, subject to any restrictions in the articles of incorporation.

- Under the Model Act, the directors may not declare a dividend if:

  (1) the corporation would not be able to pay its debts as they become due in the ordinary course of business; or

  (2) the corporation's total assets would be less than the sum of its total liabilities plus the amount the corporation would need, if it were dissolved at the time of distribution, to satisfy the preferential rights upon dissolution of shareholders whose preferences are superior to those receiving the distribution.

Contractual Rights to Dividends

- One means of assuring dividend payments is a provision in the articles of incorporation, the bylaws, or a shareholders' agreement:

  (1) making dividends mandatory when earnings are available for dividends; or

  (2) limiting the amount of earned surplus that may be accumulated.

Bad Faith Refusal to Declare Dividends

- If a shareholder can prove that the directors' refusal to declare a dividend amounted to fraud, bad faith, or an abuse of discretion, a court of equity can intervene to compel declaration.

- The court would look at all the circumstances surrounding the corporate policy decision in light of the corporation's financial condition and requirements. Relevant factors are:

  (1) intense hostility of the controlling faction against the minority;

  (2) exclusion of the minority from employment by the corporation;

  (3) high salaries, bonuses, or corporate loans made to the officers in control;

  (4) the fact that the majority group may be subject to high personal income taxes if substantial dividends are paid; and

  (5) the existence of a desire by the controlling directors to acquire the minority stock interests as cheaply as possible.

Remedies

- Once the plaintiff shareholder has proven his contractual right to dividends, or abuse of discretion of the directors, the court may issue a decree for specific performance of the contract or a mandatory injunction ordering a dividend.

Declaration and Payment of Dividends

Procedure

- Once the directors have voted to declare a dividend, they may fix a record date for determination of the shareholders entitled to receive dividends. The date is fixed in accordance with the articles of incorporation, the bylaws, or by resolution. The record date may be no more than 70 days prior to the action to be taken.

- If no record date is fixed, the record date will be at the close of business on the day the directors vote to declare the dividend.

Shareholders' Rights After Declaration

- As soon as a dividend has been declared, a debtor-creditor relationship arises between the corporation and the shareholders, and the funds to pay the dividend are considered segregated from other corporate funds.

- A valid declaration of a lawful dividend generally cannot be revoked without the shareholders' consent, unless funds are not legally available to pay the dividend. If the declaration was conditional, it may be revoked; and, a declaration not yet disclosed to shareholders may also be revoked.

- A dividend of stock may be rescinded at any time before the stock is actually issued.

- Dividends declared before a sale of stock belong to the seller, even if not paid until after transfer of the stock.

Unclaimed Dividends

- Any dividend owed by a corporation to a shareholder is presumed abandoned if, within some statutorily prescribed time after declaration, it has not been claimed or the owner has not corresponded in writing with the corporation concerning the dividend.

- Most jurisdictions have a statute which provides that unclaimed dividends escheat to the sovereign.

Liability for Improper Dividends

- Directors who vote to authorize a dividend that is in violation of the state corporation statute will be held personally liable for the amount of the dividend payment in excess of the amount that could legally have been paid, but only to the extent that it has not been repaid to the corporation.

- Directors are not liable if the dividend could properly have been paid at the time of authorization, even though circumstances later made it improper. A **good faith exception** exists where the director relied upon corporate financial records, and acted reasonably and in good faith.

- A shareholder who receives a dividend when the corporation is insolvent, or is rendered insolvent by its payment, is liable to the corporation for the amount of the dividend; or the amount of the dividend in excess of what could lawfully have been paid.

Redemption and Repurchase of Shares

DEFINITION ▶ A **repurchase** is a voluntary agreement by the corporation to buy its own shares of either common or preferred stock. Authorization in the articles of incorporation is not required; repurchase is governed by the agreement.

- A corporation cannot repurchase shares if it is insolvent, or if repurchase of common stock would impair the rights of preferred shareholders. A corporation may repurchase shares to prevent takeover by looters, but a repurchase solely to keep management in power could be enjoined, and the directors voting for it held personally liable for resulting corporate losses.

- **Redemption** occurs when a corporation has the right to compel a shareholder to sell his shares back to it. This right must be stated in the articles of incorporation. It usually applies only to preferred stock, and generally must be made ratably among all the shares in the class.

MANAGEMENT AND CONTROL

In General

- A hierarchy of authority allocates power between:

  (1) the shareholders, who own the corporation; and

  (2) the directors, who manage the corporation.

- Unless the articles of incorporation or bylaws provide otherwise, the directors elect officers of the corporation, who make the day-to-day management decisions.

- The directors are not mere agents of the shareholders, and need not follow the shareholders' wishes; rather, the directors owe a duty to the corporation to manage its affairs prudently.

■ The shareholders do, however, have indirect power to manage the corporation through their right to elect the board of directors.

Shareholder Rights and Meetings

Rights

> **SHAREHOLDER RIGHTS**
>
> • Elect and remove directors
>
> • Approve amendments to the articles of incorporation
>
> • Amend the bylaws
>
> • Approve extraordinary actions in the corporation, such as merger, consolidation, share exchange, transfer of assets, and dissolution

Meetings

RULE ▶ A corporation must hold a shareholder meeting annually for the election of directors and the transaction of any other business. The bylaws normally specify the date of the annual meeting. The hour, place, and manner of conducting the meeting are also fixed or determined by the bylaws.

■ Special meetings of the shareholders may be called by the president, the directors, or upon the written application of the holders of 10% of the shares entitled to vote. Special meetings may also be called by anyone authorized to do so by the articles of incorporation or the bylaws.

Notice of Shareholders' Meetings

■ Written notice stating the place, date, hour, and purposes of the meeting must be given by the clerk to each shareholder entitled to vote not less than 10, and not more than 60, days prior to the meeting.

Record Date and Shareholder List

■ A record date for determining the shareholders entitled to receive notice or to vote may be fixed by the articles of incorporation, the bylaws, or the board.

RULE ▶ The record date may be no more than 70 days prior to the meeting.

Shareholder Voting

Quorum

■ Unless the articles of incorporation or the bylaws provide otherwise, a majority of the shares entitled to vote at a meeting constitutes a **quorum**.

Consent in Lieu of Meeting

■ Action may be taken without a meeting if all shareholders entitled to vote on the matter act by written consent, or as otherwise provided by the articles of incorporation.

■ If provided by the articles, each eligible shareholder must be given 10 days' written notice.

Qualification of Voters

■ Unless a statute or the articles of incorporation provide otherwise, each share is entitled to one vote, and each fractional share is entitled to a proportionate vote. Only the shareholders of record are eligible to vote.

Proxy Voting

- By statute, in most states, every shareholder entitled to vote may do so by proxy. The term **proxy** means the grant of authority by a shareholder to another person to vote the shareholder's stock; it may also mean the instrument granting the authority, or the agent to whom authority is granted (also called the proxy holder).

- Most states require that the proxy be in writing, and that it be executed within a specified period of time before the meeting or vote at issue.

- Appointment of a proxy must be in writing executed by the shareholder or the shareholder's authorized agent. A proxy is generally valid for 11 months, unless it states some other duration.

- Unless coupled with an interest, a proxy is freely revocable by the shareholder unless the instrument specifically states otherwise.

Shareholder Voting Agreements

- Shareholder voting agreements are contracts designed to ensure the shareholders will vote in concert with regard to issues designated by the agreement.

- Absent fraud or other illegal object, shareholder voting agreements are generally considered valid and enforceable in court.

Voting Trusts

- A voting trust involves a transfer of legal title to the shares to a trustee who votes them for a specified period according to the trust terms.

- The duration of a voting trust is limited to 10 years; however, any of the parties may extend the trust (as to their shares) for one or more additional periods, each not to exceed 10 years.

Election of Directors

- In **straight voting**, each share has one vote for each director; thus, a majority shareholder can elect the entire board of directors.

- If permitted by the article of incorporation, representation of minority shareholders can be made more likely by **cumulative voting**, which grants each share as many votes as there are directors to be elected, and allows the shareholder to allocate his votes as he chooses.

- The formula for calculating cumulation is:

$$\frac{\text{Shares Voting}}{(\text{Directors to be Elected} + 1)} + 1$$

- The articles of incorporation may provide for staggered terms of office if there are nine or more directors. Under this provision, only one-third to one-half of the directors is up for election at any meeting.

Shareholders' Right to Information

- Shareholders have a statutory right to inspect and copy corporate records including:

    (1) the articles of incorporation;

    (2) the bylaws;

    (3) the records of all meetings of incorporators and of shareholders;

    (4) the stock and transfer records, which must contain the names and addresses of all shareholders and the amount of stock held by each;

(5)   a balance sheet as of the end of each fiscal year; and

(6)   a statement of income for that fiscal year.

■   A shareholder may inspect and copy records only if:

(1)   the demand is made in good faith and for a proper purpose;

(2)   he describes with particularity his purpose and the records he desires to inspect; and

(3)   the records are directly connected with his purpose.

■   A shareholder also has a common law right to inspect corporate records, and this may be used to examine books of account and other records unavailable under the statute.

■   The shareholders' right to information is also protected by federal securities regulations.

Directors

Number

■   The minimum number of directors is set by statute, and states vary with regard to the requisite number. Under the Model Act, only one director is required, although more may be provided for.

■   The articles of incorporation or bylaws may provide for a variable range in the size of the board of directors.

Qualifications

■   A director need not be a resident of the state of incorporation, or a shareholder of the corporation, unless required by the bylaws. The articles or bylaws may, however, prescribe further qualifications.

Election and Removal of Directors

Generally

■   The initial directors are chosen by the incorporators, and hold office until their successors are elected by shareholders at their first annual meeting.

■   Directors are usually elected at the annual meeting for a one-year term.

Vacancy

■   Unless the articles provide otherwise, any vacancy on the board of directors, is filled in the manner prescribed in the bylaws, or, in the absence of such a bylaw, by the shareholders.

Removal

■   Unless otherwise stated in the articles of incorporation, the entire board of directors, or any individual directors, can be removed, with or without cause, by a majority of the shares entitled to vote in the election of such directors. The removal of one or more directors can be accomplished only at a meeting called for that purpose, with notice given of the purpose of that meeting.

■   However, a director elected by a particular class may be removed only by a majority of the shares entitled to vote in the class that elected him.

■   If the corporation has cumulative voting and less than the entire board is to be removed, no director can be removed if the votes against his removal would be sufficient to elect him if they cumulatively voted at an election of the entire board.

Meetings of the Board of Directors

Time and Place

- Meetings of the board may be held anywhere, either within or outside the state. The bylaws may specify the time and place for meetings, but absent such a bylaw, the directors may select the time and place.

Notice

- Unless otherwise provided by the bylaws, regular meetings of the board may be held without notice if the time and place of the meetings are fixed by the bylaws or by the board.

- Special meetings may be held only upon at least two days' notice to the directors.

Quorum of Directors

DEFINITION ▶ A **quorum** is the number of directors that must be present for the board to be legally competent to transact business. Unless otherwise provided in the articles of incorporation or the bylaws, a majority of the directors then in office constitutes a quorum.

Vote of Directors

- Once a quorum is present, a vote of the majority of directors present at the meeting constitutes an act of the board, unless the articles of incorporation or bylaws require a greater margin, or even a unanimous vote.

Director Participation

- A director cannot vote by proxy, even if the proxy holder is another director. In order to vote, a director must be present at the meeting.

Defects in a Meeting

- Defects in quorum, notice, or voting may be cured by post-meeting ratification, where a majority of the directors:

    (1) signs a writing that approves the resolution; or

    (2) fails to object after knowledge of the resolution is acquired.

Action by Committee

- The board does not ordinarily run the corporation on a day-to-day basis; it may delegate its powers to officers and executive committees.

Directors' Objections to Actions

- A director who objects to a course of action to be taken by the board of directors or a committee of the board of directors must dissent by an affirmative act at the time of the meeting at which the vote on the action is taken.

Officers

In General

- Directors delegate the day-to-day management of the corporation to officers.

- A previous version of the Model Act required that a corporation have at least four officers: a president; one or more vice presidents; a secretary; and a treasurer. However, the latest versions of the Model Act does away with these requirements, and provide that a corporation shall have the officers described in its bylaws or appointed by the board of directors in accordance with the bylaws.

Authority of Corporate Officers

- The powers of a corporate officer are, like the powers of an agent, either actual or apparent.

- **Actual authority** may be either expressly delegated or implied. Express actual authority of an officer may originate in board approval of actions by resolution at a board meeting. Corporate officers have the implied authority to enter into any transaction for which he has been expressly or implicitly authorized under the certificate of incorporation, the bylaws, an employment contract, or a corporate resolution, and those transactions that are reasonably related to performing the duties for which they are responsible.

- Where a corporation should have recognized that a third party would be likely to view the officer or agent in question as possessing the authority to bind the corporation to the agreement in question, it cannot avoid the transaction based on the concept of **apparent authority**.

Ratification

- Acts of a corporate officer or agent that have not been properly authorized may be ratified by the board.

- Ratification may be explicit (i.e., by passing a resolution that confirms the transaction) or implied (i.e., by acceptance of the benefits of an agreement).

Officer Liability

- Officers are agents of the corporation and will be liable for contracts and obligations incurred by them in violation of their agency authority.

Vacancies and Removal

- Any vacancy in an office may be filled in the manner prescribed in the bylaws, or, absent such a bylaw, by the directors.

- Any officer or agent may be removed by the board of directors at any time with or without cause.

FIDUCIARY AND OTHER DUTIES OF MANAGEMENT AND CONTROLLING SHAREHOLDERS

Duty of Care

Standard of Care

- In general, directors, officers, and incorporators of a corporation must perform their duties:

    (1)   in good faith;

    (2)   in a manner reasonably believed to be in the best interests of the corporation; and

    (3)   with such care as a person in a like position would use under similar circumstances.

Business Judgment Rule

RULE ▶ The **business judgment rule** shields directors from liability and insulates board decisions from review. The business judgment rule creates a rebuttable presumption that directors are honest, well-meaning, and acting through decisions that are informed and rationally undertaken in good faith.

- Usually, a director or officer who makes a good faith error of business judgment will not have breached his duty of care.

- A director is entitled to rely on information, opinions, reports, records (including financial statements), and other financial data presented or prepared under authority delegated by the board of directors, by:

    (1)   one or more officers or employees of the corporation whom the director or officer reasonably believes to be reliable and competent in the matter;

(2) legal counsel, public accountants, or other persons as to matters that the director or officer reasonably believes to be within that person's professional or expert competence, or as to which the person merits confidence; or

(3) a duly constituted committee of the board upon which he does not serve.

Statutory Liabilities

- In the absence of good faith action or reliance on the enumerated items, directors are subject to the following liabilities under the Model Act:

    (1) **Improper Declaration of Dividend:** A director who votes for or assents to the declaration of any dividend or other distribution of the assets of a corporation to its shareholders contrary to statutory provisions or any restrictions contained in the articles of incorporation is liable, together with all other assenting directors, to the corporation for the amount of the distribution.

    (2) **Distributions During Liquidation:** A director who votes for or assents to any distribution to the shareholders during the liquidation of the corporation without payment of or adequate provision for all known debts, obligations, or liabilities of the corporation will be liable, with the other assenting directors, for the value of the assets so distributed.

    (3) **Improper Redemption and Repurchase of Shares or Purchasing Corporation's Shares:** A director who votes for, or assents to, the purchase of the corporation's own shares, contrary to the statutory provisions, is liable, together with the other assenting directors, to the corporation for the amount of consideration paid for those shares.

    (4) **Failure to Give Notice to Barred Creditors:** If a dissolved corporation proceeds to bar any known claims against it, directors who fail to take reasonable steps to cause the required notice to be given to any known creditor of the corporation will be jointly and severally liable to the creditor for all loss and damage caused.

- Any director against whom such a claim is successfully asserted is entitled to contribution from the other directors who voted for, and the other officers who participated in, the wrongful action, and who did not meet the good faith standard.

Responsibility for Acts of Others

- A director or officer can be liable for negligently selecting or supervising subordinates.

- He would not be liable, however, for the negligence of a person at the same level of responsibility, unless he participated in the negligence, or was negligent in not discovering and correcting the problem.

Burden of Proof

- In a suit for breach of duty of care, the plaintiff has the burden of rebutting the business judgment rule.

Duty of Loyalty

In General

- The fiduciary duty of officers, directors, and employees requires that they be loyal to the corporation and not promote their own interests in a manner injurious to the corporation.

- A conflict of interest constituting a breach of the duty of loyalty may arise where the individual:

    (1) has business dealings with the corporation;

    (2) takes advantage of a corporate opportunity; or

    (3) enters into competition with the corporation.

Business Dealings with the Corporation

- A conflict of interest is inherent whenever a director or officer contracts with the corporation to buy or sell goods or services, or has a personal or financial interest in the transaction.

Corporate Opportunity

- The fiduciary duty of loyalty prohibits directors and officers (and sometimes employees) from taking for their own benefit any business opportunity that properly belongs to the corporation, unless:

  (1) the opportunity is fully disclosed to the corporation, the corporation is first given a chance to pursue the opportunity, and the corporation decides not to pursue the opportunity; or

  (2) the corporation could not have taken the opportunity.

- Factors considered in determining whether a corporate opportunity exists, include:

  (1) whether the business constituting the opportunity is closely related to that of the corporation;

  (2) whether the board had expressed an interest in acquiring that type of business;

  (3) whether the individual became aware of the opportunity while acting in his capacity as a director or officer; and

  (4) whether he used any corporate funds or facilities in discovering or developing the opportunity.

Competition with Corporation

- Competition by a director or officer will not necessarily be a breach of fiduciary duty if he acts in good faith.

- As a general rule, directors and officers may engage in independent business, but if the independent business competes with the corporation, equitable limitations will apply.

- The remedy for such a breach would be:

  (1) the profits earned in competition;

  (2) a constructive trust on the competitor's property; or

  (3) damages for injury to the corporation.

Burden of Proof

- In a suit for breach of duty of loyalty, the defendant has the burden of disproving a breach of loyalty.

Duties of Controlling Shareholders

In General

- A majority shareholder's fiduciary duty is usually enforceable by the corporation, by means of a shareholder's derivative action, or by an individual shareholder's action for a direct breach of fiduciary duty to him.

- The controlling shareholder has the burden of proving the entire fairness of the transaction.

Federal Securities Law

Rule 10b-5

 DEFINITION Rule 10b-5 is an anti-fraud rule that prohibits false or misleading statements in connection with the purchase and sale of any security (whether or not such security is listed on a national exchange).

- The elements of a 10b-5 action are:

  (1) a misrepresentation or omission of a material fact;

  (2) knowledge by the defendant of the misrepresentation or omission, or reckless disregard of the truth (negligent misrepresentation is not sufficient);

  (3) scienter (intent to deceive, manipulate, or defraud);

  (4) reliance of the plaintiff, which is generally assumed if the fact was material; and

  (5) damages.

Insider Trading Action

RULE ▶ Rule 10b-5 has been applied to insider trading actions. An insider who learns of material, non-public information about the corporation as a consequence of his corporate position cannot make a secret profit by dealing in that stock before public disclosure.

- An insider trading action requires merely materiality or scienter.

- **Tippers**, or insiders who make selective disclosures of material inside information, can be liable for the profits of their **tippees** if they (the insiders) made the disclosure for the purpose of obtaining direct or indirect pecuniary gain (money, gift, benefit, etc.).

Misappropriation of Inside Information

- Under the **misappropriation theory**, a person may be prosecuted by the government under 10b-5 even when he has no duty to the issuer, or shareholders of the issuer, when he has traded on market information in breach of the duty of trust and confidence owed to the source of the information.

Section 16(b)—Recovery of Short-Swing Profits

- A *per se* rule of invalidity is applied to short-swing profits made by insiders on in-and-out transactions within a short period of time.

- Under Section 16(b), any profit is recoverable if:

  (1) made by an officer, director, or beneficial owner of more than 10% of a class of equity security;

  (2) derived from any sale of a security; and

  (3) occurring no more than six months from a purchase of the same security.

DIFFERENCES BETWEEN 10b-5 ACTION AND RULE 16(b) ACTION	
10b-5	**16(b)**
Applies to all corporations	Applies only to publicly traded companies
Applies to all purchases and sellers	Applies only to directors, officers, and 10% beneficial owners
Requires a purchase or sale	Requires a purchase and sale
Requires intent to deceive	No intent required; strict liability
Direct and derivatives actions; SEC action	Derivative action

CLOSE CORPORATIONS AND SPECIAL CONTROL DEVICES

In General

DEFINITION A **close corporation**, or closely held corporation, is defined as one having a small number of shareholders; no ready market for the corporate stock; and substantial majority shareholder participation in the management, direction, and operations of the corporation.

Statutory Provisions

- The articles of incorporation or bylaws may set a voting requirement of a percentage greater than a majority (a **supermajority**), or a unanimous vote. Such higher requirements protect the minority, but can create a danger of deadlock by minority veto.

- To equitably balance ownership and voting in a close corporation, shareholders may want to avail themselves of statutory provisions permitting classification of stock, preemptive rights, and preferred stock.

Resolution of Disputes and Deadlock

- Because close corporations are likely to suffer from deadlock of shareholders or directors, the articles of incorporation may provide for a remedy, such as arbitration or a buyout agreement in the event of irreconcilable conflict. The articles may also provide for dissolution at the option of a specified percentage of the shares, or upon some other contingency, which must be conspicuously noted on the shares.

Stock Transfer Restrictions

- Any restriction on transfer must be set forth in the articles of incorporation, the bylaws, or a separate agreement, and must be noted conspicuously on the share certificates.

- The **right of first refusal** obliges a shareholder to offer shares first to the corporation or other shareholders before they may be sold to outsiders.

- A **buy-sell agreement** is similar to a first option, but is mandatory, requiring the offeree shareholders or corporation to buy the stock upon the triggering event (e.g., death, disability, termination of employment, or proposed sale).

Fiduciary Duty of Shareholders in a Close Corporation

- In a close corporation, courts are willing to say that managing shareholders owe a fiduciary duty to the corporation and possibly directly to other shareholders.

- The fiduciary duty may be applied to all shareholders alike, and thus prohibits a minority shareholder from acting to harm the corporation.

FUNDAMENTAL CHANGES IN CORPORATE STRUCTURE

> **FUNDAMENTAL CHANGES TO THE CORPORATE STRUCTURE**
>
> - Amendment of the articles of incorporation
> - Mergers and share exchanges
> - Transfers of corporate assets
> - Dissolution

Amendment of Articles of Incorporation

When Permitted

- A corporation may amend its articles of incorporation in any respect if the amendment would be a legal provision in original articles filed on the date of amendment. The Model Act requires only a majority vote to effect a change.

Board Resolution

- The board of directors must adopt a resolution setting forth the proposed amendment and direct that it be submitted to a vote at a meeting of the shareholders.

Amendments Authorized by Majority Vote of Board of Directors

- Without the approval of shareholders, a corporation may authorize amendments of its articles of incorporation:

    (1) to extend the duration of the corporation;

    (2) to delete the names and addresses of the initial directors, initial registered agent, or registered office;

    (3) if the corporation has only one class of shares outstanding, to change each issued and unissued authorized share of the class into a greater number of whole shares of the class; or increase the number of authorized shares of the class to the extent necessary to permit the issuance of shares as a share dividend;

    (4) to effect a change to the business designation or geographic designation of its corporate name;

    (5) to reflect a reduction of the authorized shares of any class;

    (6) to delete a class of shares from the articles when there are no remaining shares of the class (because the corporation has acquired all the shares of the class and the articles prohibit the corporation to reissue the shares); or

    (7) as otherwise provided in the articles of incorporation.

Dissenters' Appraisal Rights

- A shareholder who is adversely affected by an amendment of the articles and who objects to the action is entitled to an appraisal and payment for his stock.

- Unless the articles provide otherwise, a shareholder's rights are deemed adversely affected only when the amendment:

    (1) alters or abolishes any preferential right of his stock;

    (2) creates, alters, or abolishes any right in respect of redemption of his stock;

    (3) alters or abolishes any preemptive right in respect of his stock; or

    (4) excludes or limits his right as a shareholder to vote on a matter, except as such a right may be limited by voting rights given to new shares then being authorized of an existing or new class.

Mergers, Consolidations, and Share Exchanges

In General

DEFINITION   In a **merger**, one corporation is absorbed into another corporation, which survives.

DEFINITION   In a **consolidation**, two corporations combine to form a new corporation, and both of the former corporations cease to exist.

DEFINITION In a **share exchange**, one corporation acquires all of the outstanding shares of one or more classes or series of another corporation, pursuant to a plan of exchange adopted by the board of directors of each corporation.

Board Resolution for Merger

- Two or more domestic corporations may merge into one of the corporations under a plan of merger that must be approved in accordance with statutory procedures.

- The board of directors of each corporation must adopt a plan of merger that sets forth:

  (1) the names of the corporations preparing to merge, and the name of the surviving corporation;

  (2) the terms and conditions of the proposed merger;

  (3) the manner and basis for converting shares, obligations, and securities into cash or other property; and

  (4) a statement of changes in the articles of incorporation of the surviving corporation.

Board Resolution for Share Exchange

- When a corporation desires to acquire the shares of another corporation in a share exchange, the board of directors of each corporation must adopt resolutions setting forth:

  (1) the names of the corporations whose shares will be acquired, and of the corporation that will acquire those shares;

  (2) the terms and conditions; and

  (3) the manner and basis of exchanging shares.

- In the resulting organizational scheme, the acquirer will be the parent of a wholly owned subsidiary.

Shareholder Approval

- For mergers, consolidations, and share exchanges, the plan must be submitted to a shareholder vote for approval unless such approval is not required. The Model Act requires a vote of the majority of the shareholders.

Short-Form Merger

- A parent owning at least 90% of the outstanding shares of each class of its subsidiary may merge the subsidiary into itself without the approval of shareholders of either the parent or the subsidiary.

- The board of the parent must approve a plan of merger, stating the terms and conditions of the merger and the manner of determining its effective date, and a copy of the plan must be mailed to each shareholder of record of the subsidiary corporation.

- Articles of merger, signed by the president or vice president and the secretary or assistant secretary must be filed with the Secretary of State, and become effective upon the issuance of a certificate of merger.

Effect of Merger or Consolidation

- Upon the effective date, the participating corporations become a single corporation, and the surviving or new corporation succeeds to all the rights, privileges, immunities, powers, liabilities and duties of the former corporations.

Sale of Substantially All Assets

- Instead of merging with another corporation, a corporation may choose to acquire the other corporation by buying all its assets.

- Shareholder approval is required for sale of all, or substantially all, assets not in the ordinary course of business.

- Shareholders dissenting from a sale, lease, or exchange of all, or substantially all, property and assets are entitled to the same appraisal rights as dissenters from a merger or consolidation, and must follow the same procedures.

Recapitalizations

- An existing corporation may choose to change its capital structure by adjusting the amount or priority of the debt and equity securities of the corporation. Recapitalization may be accomplished by adjusting the amount of each type of security, or changing the priority of different classes of stock.

Dissenting Shareholders' Appraisal Rights

- Shareholders may dissent from:

    (1) an amendment of the articles of incorporation that materially and adversely affects their rights;

    (2) a sale of all assets other than in the ordinary course of business; or

    (3) a merger or consolidation if the shareholder has the right to vote or is a shareholder in a subsidiary being merged with its parent.

- Dissenting shareholders have the right to require the corporation to appraise their shares and buy them at fair market value.

Dissolution

Voluntary Dissolution

- A corporation may be voluntarily dissolved by:

    (1) the written consent of all of its shareholders by executing and filing a statement to that effect with the Secretary of State; or

    (2) the corporation's filing of articles of dissolution with the Secretary of State pursuant to a vote of two-thirds of each class of stock outstanding and entitled to vote thereon, and with the approval of the board of directors, or pursuant to provisions in the articles of incorporation.

Judicial Dissolution

- A court may dissolve a corporation in a proceeding by the attorney general, if it is established that:

    (1) the corporation obtained its articles of incorporation through fraud; or

    (2) the corporation has continued to exceed or abuse the authority conferred upon it by law.

- A court may dissolve a corporation in a proceeding by a shareholder, if it is established that:

    (1) the directors are deadlocked and irreparable injury to the corporation is threatened or being suffered, or the business and affairs of the corporation can no longer be conducted to the advantage of the shareholders;

    (2) the directors, or those in control, have acted in a manner that is illegal, oppressive, or fraudulent;

    (3) the shareholders are deadlocked in voting power and have failed for at least two consecutive annual meetings to elect successors to directors whose term has expired; or

    (4) the corporate assets are being misapplied or wasted.

- A court may dissolve a corporation in a proceeding by a creditor, if it is established that:

    (1) the creditor's claim has been reduced to judgment, the execution on the judgment has returned unsatisfied, and the corporation is insolvent; or

    (2) the corporation has admitted in writing that the creditor's claim is due and the corporation is insolvent.

- A court may dissolve a corporation in a proceeding by the corporation to have its voluntary dissolution continued under court supervision.

Administrative Dissolution

- The Secretary of State can commence a proceeding to administratively dissolve a corporation if:

    (1) the corporation does not pay franchise taxes or penalties within 60 days after they are due;

    (2) the corporation fails to deliver its annual report within 60 days after it is due;

    (3) the corporation is without a registered agent or office for 60 days or more;

    (4) the corporation does not notify the Secretary of State within 60 days that its registered agent or office has been changed, the agent resigned, or the office discontinued; or

    (5) the corporation's period of duration in the articles has expired.

- The corporation must receive notice of the administrative dissolution and it has a right to correct the ground for such dissolution.

The Corporation After Dissolution

- After dissolution, or expiration of the duration stated in the articles of incorporation, the corporation's existence continues to allow it to:

    (1) prosecute and defend lawsuits;

    (2) gradually settle and close its affairs;

    (3) dispose of and convey its property; and

    (4) make distributions to its shareholders of any assets remaining after the payment of its debts and obligations.

- The corporation may not, however, continue the business for which it was established.

- The Secretary of State normally has the power to revive a corporation after dissolution for any purpose, irrespective of the period of time having elapsed since dissolution and of the method of dissolution.

TAKEOVERS AND CORPORATE CONTROL TRANSACTIONS

Tender Offers

DEFINITION ▶ A **tender offer** is a public (usually published) solicitation by a bidder (the individual, group, or corporation) of the publicly held shares of the corporation to be acquired (the **target**).

- Target companies have developed a number of defensive tactics against takeover attempts. One technique involves finding a more acceptable bidder (**white knight**). Another is creating classes of stock that increase in rights if any person acquires more than a specified percentage of shares, making the acquisition more expensive to the bidder (**poison pills**).

State Regulation

- Anti-takeover statutes prevent the acquirer from exercising control of the shares unless the prior shareholders approve, despite the acquirer's possession of a controlling block of shares. If the acquirer fails to win voting rights from the prior shareholders, the target corporation may redeem the control shares.

Federal Regulation of Tender Offers

In General

- A party that directly or indirectly acquires more than 5% ownership of a corporation must disclose, within 10 days of passing the 5% threshold, certain information, such as:

  (1) the party's identity and number of shares held;

  (2) the source and amount of funds for making share purchases;

  (3) any arrangements the party has with others concerning shares of the target; and

  (4) the party's purposes in acquiring the shares, and intentions regarding the target.

- A bidder must disclose, on the day it commences its tender offer, the information required by 5% owners and:

  (1) the purpose of the tender offer;

  (2) the bidder's plans for the target;

  (3) past negotiations between the bidder and the target;

  (4) the bidder's financial statements (if material);

  (5) regulatory approvals that may be necessary; and

  (6) any other material information.

- The SEC requires tender offers to be kept open for at least 20 business days. If the offeror increases the price, then the offer must be kept open for at least 10 days after the announcement of the increase.

- Section 14(e) prohibits any false or misleading statements or omissions, as well as any fraudulent, deceptive, or manipulative acts, in connection with any tender offers.

Requirements for Section 16(b) Actions

- In a Section 16(b) action, both the target corporation and the tendering and non-tendering shareholders may sue for damages.

- The plaintiff must prove injury caused directly by the defendant, or through reliance on the defendant's misrepresentations or omissions.

- To obtain injunctive relief under Section 16(b), the plaintiff must show a substantial probability that a violation has occurred, or that an irreparable injury will occur.

SHAREHOLDER LITIGATION

Direct Suits

> **RULE**   In a **direct suit**, a shareholder sues on his own behalf to redress an injury to his interest as a shareholder.

- Causes of action held to be direct include suits to:

  (1) compel payment of dividends;

  (2) enforce the right to inspect corporate records;

(3) protect preemptive rights;

(4) enforce the right to vote; and

(5) recover for breach of a shareholders' agreement, a preincorporation agreement, or a contract with a shareholder.

■ In a direct suit, the damages go to the shareholder bringing the suit; in a derivative suit, the damages go to the corporation.

Derivative Suits

 In a **derivative suit**, a shareholder sues on behalf of the corporation to redress a wrong to the corporation when it fails to enforce its right. A derivative suit is an equitable action, and often involves breach of fiduciary duty.

■ A derivative action may not be maintained if it appears that the plaintiff does not fairly and adequately represent the interests of the shareholders similarly situated in enforcing the right of the corporation.

■ In a derivative suit, the plaintiff must allege in his complaint that:

(1) he was a shareholder at the time of the transaction complained of, or that his shares thereafter devolved upon him by operation of law (e.g., inheritance) from a person who was a shareholder at that time; and

(2) the action is not a collusive one to confer jurisdiction on a court of the United States that it would not otherwise have.

■ A shareholder must first attempt to persuade the board of directors to enforce the corporation's right, by making a written demand upon the board. A shareholder's complaint must allege with particularity his efforts to secure from the board of directors such action as he desires.

■ Upon a motion by the corporation, a court will dismiss a derivative proceeding if a majority of independent directors, or a majority of a committee consisting of two or more independent directors (a special litigation committee appointed by the board of directors), has determined in good faith, after conducting a reasonable inquiry upon which its conclusions are based, that a derivative proceeding is not in the best interests of the corporation.

■ Since shareholders in a derivative suit stand in the shoes of the corporation, they are subject to the same defenses that could have been raised against the corporation.

■ Other shareholders may wish to intervene in either direct or derivative suits involving their corporation. A person is entitled to intervene when he claims an interest relating to the property or transaction that is the subject of the action and is so situated that the disposition of the action may as a practical matter impair or impede his ability to protect that interest, unless the applicant's interest is adequately represented by existing parties.

LIMITED LIABILITY COMPANIES

Purpose and Characteristics

DEFINITION A **limited liability company** is an unincorporated association, without perpetual duration, having one or more members, and is organized and operated pursuant to a state's LLC statute.

■ A limited liability company is treated like a corporation for limited liability purposes in protecting its members, managers, and agents from liability for the obligations of the company, but if properly organized, it has the attributes of a partnership for federal income tax purposes.

DEFINITION A **professional limited liability company** is organized for the sole purpose of rendering those professional services enumerated, and has, as its members, individuals who are licensed or otherwise duly authorized to render the professional services for which the limited liability company is organized.

■ A member will not be liable for any debts or claims against the professional limited liability company, or the acts or omissions of the professional limited liability company or any other member or employee not under the member's supervision.

Organization and Permitted Ownership

■ A limited liability company must file **articles of organization** with the Secretary of State in which it is organized.

■ LLC names, which must be distinguishable from the name of any other LLC organized or doing business, must contain the word "limited company" or "limited liability company," or the abbreviations "L.C." or "L.L.C." In addition, the name must not include any word or phrase (a long list is set forth in the act) that implies or infers association with a government entity.

■ LLCs are governed by the **operating agreement**, a document similar to a corporation's bylaws that governs the LLC's internal affairs.

■ One or more individuals or entities are required to form a limited liability company.

Control and Management

■ Absent an operating agreement or a controlling provision in the articles of organization to the contrary, control of a limited liability company lies with the members in proportion to their equity in the LLC at the time a vote is taken.

■ The members of a limited liability company may agree to appoint one or more managers to operate the business, in which case the limited liability company is **manager-managed**. If the members decide not to appoint managers, the limited liability company is **member-managed**.

Owner Liability and Ownership Rights

■ No member, manager, or agent of a limited liability company will have any personal obligation for the liabilities of the company, whether such liabilities arise in contract, tort, or otherwise.

■ Courts may pierce the veil of a limited liability company, however, under circumstances similar to those of a corporation: alter ego liability (when the LLC is a mere instrumentality), inadequate capitalization, and failure to comply with corporate formalities.

■ Members may bring direct actions against the LLC when injured personally by the LLC or derivative actions on behalf of the LLC in the same way that a shareholder may bring a derivative action on behalf of the corporation.

■ A limited liability company has complete flexibility in structuring classes of membership interests, each with different management and control rights, capital and other obligations, preferences with respect to distributions and other economic benefits, voting privileges, and other privileges the members wish to address.

Family Law

Family Law

DEFINITIONS

Marriage: the civil status or relationship created by the legal union of two persons as a married couple which imposes on the spouses certain duties and responsibilities that are in effect during the marriage, with certain rights accruing at legal termination of the marital relationship and upon the death of one of the spouses

Premarital Agreement: contracts made by the parties prior to and in contemplation of marriage, generally attempting to alter or extinguish the spouses' property and/or support rights otherwise recognized by law

Annulment: a judgment declaring the invalidity of a void or voidable marriage

Void Marriage: a marriage that is of no legal effect and never was

Voidable Marriage: a marriage that results from an impediment intended for the protection of a disadvantaged party; it is valid until the aggrieved party obtains an annulment

Separation Agreement: an agreement between the parties which is executed in contemplation of separation or divorce, which may settle issues of property division and alimony

Separate Property: property that is not subject to equitable distribution because it is premarital property; exchange property; income from and appreciation of premarital property; property acquired by gift, bequest, devise, or descent; an award; or property acquired by a spouse pursuant to an order of legal separation

Marital Property: all property that is not separate property acquired by either or both spouses during the marriage up to the date of the final divorce hearing and owned by either or both spouses as of the date of filing of the complaint

KEY TOPICS

- Annulment
- Creation of the Marriage Relationship
- Divorce Decree
- Divorce Proceedings
- Interstate Aspects of Decrees and Orders
- Legal Effects of the Ongoing Marital Relationship
- Parents and Children

IMPORTANT RULES OF LAW

- In addition to terminating the marital relationship and related legal effects, a divorce decree may determine the respective rights of the parties with regard to division of property, spousal support or alimony, and child support, custody, and visitation.

- The United States Constitution requires domicile of one of the parties as a basis for a state court to exercise divorce jurisdiction. Domicile generally requires both physical presence in the state and the intent to make the state a permanent home. Subject matter jurisdiction is established over the marital status by virtue of the domicile of one of the parties within the state at the time of filing the action, whether or not the parties lived there as a couple.

- Custody and visitation will be determined according to the best interests of the child. The prevailing view is that a court may modify a custody order upon proof of a material and substantial change in circumstances such that a change in custody will be conducive to the best interests of the child.

GETTING MARRIED

Marriage

Nature of Marriage

DEFINITION ▷ A **marriage** is the civil status or relationship created by the legal union of two persons. The relationship imposes on the spouses certain duties and responsibilities that are in effect during the marriage, with certain rights accruing at legal termination of the marital relationship and upon the death of one of the spouses.

- The law of domestic relations today is actually a complex mixture of rights and duties arising from:

  (1) the "status" of the spouses as married persons, with many rights and obligations dictated by statute and case law;

  (2) the spouses' voluntary contractual agreements with each other as independent parties; and

  (3) the sharing of life and life's work that occurs in marriage, which has given rise to an understanding of marriage as a merger or intimate partnership relationship.

RIGHTS GRANTED BY THE U.S. CONSTITUTION	
Right to Marry	The right to marry is fundamental in nature and subject to protection under both the **Equal Protection Clause** and the **Due Process Clause**.
Right to Engage in Intimate Relationships	Under the Due Process Clause, states may not criminalize consensual sexual relationships between adults.
Right to Use Contraception	The Supreme Court has long protected the right of adults—whether married or single—to use contraception and otherwise make decisions about whether to bear or beget children.
Right to Have an Abortion	States may not impose an undue burden on a woman's right to terminate a pregnancy.
Right to Make Family-Based Decisions	Fit parents have the right to make decisions about the care, control, and upbringing of their children. The state may not interfere with that right unless necessary to protect children from harm.
Right to Live with Family Members	States or localities cannot enact zoning ordinances or other regulations that ban individuals who are related by blood, marriage, or adoption from living together.
Right to Have a Meaningful Relationship with One's Child	Biological parents have the right to pursue a meaningful parent-child relationship with their offspring. For mothers, this right is more or less absolute. Fathers must have the opportunity to establish a meaningful parent-child relationship, but if they do not avail themselves of the opportunity to establish parent-child ties, they may be held to forfeit their rights.

Breach of Promise to Marry

- Generally, there is no cause of action in tort for breach of a promise to marry (or for "seduction"), and likewise, tort claims for deceit, misrepresentation, or to recover for emotional distress in connection with a breach of a promise to marry, are not actionable.

RULE ▷ At common law, a promise to marry was legally enforceable, with damages for breach. However, this cause of action has been abolished in most jurisdictions by statutes known as **anti-heart balm acts**.

Gifts in Contemplation of Marriage

- A gift is complete and **irrevocable** so that the gift recipient becomes the new owner of the asset if:

  (1)   the donor intends, unconditionally, to make a gift to the donee at that time;

  (2)   the property is delivered to the donee; and

  (3)   the donee accepts the property.

- A gift is made **in consideration (or contemplation) of marriage** under circumstances indicating that the donor intended the gift:

  (4)   to be subject to a condition subsequent, namely, that the donor and donee later marry; and

  (5)   would not have been made without expectation of marriage.

Premarital Agreements

Nature and Validity

DEFINITION ▶ **Premarital agreements** (also called prenuptial or antenuptial agreements) are contracts made by the parties prior to marriage and in contemplation of marriage, generally attempting to alter or extinguish the spouses' property and/or support rights.

- A valid premarital agreement becomes effective upon a formal marriage between the parties. If the marriage is later declared void, the agreement remains effective to the extent necessary to avoid an inequitable result.

- Premarital agreements are generally valid devices to resolve disputes between spouses in the event of divorce, as well as a means for estate planning in the event of death.

- Generally, the issues considered for enforcement are:

  (1)   Have basic contract formation rules been satisfied?

  (2)   Was there procedural fairness (disclosure of certain financial information) when the contract was formed?

  (3)   Are the terms in the agreement substantively fair?

- In general, it is difficult to successfully challenge the enforcement of a premarital agreement, as modern law emphasizes the importance of freedom to contract.

Voluntariness

- All states and the UPAA allow a challenge to enforcement of the contract if a party can prove that he or she did not execute the agreement voluntarily.

- Voluntariness is evaluated under the usual common law standard in contract situations. The agreement will be enforced unless the challenger can show that the agreement was the product of fraud or duress.

- Courts generally have not found that presenting the agreement to the spouse on the eve of the wedding, and threatening to call it off if the agreement is not signed, constitutes sufficient duress to invalidate the agreement for lack of voluntariness. However, pressured timing is relevant and may contribute to a duress claim if combined with other facts.

- Most states do not require independent counsel as a precondition to enforcing an agreement against an objecting party, but the assistance or at least availability of counsel may be a factor in the assessment of voluntariness. The UPAA does not require the assistance of independent counsel for each party. Limited language skills and lack of practical alternatives for one party may be factors showing unconscionability, however, in the absence of independent counsel.

Lack of Adequate Disclosure

- Prenuptial agreements can also be challenged for lack of adequate financial disclosure. The disclosure standard, as set forth in the UPAA and typically followed under state laws, is that before execution of the agreement, the challenger:

  (1) was not provided a fair and reasonable disclosure of the property or financial obligations of the other party;

  (2) did not voluntarily and expressly waive, in writing, any right to disclosure of the property or financial obligations of the other party beyond the disclosure provided; and

  (3) did not have, or reasonably could not have had, an adequate knowledge of the property and financial obligations of the other party.

- While full financial disclosure is not required in every case, such as where the parties have a fairly accurate knowledge of each other's financial condition, a party may demand it. Many jurisdictions have indicated that a "fair and reasonable disclosure" requires the parties to provide each other with a general approximation of their income, assets, and liabilities, preferably in a written schedule.

Substantive Unfairness or Procedural Unfairness: The Majority Approach

- In most states, courts will evaluate a premarital agreement for the substantive fairness of its provisions. Accordingly, in most states, an antenuptial agreement can be invalidated based on a finding of either procedural or substantive unfairness.

- In contrast, the language of the UPAA itself requires both procedural and substantive unfairness in order to invalidate a premarital agreement. States generally have not followed this aspect of the UPAA. This important difference is one example of how, even among the jurisdictions that have adopted the UPAA, there are differing versions of some provisions, and differing interpretations on many of the issues related to substantive and procedural fairness.

- Although it is unlikely as the standards are similar and overlapping, the UPAA unconscionability standard tracks contract law and may be more difficult to prove than the arguably lesser demands of a substantive unreasonableness standard. In other words, it is possible that a fact situation could be substantively unfair but not necessarily rise to the level of unconscionability.

- In contrast to the UPAA, some states will evaluate the agreement at the time of enforcement, allowing the court to take into account changed circumstances such as changes in employment prospects, health, or the birth of children, since the time of signing.

- The American Law Institute's Principles of the Law of Family Dissolution ("ALI Principles") have not been officially adopted, but reflect aspects of the law of many states. The ALI Principles attempt to clarify some of the issues that have remained most unsettled under the UPAA.

- The ALI Principles, which apply to both prenuptial and post-nuptial agreements, articulate a balance between the parties' autonomy and concerns for fairness at the time of execution as well as at the time of enforcement. In a departure from the norm, the ALI Principles place the burden of proof on the party seeking enforcement, not on the challenger.

Subject Matter

- The subject of the agreement may include any provisions that do not violate public policy.

- Agreements concerning property division are permissible.

- The majority view, and modern trend, permits waiver of alimony by agreement. Even when permissible, states tend to more closely scrutinize agreements waiving spousal support upon divorce.

- In virtually all states, an agreement that abrogates, or even limits, the obligation of a parent to support his or her minor children during or after the marriage, is against public policy and is invalid.

- A premarital agreement may alter the spouses' ownership and powers of management of property during marriage and the expectations of creditors with respect to debts of the spouses and access to what would otherwise be marital or community property.

Legal Requirements for Marriage

Formal Marriage

- The majority of states require a formal marriage, meaning that there must be a state-issued marriage license and solemnization (a ceremony) by a state-authorized official.

Marriage License Requirements

- Both parties must generally appear before the clerk of the local probate or family court to obtain a marriage license.

- Most states no longer require a premarital blood test to show the absence of sexually transmitted diseases, but they may require that the applicants receive information about sexually-transmitted and/or genetically-transmitted diseases.

- Many states impose a short waiting period between the filing of the application for a marriage license and the issuance of the license.

Solemnization; Performance by Authorized Official

- Once a marriage license is issued, the ceremony may be performed by an authorized official prior to the expiration of the license. State law determines who may solemnize a marriage.

Failure to Comply With Formalities

- Lack of authority on behalf of the official performing the ceremony generally does not render the marriage invalid. Most states will forgive the mistake under a substantial compliance doctrine.

RULE ▶ In many states, even failure to obtain a marriage license will not invalidate the marriage, as long as the parties are eligible to marry and married in good faith that the marriage was valid. Other states will insist on strict formalities. Even so, the would-be spouses may yet get relief as **putative spouses**.

Informal or Common Law Marriage

In General

- Most states today do not recognize common law marriages. Yet even those that do not themselves recognize common law marriages created within the state will nonetheless recognize a common law marriage validly created in another state, unless the circumstances violate an important state public policy.

- The requirements for such marriages are generally as follows:

  (1) expression of intent;

  (2) cohabitation (that the parties must live together on an ongoing basis and consummate the relationship);

  (3) holding out (the parties represent themselves to others as a married couple);

  (4) legal capacity; and

  (5) burden of proof (generally, the burden of proving a common law marriage is on the party asserting it, and must be proven by clear and convincing evidence).

- **Expression of Intent:** Intent to be married can be demonstrated expressly, such as in an exchange of words or vows. Alternatively, intent can be implied based on upon the parties' behavior—i.e., acting like a married couple.

- **Cohabitation:** Cohabitation has been defined in various domestic relations contexts as consisting of more than a common residence and a sexual relationship. It requires carrying out certain mutual responsibilities in the everyday maintenance of the home and a financial relationship, as well as the intimate relationship between the parties.

- **Legal Capacity:** Legal capacity may arise subsequently, when an existing impediment is removed, such as by the death or divorce of the spouse of the prior marriage. Once legal capacity exists, a common law marriage may then arise if all of the other elements exist (i.e., intent, cohabitation, holding out).

Legal Impediments to Marriage

Nonage

- In most states today, a marriage license will not issue without the consent of a parent or guardian if either party is under 18.

Consanguinity and Affinity

- A marriage license generally will not be issued for marriages between relatives who are ancestor and descendant, brother and sister, uncle and niece, or aunt and nephew, whether of the whole blood or half blood.

Mental Incapacity, Lack of Consent, Fraud

- The inability of a party to consent to a marriage due to mental incapacity or infirmity will render the marriage invalid.

- Fraud must be proven in the same manner as fraud in other contexts under state law. Thus, the misrepresentation or failure to disclose must be intended to induce the other party to enter the marriage, and must be material, i.e., must cause reliance, or in some states, go to the "essence" of the marriage contract in order to invalidate a marriage.

- To invalidate a marriage, duress must be sufficient to override a party's free will. Threats of physical force may be required, and courts are reluctant to invalidate a marriage on this ground if the party had opportunity to escape the situation.

Physical Incapacity

- The ability to consummate the marriage is a common law requirement for marriage.

Prior Marriage Still in Force

- A person who has already been married is incapable of entering into another valid marriage unless the former spouse has died or the prior marriage has been judicially terminated.

- The fact that the second marriage was made in good faith under a reasonable belief that the former spouse was dead, will not render the marriage valid.

- Where a party has entered more than one marriage, there is a strong presumption in most states that the party's latest marriage is valid, and any earlier marriage was dissolved.

- By statute or case law in many states, in accord with the Uniform Marriage and Divorce Act view, a subsequent marriage that is initially invalid because one of the parties had a prior marriage in force, will become valid upon removal of the impediment of the prior marriage by death or dissolution. The following requirements typically must be met for this to occur:

  (1) at the time of the subsequent marriage, one of the parties to it believed, in good faith, that:

      (a) the other spouse to the former marriage was dead;

      (b) there had been a divorce; or

    (c)   there had been no former marriage;

  (2)   after the subsequent marriage, the parties lived together as a married couple; and

  (3)   they continued to live together as a married couple after the impediment had been removed.

- Bigamy is a crime in many states. A ban on polygamy has been upheld as constitutional even where it is a widely-held religious belief.

Putative Spouses

RULE ▶ Many states recognize a **putative spouse doctrine**, under which a putative spouse is granted divorce-like remedies at the dissolution of the relationship, even if the marriage is void because of a flaw in the marriage formation process. The doctrine provides an alternative when no marriage has been validly created.

Annulment

Challenges

- If the validity of a marriage is questioned, a party, and in some instances a third party, may seek a judgment declaring the invalidity of (annulling) the marriage. A marriage generally may be annulled whether the marriage is void or voidable.

- The primary difference between a void marriage and a voidable one is that only the aggrieved party may bring the action to annul a voidable marriage, during the life of both parties.

Grounds

- Most states distinguish between invalid marriages that are void and those that are voidable, but they may differ on which grounds fall into each category, particularly in instances of nonage.

- In either case, the grounds for annulment must have existed at the time of the marriage ceremony, not arising later.

Void Marriages

- A void marriage is of no legal effect.

- Although there is technically no need for a court decree of annulment in the case of a void marriage, a party may request a judicial determination of invalidity by means of an annulment action in order to clarify the rights of the parties.

Voidable Marriages

- A voidable marriage is valid until and unless the aggrieved party obtains an annulment.

- If a voidable marriage is confirmed or ratified by the aggrieved party or if one of the parties to the marriage dies, the validity of the marriage may not be questioned or attacked by any person.

Validity of Out-of-State Marriages

Principles of Comity

- Most states have adopted the view that a marriage which satisfies the requirements of the state where contracted "will everywhere be recognized as valid, unless it violates the strong public policy of another state which had the most significant relationship to the spouses and the marriage at the time of the marriage."

Evasion of State Law

- Most states do not recognize marriages entered into by their residents who leave the state to contract a marriage that would not be valid if contracted within the state, with the intention of continuing to reside in the state while attempting to evade its public policy against such marriages.

Rights of Unmarried Partners

Express and Implied Contracts

- Most states have followed the principle of Marvin v. Marvin in recognizing express and implied contracts between cohabiting persons by which they agree to support each other (pay "palimony") or share property, so long as there is consideration to support the contract other than the furnishing of sexual services because that would constitute an illegal contract. Marvin held that:

    (1) courts should enforce express oral or written contracts between nonmarital partners;

    (2) in the absence of an express contract, a court should inquire into the conduct of the parties to determine whether that conduct demonstrates an implied contract, partnership agreement or joint venture, or some other tacit understanding between the parties; and

    (3) courts may also employ the doctrine of *quantum meruit*, or equitable remedies such as constructive or resulting trusts, when warranted by the facts of the case.

- Some states are willing to enforce cohabiting partners' agreements or expectations so long as they are able to sever the "illegal," or sexual, components of the agreement from those that could be enforced between any two unrelated parties.

Domestic Partnerships and Civil Unions

- Some states have enacted a form of "domestic partnership" or "civil union" act under which domestic partners acquire rights similar, but not identical, to those of married partners.

Tort Recovery

- A majority of jurisdictions would be unlikely to extend tort recovery for emotional distress to a cohabitant, even a cohabiting fiancée, who witnesses a serious accident injuring or killing the other cohabitant.

- Compensation for loss of consortium is likewise available only to the legally recognized spouse of the injured party, not to a fiancée or cohabitant.

EXAM TIP To distinguish a common law marriage from a putative marriage or from an unmarried cohabiting relationship, consider the parties' state of mind.

- A **common law marriage** cannot be entered without present ability and intent. (The requirements closely mirror those for a formal marriage, but the official ceremony and license is missing. If valid, when and where entered, a common law marriage creates full marital rights.)
- A **putative spouse** legitimately thinks he is legally married because there was a ceremony, and he is unaware of an impediment or procedural flaw. (The putative spouse may have equitable spousal inheritance rights at the death of the other party, but rights of property division and support are generally determined by annulment remedies.)
- **Unmarried partners** know they are not married because there has been no legal ceremony and either they cannot marry or at least one of them doesn't intend to. (They may have statutory, contractual, or equitable rights that vary greatly in different states.)

LEGAL EFFECTS OF THE ONGOING MARITAL RELATIONSHIP

Family Privacy

- **Common Law Doctrine:** Under the common law, a family's home is subject to privacy, and its internal affairs generally cannot be regulated or interfered with by the government or the courts.

Spousal Property Rights During Marriage: During Life

Title Rules

- Most states are so-called "separate property" states where the spouse with title to property is the legal owner. Neither spouse has a vested interest in property over which they do not have formal title. During ongoing marriage there is no "marital property" that would prevent a title-holding spouse from conveying marital property to a third party during the marriage.

- In contrast, spouses in one of the nine community-property states have a present interest in community property before termination of the marriage. Community property states also have special rules on the spousal power to manage community property during the marriage that affect the power of conveyance, but where the property is held in one spouse's name alone, there may be a presumption that that spouse has the power to convey the property without joinder by the other spouse.

Married Women's Property Rights

- Today a married woman retains her rights to her separate property held before or acquired after her marriage. She has the power to contract with her spouse or with third parties, to grant or receive conveyances of real or personal property, and to sue and be sued in her own right.

Co-Ownership

- Often spouses choose to own property jointly in a form that may avoid potential difficulties upon the death of one of the parties. Concurrent estates recognized at common law include joint tenancies, tenancies in common, and tenancies by the entirety.

- The tenancy in common does not carry inherent survivorship rights. Generally, rights of survivorship are implied if the grant specifies a "joint tenancy."

- A tenancy by the entirety, recognized in a significant minority of states, is the only form of joint ownership that requires an existing marital relationship between the co-owners. Unlike joint tenants, a tenant by the entirety cannot unilaterally destroy the other tenant's right of survivorship nor alienate his interest in the property without the other spouse's consent.

- Some states have enacted statutes that convert a conveyance to a married couple in the form of a tenancy by the entirety into a joint tenancy with rights of survivorship or a tenancy in common. In many common law states today, the default for transfers of real property to a married couple is a tenancy in common, unless a joint tenancy is expressly declared.

- A tenancy by the entirety is converted into a tenancy in common by a judgment terminating a marriage, unless the court orders otherwise through an order of equitable distribution.

Transfers Between Spouses

- Transfers of real and personal property between spouses are generally valid to the same extent as if they were unmarried. When one spouse transfers money or other property to the other without consideration, there is a rebuttable presumption that it is a gift.

- For the protection of third parties, however, statutes may provide that when a married couple live together, no transfer or conveyance of goods and chattels between the spouses will be valid against any third person, unless the transfer is in writing and filed in the same manner as security interests where possession of the property is to remain with the person giving security.

Transfers to Third Parties

- A married person may transfer real or personal property that he owns separately.

- Property owned as tenants by the entirety cannot be transferred without the consent of the spouse, but other jointly owned property generally can be. The spouse can transfer only his own interest in such property, however, severing the joint ownership.

- In community property states, property that is subject to joint management requires both spouses to join in the conveyance, so creditors generally require this for their protection, although some community property may be eligible for conveyance by one spouse alone.

Spousal Property Rights During Marriage: Upon Death

- Virtually all non-community property states today have effectively abolished dower and curtesy, which provided certain property rights to a surviving spouse. Now, instead, there are family protection devices, such as homestead and an elective share for a spouse who is not provided for, or feels inadequately provided for, in the deceased spouse's will. Dower and curtesy were not needed in the community property states.

Support Obligations

Duty of Both Spouses

- Spouses have a legal duty to support each other. Courts first ascertain which of the spouses or parents is able to provide support, and then place the obligation on that person without regard to gender-based distinctions.

- The duty of support is generally not enforceable by a spouse directly during the marriage, however. Most states provide civil remedies and criminal penalties for nonsupport and desertion, allowing the state to enforce family support obligations so that needy individuals do not become public charges.

Liability for Debts and Necessaries Contracted for by Needy Spouse

- A corollary to the duty of support is the **necessaries doctrine**, which is a tool for creditors. There is a reciprocal obligation on the part of each spouse to provide for necessaries furnished to the other spouse based on the respective spouses' needs and financial ability.

- The majority of states recognize a doctrine of necessaries whereby a spouse's liability for obligations incurred by the other spouse arises in three primary situations:

    (1) where the debtor-spouse has express or apparent authority to pledge the other's credit for household expenses;

    (2) where the non-needy spouse neglects, fails, or refuses to furnish the needy spouse with necessaries which are then supplied to that spouse by a third person with expectation of payment; and

    (3) where one spouse has incurred medical expenses beyond his sole ability to pay.

- Some states have "family expense" statutes that impose joint liability on both spouses. Others impose primary liability on the spouse who directly incurred the debt or liability and secondary liability on the other spouse.

- A few states have abrogated the doctrine of necessaries entirely, holding neither spouse liable for debts incurred by the other spouse, absent an express agreement with the creditor.

- Once there is a separate support decree in most states, a spouse's legal obligation is set by the decree, and the spouse would no longer be liable to third persons for necessaries furnished to the other spouse.

Contract Liability

- Contract liability is generally based on which spouse contracted the debt, unless it is a contract for necessaries. Contracts may be made and liabilities incurred by either spouse and may be enforced against that person to the same extent as if unmarried. Generally, the liabilities of each spouse are determined by the express terms of their agreements with creditors and other third parties.

Tort Liability

Interspousal Immunity

- The modern view favors complete abolition of interspousal immunity, such that certain suits between spouses are generally permitted. Virtually all states have at least partially abolished the doctrine.

- States have taken different positions on whether such suits should be allowed for intentional torts committed by one spouse upon another, or for negligence actions, particularly involving insured motor vehicles. Such situations have typically been assessed with regard to whether abolition of immunity would tend to disrupt the peace and harmony of the marital home or possibly encourage collusive fraud upon insurance companies.

Torts Against the Marital Relationship

- Most states have abolished:

  (1) the common law tort of alienation of affections against a third party who causes separation from the plaintiff's spouse resulting in loss of consortium; and

  (2) the common law tort of criminal conversation against a third party who has sexual intercourse with the plaintiff's spouse.

- **Elements of Tort Recovery:** A spouse may recover consequential damages that derive from an underlying tort against the other spouse.

- **Loss of Consortium:** Loss of consortium refers to the loss of benefits that one spouse is entitled to receive from the other, including companionship, cooperation, aid, affection, and sexual relations. Today, most states permit this form of recovery for either spouse as an element of damages in a negligence action for injuries to the other spouse.

Vicarious Tort Liability

- A spouse is not vicariously liable for torts committed by the other spouse. This is a departure from prior law, under which a husband was liable for his wife's torts.

Criminal Liability and Domestic Violence

- Spouses can be held accountable for criminal conduct, including rape. All 50 states and the District of Columbia make protective orders available as a civil remedy to victims of domestic violence.

- Typically, the following acts may give rise to a protective order:

  (1) attempting to cause, or intentionally, knowingly, or recklessly causing bodily injury or a sexual offense;

  (2) placing another in reasonable fear of imminent serious bodily injury;

  (3) false imprisonment; or

  (4) physical or sexual abuse of minor children.

Postnuptial Property Agreements

- The rules applying to postnuptial agreements are generally the same as those applicable to prenuptial agreements. The UPAA, governing premarital agreements, does not, by its terms, apply to postnuptial agreements, but some states have extended the same principles to postnuptial agreements.

- The law encourages spouses who have decided to change or end their marital relationships to use separation agreements to settle their affairs. An agreement is generally negotiated after the cause for separation has occurred and while the parties are separated.

- States differ as to whether they find a confidential relationship between the parties before marriage as they do after marriage. Separation agreements must be fairly and voluntarily made and will be upheld in the absence of fraud, duress, concealment, or overreaching. In addition, there may be a requirement of full and fair financial disclosure between the parties.

- **Contract Principles Govern:** The agreement is a contract between the parties and is governed by ordinary contract principles. If intended as a complete and final settlement (i.e., fully integrated) it will bar all further claims by either party. It must be supported by consideration, and each party's waiver of rights in the property or estate of the other spouse is sufficient consideration.

- **Modification or Termination of Agreement:** The agreement may only be modified by mutual consent of the parties. The parties may expressly or impliedly agree to terminate or revoke the agreement. If both parties act in a manner inconsistent with the terms of the agreement, a court may find mutual consent to terminate the agreement. Subsequent cohabitation by the parties after reconciliation will void the agreement, but only if such intent is manifested by the parties.

PARENTS AND CHILDREN

Establishing Parenthood

Presumption of Marital Legitimacy / Paternity

- Paternity may be established because of marriage. Common law rules, supplemented by statutes in many states, reflect a strong presumption that children born to or conceived by a woman while she is married are the children of the woman and her husband.

- This presumption may only be rebutted on facts proving, by clear and convincing evidence, that the mother's husband was not the father. There are varying state laws on whether and when evidence of biological paternity will be allowed to rebut the presumption. Many states will allow DNA evidence to challenge the husband's paternity within a few years of the child's birth.

- The doctrine of estoppel may operate to confirm the marital presumption of paternity.

- Most states have enacted statutes providing that children born to parents whose marriage was invalid are, nevertheless, legitimate. Under the Uniform Parentage Act ("UPA"), as adopted in some states, every child is deemed to be the legitimate child of both natural parents, regardless of the parents' marital status.

- The UPA provides presumptions of paternity, which may only be rebutted by results of genetic testing introduced in a paternity proceeding, if the man and the child's natural mother:

  (1) are or have been married to each other, regardless of whether the marriage is or could be declared invalid, and the child was conceived or born during such marriage or within 300 days after its termination;

  (2) married each other after the child's birth and the man voluntarily asserted his paternity, such as by agreeing to be named as the child's father on the birth certificate; or

(3)   for the first two years of the child's life, resided in the same household with the child and the man openly held out the child as his own.

Actions Brought by a Putative Father

- In the interest of preserving intact families, states may take a different view of assertions of parenthood by an alleged ("putative") father when the child has a presumed father. In Michael H. v. Gerald D., the U.S. Supreme Court upheld a California statute that precluded a biological father from bringing a paternity action when the mother of his child was married at the time of the child's birth, and she did not join in the paternity petition.

- In the wake of the Michael H. opinion, many states have enacted statutes that give an unmarried father no more than two years to establish his paternity when his alleged child has a presumed father, deeming a two-year period sufficient to resolve the issue without subjecting the child to a long period of possibly unsettled circumstances.

Establishing Maternity

- Due to issues arising from assisted reproduction methods and surrogacy arrangements, the UPA now recognizes that maternity may also be established by adjudication.

Actions to Establish Paternity

- **Statute of Limitations:** Most states allow paternity actions to be brought at any time prior to the child reaching the age of 18. However, many states require that a paternity action be instituted prior to the death of the putative father.

- **Evidence of Paternity:** Evidence to establish paternity may include the following:

    (1)   evidence that there was sexual intercourse between the mother and the defendant at or near the time of conception and that the child was likely born as a result;

    (2)   medical evidence regarding the defendant's paternity based upon genetic tests performed by experts; and

    (3)   any other relevant evidence.

- **Level of Accuracy of Test Results:** The test results are admissible only where they definitely exclude the defendant as the father. Under the UPA, genetic testing results create a rebuttable presumption of paternity if the results show that the man has at least a 99% probability of being the father.

- **Burden of Proof:** Many states permit a finding of paternity to be made by a preponderance of the evidence, although some require a higher standard of "clear and convincing evidence." Where a married woman is seeking to prove that someone other than her husband is the father of her child, a higher standard of proof must be met because of the presumption of legitimacy. This presumption can only be overcome by clear and convincing evidence that someone other than her husband is the child's father.

Acknowledgment or Legitimation

- Federal law provides that a valid, unrescinded, unchallenged acknowledgment of paternity is to be treated as equivalent to a judicial determination of paternity.

- The father may voluntarily legitimize the child in various ways under state laws. Most states permit the establishment of paternity by the filing of an acknowledgment of paternity executed by both parents and filed with a court or other office.

Rights of Children Born Out-of-Wedlock

- **Support:** Nonmarital children are constitutionally guaranteed equal rights to support as marital children.

- **Inheritance:** In addition, by statute in most states today, a nonmarital child is given the same rights to inherit from the intestate estate of the mother as a marital child, and also from the child's natural father if the decedent's paternity of the child is properly shown. The state may require, however, that paternity have been proved during the life of the alleged father in order to inherit from him.

■ **Wrongful Death:** Nonmarital children also have equal rights to sue for a parent's wrongful death and recover applicable wrongful death benefits.

Nature of Parental Rights

Custody and Control of Children

■ If both parents are living, competent, and have not been found to be unfit, they are entitled to custody of the minor and to direct his education and medical care. If one parent dies and the remaining parent is competent and not unfit, the remaining parent has these rights, superior to all others.

■ For a non-parent to seek custody or visitation rights over a child with living parent(s), significant deference must be given to a legal parent's objection to visitation. However, the Supreme Court has not specified what weight must be given to a parent's decision. The court suggested that a requirement of a finding of parental unfitness or harm to the child to override a parent's decision likely would satisfy the constitution's demands.

■ Third parties seeking custodial or visitation rights who show a substantial, *in loco parentis* relationship with the child, i.e., in the nature of a surrogate parent who has exercised custody over the child in place of the legal parent, are treated more favorably, and may have standing to sue for custody, but still have to overcome the parental preference.

Education of Children

■ The Supreme Court has found that:

(1) states may require up to an eighth-grade education but not more, where the parents' religious beliefs require the children to be kept home;

(2) states may not forbid the teaching of languages other than English to children in the eighth grade or below; and

(3) parents have a right to choose between public and private school for their children to satisfy compulsory education requirements.

Medical Decisions

■ Statutes in all states require the consent of parents to medical care for their children, except in emergency situations. Parents who refuse to allow "necessary" medical procedures to save the life of their child may be found guilty of neglect and a guardian may be appointed to make medical decisions.

Support Rights and Obligations

Parental Obligation to Support Child

■ As a general rule, a parent's obligation to support a child is terminated when the child reaches the age of majority (18 in most states). Some states require parents to continue to support a child beyond the age of majority where the child is incapable of self-support by reason of mental or physical disability.

■ **Emancipation:** A minor child who is legally "emancipated" need not be supported by the parent. See further discussion of emancipation below in connection with termination of parental rights.

Obligation to Support Parent

- Some states impose a statutory duty on adults to support their parents or other close relatives who are in danger of becoming public charges. Support obligations of this nature are typically not enforceable directly by the individual relative but are for the benefit of government agencies that have expended funds for the individual's support.

Tort and Contract Liability

Torts Committed by Child

- **Liability of Child:** Except where the age of a child prevents the child from forming the state of mind necessary for the commission of the tort, a child is generally liable for his torts. A child is liable for negligence where the child has failed to exercise the degree of care expected of the ordinary child of comparable age, knowledge, and experience.

- **Liability of Parent:** All states have enacted "parental responsibility" laws that make parents either civilly or criminally liable for the acts of their children. While all states have some form of statutory civil remedy against parents, states vary greatly in their restrictions on liability. Most states limit responsibility to situations of malicious or intentional acts by the child, and more than 25% of states restrict liability only to property damage. Some states impose strict liability on the parents for willful damage to property of another by an unemancipated minor, up to a specified dollar amount.

Torts Committed Against a Child

- **Parent-Child Immunity:** Most states have abolished the common law parent-child immunity doctrine such that it is not an absolute bar to suits against the parent by the child. However, states vary in the types of suits that are permitted.

- Some states have abolished parent-child immunity only for intentional personal injuries to the child, some for any negligently caused injuries, and some have done so only with regard to motor vehicle negligence actions or other actions covered by insurance.

- **Recovery for Injury to the Child:** An action by a minor who is injured by the negligence of another may typically be commenced by a parent or next friend or guardian who brings suit on behalf of the minor. A second cause of action may arise in favor of the parent to recover for consequential damages as a result of the injury to the child. The parent may sue for loss of the services of the child, loss of consortium, medical expenses paid by the parent, and related matters.

Minor's Contract Liability

- The age of majority in most states today, for most purposes, is 18 years. Persons over 18 thus have full legal rights—e.g., they can marry without parental consent, make a will, form a contract, and select their own domicile apart from their parents.

- Conversely, minors under age 18 do not have full capacity to contract. There is no "mature minor" exception to distinguish adolescents from younger children in this regard. Under the common law, a contract entered into by a minor is, in general, voidable at the option of the minor. This rule of law was designed to protect minors from improvident bargains and injustice, but the contract may be disaffirmed even if the minor is sophisticated, and the contract is highly beneficial to the minor.

- Contracts for necessaries may not be avoided by the minor, but the minor is liable for the reasonable value of the necessaries, rather than the contract price.

- A minor has until a reasonable time after reaching the age of majority to disaffirm the contract. Failure to disaffirm the contract during this time period may constitute a ratification of the contract.

Termination of Parental Rights

Introduction

- Parental rights and obligations involving a child may be terminated by actions of the child (**emancipation**), the parent (**relinquishment**), and/or the state (**involuntary termination**).

Emancipation

- The financial independence and maturity of the child are generally important considerations in a finding of emancipation. A child who voluntarily leaves the custodial parent's home, or who willfully fails to abide by the reasonable rules of the custodial parent, however, may be found to have forfeited the right to support. More recent cases tend to focus more on the dependency of the child for support than on whether the parents disapprove of their child's behavior, such as bearing a child out of wedlock.

- A minor who marries before the age of majority is generally emancipated under state law unless, in some states, neither the minor nor the minor's spouse can provide sufficient support.

Voluntary Relinquishment of Parental Rights

- Parental rights may be lost by the parent's voluntary relinquishment of parental rights. States typically have statutory formalities such as that an affidavit for voluntary relinquishment of parental rights must be:

  (1) signed by the parent after the birth of the child, but usually not earlier than a specified period after the birth (such as 48 hours), to give the parent some time for reflection after the birth;

  (2) objectively confirmed such as an oath in front of witnesses; and

  (3) the affidavit may be required to state whether the relinquishment is revocable, irrevocable, or irrevocable for a stated period of time, or the state may permit only irrevocable relinquishment.

Involuntary Termination

Due Process Concerns

RULE ▶ **Notice of Termination of Parental Rights:** Parental rights cannot be terminated without notice and hearing. Such due process protections are extended only to legal and biological parents, not foster parents. An unwed father has a right to notice and hearing before termination of his parental rights, but these rights depend on his having made some efforts to establish a relationship with or take responsibility for the child.

- **Standard of Proof:** The involuntary termination of parental rights generally puts the parental right to custody and care of the child before the issue of the child's "best interest." Termination must be based upon a finding of parental unfitness proved by clear and convincing evidence.

- **No Right to Appointed Counsel:** The Supreme Court has declined to find a constitutional right to counsel for indigent parents contesting termination of parental rights.

Considerations

- A finding of parental unfitness may result from proof of at least one of the following conditions:

  (1) **abandonment**—the parent has failed to maintain a reasonable degree of interest, concern, or responsibility for the child's welfare for a specified period of time;

  (2) **neglect**—the child has been neglected, i.e., denied the care, guidance-or control necessary for his physical, educational, moral, or emotional well-being; or

  (3) **abuse**—inadequately explained serious physical injury to a child may constitute evidence sufficient for the termination of parental rights, and expert testimony may be required regarding the causes of the child's injuries or behavior and effects of emotional or physical abuse.

- In determining whether to terminate parental rights, a court may also consider, in addition to the negative factors justifying a finding of unfitness:

  (1) the child's positive emotional ties to his or her parents and to anyone else who has had custody of the child;

  (2) the parent's efforts to adjust his or her circumstances or conduct to make it in the child's best interests to remain in, or return to, the parent's home, including regular contact with the child and with the child's custodian; and

  (3) the extent to which a parent has been prevented from maintaining a meaningful relationship with the child by the unreasonable actions of the other parent or any other person or by the economic circumstances of the parent.

Adoption

Who May Be Adopted

RULE ▶ Usually, the object of adoption is a minor. A minor child is considered free for adoption if the child has no living parents or the rights of the parents have been terminated. Many states require the consent of the minor, where the minor is above a particular age, such as 12, although a court may override a minor's refusal to consent upon a finding of good cause.

- In many states, an adult may adopt another adult, but there may be restrictions on adopting close blood relatives. The Uniform Adoption Act recognizes adoptions of adults, but does not permit an adult to adopt his spouse.

Who May Adopt / Standing

- Persons who have the right to adopt have a legally protectable interest in the adoption, and therefore, also have the right to object to another person's petition to adopt.

- In order to adopt another, the adopting person generally must be of the age of majority.

- In most states, a married person may not adopt a child unless both spouses join in the adoption petition, unless the court excuses this requirement (or unless the other spouse is already the parent of the child).

Parental Consent

- Consent of the natural parents is generally required for adoption, unless they have waived their rights or been deemed "unfit" by clear and convincing evidence. In the case of a child born to unmarried parents, the consent of the biological father may be required (in addition to the consent of the mother) as a matter of equal protection where the father has established an ongoing parent-child relationship with the child.

- **Revocation of Consent:** The consent of a parent generally may be revoked upon proof of fraud or duress prior to the adoption decree. Some states impose time limits on revocation for other reasons. The Uniform Adoption Act would allow revocation of consent within 192 hours (eight days) after the child's birth.

- After the decree has been entered, revocation is generally limited to instances where there has been some substantial defect in the adoption process (such as a lack of the required notices or consents).

Procedure

- Where a child has living parents, the rights of the natural parents must first be terminated, either voluntarily or involuntarily, prior to adoption. In some states, termination of the rights of the natural parents and the approval of the adoption may be accomplished in one judicial proceeding.

- Replacement of the bond of natural parenthood with that of adoptive parents is subject to considerable scrutiny by the state, whether the adoption is handled by a state-run agency, a private agency, or private individuals.

Standard for Adoption

- A court will decide whether to grant a petition for adoption based on a determination of the child's best interests.

- Neither the State nor any other entity in the State that receives funds from the Federal Government and is involved in adoption or foster care placements may:

    (1) deny to any person the opportunity to become an adoptive or foster parent on the basis of the race, color, or national origin of the person or of the child involved; or

    (2) delay or deny the placement of a child for adoption or into foster care on the basis of the race, color, or national origin of the adoptive or foster parent or the child involved.

- Religion may be a consideration but typically not an exclusive one.

Effect of Decree

- A decree of adoption generally has the following effects:

    (1) it creates the relationship of parent and child between the adopting parent or parents and the adopted person, as if the adopted person were the natural child of such adopting parent or parents for all purposes, including inheritance;

    (2) it ends all legal relationships between the adopted person and the natural parents for all purposes, including inheritance, except for prohibitions against marriage, incest, and cohabitation;

    (3) the adopting parents or their relatives inherit the estate of an adopted child if he dies intestate; and

    (4) the adopted child's name will be changed and a new birth certificate will issue, including the names of the adopting parents and deleting the names of the natural parents.

- Some jurisdictions have refused to permit an adult adoptee to inherit through his adopted parent where it would frustrate the probable intent and expectations of a testator or settlor.

- The decree is not revocable or modifiable unless parental rights are terminated. Thus, a stepparent who adopts the spouse's child does not lose rights or responsibilities upon divorce from the spouse.

Confidentiality of Records

- Adoption records are generally confidential and may not be opened unless leave of court, for cause shown, is obtained. Many states today, however, allow an adopted person and the adopting parents access to certain types of information concerning the natural parents (such as medical information) without revealing the identity of the parties, or may even have procedures for accessing information as to identity after the child reaches adulthood.

Equitable Adoption or Parenthood by Estoppel

- The issue generally arises when at least one of the would-be adoptive parents dies, and the child, perhaps now grown, seeks to share in the estate (in abrogation of the statutory requirements for both adoption and inheritance). The effects of equitable adoption are generally limited to recognition of the child's inheritance rights. Courts have been reluctant to find equitable adoption in non-inheritance instances, including those:

    (1) involving claims of child support upon a stepparent who did not legally adopt the spouse's child; and

    (2) claims by a "de facto" parent to custody or visitation.

- The ALI Principles would recognize as a **parent by estoppel** a nonparent who has lived with the child since the child's birth, holding out and accepting full and permanent responsibilities as parent, as part of a prior co-parenting agreement with the child's legal parent to raise a child together, "each with full parental rights and responsibilities, when the court finds that recognition of the individual as a parent is in the child's best interests."

Alternatives to Adoption

Artificial Insemination

 Artificial insemination is a technique by which semen is artificially transferred to the body of a woman in order to make her pregnant.

- **Husband as Donor:** Where artificial insemination occurs by means of the husband's semen, few legal issues should develop, as the husband would be the biological father of any child conceived and, thus, subject to all rights and obligations of a father.

- **Third-Party Donor:** Where the woman is married but a third-party donor is used, the UPA provides that the child is the legal child of the mother's husband if he consented in writing.

- The latest version of the UPA also covers the situation where the mother is not married by providing that the donor is not a parent of a child conceived by means of assisted reproduction. The commentary further explains that the donor cannot sue to establish his parental rights nor can he be required to provide child support. However, in a state that has not adopted the UPA, there could be a different result.

Surrogacy

- **Nature of Motherhood:** As various means of assisted reproductive technology have developed, establishing the rights of motherhood, like fatherhood, has become more problematic where one woman gives birth and another intends to raise the child. It is generally agreed that a child can have only one "legal" mother (except perhaps in cases of lesbian couple adoptions), just as there can be only one legal father.

- **Role of Surrogate Mother:** The term **surrogate mother** generally refers to a woman who is artificially inseminated with the semen of a person to whom she has agreed to relinquish the child after birth. Thus, the surrogate mother is the biological or "natural" parent of the child because her egg is used. Surrogate mother may also be used to describe the situation where an egg is taken from party A, fertilized outside of the body, and then implanted into party B, as discussed below under the topic of in vitro fertilization. In this case, the birth mother has no genetic relationship to the child.

Legal Effects of Surrogacy Contract

- Whether a surrogacy contract is legally enforceable is unclear in many states. The contract may simply be viewed as an illegal contract to sell a child for adoption, violating public policy. More likely, courts will consider the genetic relationships and/or the parties' intent in sorting out their rights.

- The UPA takes the unequivocal position that "gestational agreements" should be recognized, under judicial supervision, with consents handled in a manner similar to adoption.

In Vitro Fertilization

- *In vitro* fertilization refers to the medical procedure by which a woman's egg is removed from her body, fertilized outside of her body in a test tube by means of a man's semen, and then implanted into a woman. It should be noted that the recipient of the fertilized egg may be the same woman whose egg was originally removed for fertilization purposes or the recipient may be a different woman (the latter situation sometimes is referred to as "gestational surrogacy").

- The law in this area is developing and the legal issues are murky. The following possibilities arise:

    (1) where the process occurs with the egg and semen of a wife and husband, and the fertilized egg is implanted into the wife, the child ought to be viewed as the legitimate child of the wife and husband;

    (2) where the semen is that of a third party donor and the egg is implanted into the woman from whom it was taken, the process ought to be treated in the same way as artificial insemination by donor; and

    (3) where an egg of one woman is fertilized and then implanted into a different woman with the agreement that the woman will serve as a "gestational surrogate," the law of surrogacy applies.

Embryos Implantation

- Alternatively, the fertilized egg may even be frozen for future use. Where *in vitro* fertilization has occurred using the eggs of a wife and the semen of her husband, and the fertilized eggs ("preembryos") were frozen for future use, a subsequent divorce between the parties may result in a dispute over "rights" to the frozen preembryos. Presumably, the disposition of the preembryos should be governed by any prior agreement of both parties.

- Where the parties have made no agreement concerning the disposition of their unused preembryos, either potential parent's interest in avoiding procreation (an interest of constitutional dimension) may prevent their transplantation into a third person or require their destruction.

DIVORCE PROCEEDINGS

Jurisdiction and Venue

Subject Matter Jurisdiction: Domicile and Residency Requirements

RULE ▶ **Domicile:** The United States Constitution requires domicile of one of the parties as a basis for a state court to exercise divorce jurisdiction. Subject matter jurisdiction is established over the marital status by virtue of the domicile of one of the parties within the state at the time of filing the action, whether or not the parties lived there as a couple.

- **Domicile** generally requires both physical presence in the state and the intent to make the state a permanent home. The parties cannot confer jurisdiction by consent on a state in which neither party is domiciled.

- **Residency:** In addition, some states impose a jurisdictional requirement that one of the parties must have resided in the state for a specified period of time prior to the filing of the divorce action. Residency is different than domicile. Residency refers to living in a particular place for a period of time, whereas domicile is established where a person lives in a state with the intent to make it his permanent home, with no present intent to live permanently elsewhere.

Personal Jurisdiction

- Although domicile establishes subject matter jurisdiction for purposes of granting the divorce, personal jurisdiction over the defendant is necessary for the court to enter or enforce any decrees *in personam*, including the entry of orders imposing support obligations, orders relating to out-of-state property, or the institution of contempt proceedings to enforce such orders.

- Personal service on the defendant within the state hearing the case is one way of establishing in personam jurisdiction. Substituted service (such as service by publication in cases where the whereabouts of the defendant is unknown), where necessary, may be sufficient under state long-arm statutes.

- Personal jurisdiction can also be obtained by use of a long-arm statute against a nonresident defendant spouse. In addition to proper service of process, in order for the court to enter an *in personam* order, the defendant spouse must have sufficient minimum contacts with the state such that entry of such an order is consistent with due process principles (i.e., sufficient minimum contacts such that the suit does not offend traditional notions of fair play and substantial justice).

Venue

- Proper venue is set by statute, generally in the county where either party resides. Venue is not jurisdictional and objection is generally waived if not made within the time for the defendant's response.

Procedure

Comparison of Legal Separation and Divorce

■ Legal separation, sometimes also called a "divorce from bed and board," a "divorce *a mensa et thoro*," or a limited divorce, was permitted in many states before full divorces were recognized. Fault grounds needed to be proven, but the grounds might be somewhat broader than for a full or "absolute" divorce.

■ Separation statutes typically give courts the authority to divide property, order payment of spousal and child support, and award custody. The only true difference between legal separation and divorce, then, is that only an absolute divorce bestows on the former spouses the right to remarry.

Commencement of Action

■ Actions for dissolution of marriage or legal separation are generally commenced and conducted as in other civil cases. States may have particular pleading requirements, particularly for the complaint, in domestic relations actions, however.

Financial Disclosure

■ Where a spouse seeks alimony, child support, property division, counsel fees, or expenses, a statement of income, expenses, assets, and liabilities generally must be filed by both parties with the court. States may differ on the specifics of when and how such information must be produced.

Default or Summary Judgment

■ Generally, no judgment may be entered by default or on the pleadings in a marital action. The moving party must generally testify as to the grounds for dissolution of the marriage.

■ However, as a matter of due process, a default may be entered if the defendant fails to appear after adequate notice and the moving party has established the required jurisdictional and substantive basis for a divorce.

Mediation

■ State statutes may recommend or require that the parties use a form of alternative dispute resolution before entry of a final divorce decree. Even if the parties decide to continue to pursue the divorce, a mediator can help them reach a settlement agreement with a minimum of rancor, which is particularly important when children are involved.

■ The ABA publishes Model Standards of Practice for Family and Divorce Mediation. A mediator's substantial misconduct is a basis for setting aside a settlement agreement. A mediator:

  (1) must be impartial and disclose potential conflicts of interest;

  (2) must explain the mediation process and make sure that the parties have enough information to ensure informed decision making;

  (3) may not coerce or improperly influence any party to make a decision; and

  (4) should recognize and control any situation, such as domestic violence, that would result in unfairness or prejudice to one of the parties.

Consultation with and Counsel for the Child

■ The judge may interview the child in chambers to determine the child's wishes regarding custody. States may vary in the age at which the child's wishes are taken into account, but often the age is 12. However, the child's wishes are only one of many factors that must be considered by the judge in determining the best interests of the child.

Interim Rights During Pendency of Proceedings

- While a marital action is pending, the court can make temporary orders for custody or support and has general equity powers to issue temporary restraining orders or preliminary injunctions or other orders necessary to protect the parties' interests.

- In addition, during the pendency of an appeal, the court may grant and enforce the payment of maintenance as it deems reasonable and proper. Also, the court may be asked to provide protection from threats or harassment by one of the parties. Many states provide statutory remedies for a family or household member who has been threatened by, or been the victim of, physical abuse by another family or household member, including money damages or a restraint order.

Grounds

Fault

- Today, many states permit divorce on no-fault grounds but have retained fault grounds as well. Fault grounds still recognized in many states include: desertion, adultery, impotence, cruelty, imprisonment, habitual intoxication, or drug addiction.

- **Desertion:** A spouse may obtain a divorce when the other spouse, without reasonable cause, abandons marital cohabitation with the intent to desert and willfully persists for a continuous and set period of time, including any period during which an action was pending between the spouses for dissolution or legal separation. Voluntary or consensual separation negates the requisite intent.

- **Constructive desertion** may be established where one spouse forcibly and without consent puts the other out of the house, or the latter leaves because of justifiable fear of immediate bodily harm, and the separation continues for the requisite period of time.

- **Adultery:** Adultery is a ground for dissolution of marriage in all states that recognize fault-based grounds. Because there is a natural secrecy to the act of adultery, circumstantial rather than direct evidence is usually permissible.

- **Impotence:** Impotence is the inability of one party to perform the act of sexual intercourse. It may also be a ground for annulment if the fact was concealed before the marriage. Sterility, the inability to conceive or to father children, is not a fault ground for divorce in most states.

- **Cruelty:** Most commonly, cruelty as a ground for divorce consists of a pattern of physical abuse committed by one spouse upon the other which causes physical injury. Yet, a single egregious act of physical violence may be sufficient. An activity carried on by one spouse (such as harsh words), which is designed to hurt the other spouse's health and does, in fact, impair health, may warrant a finding of mental cruelty even though no physical abuse is involved.

- Some states make mental cruelty a separate fault ground from physical cruelty, under a term such as "indignities." This generally requires a course of conduct that makes life "unbearable" or "intolerable." This can overlap with, but is distinct from, no-fault grounds of "irretrievable breakdown."

- **Felony Conviction:** In some states, a period of incarceration of a year or more is required.

No-Fault Divorce

- All states today provide no-fault grounds for divorce in some form, but they differ on the extent to which these have replaced the fault grounds. Many states retain both fault and no-fault schemes.

- Some states allow a divorce upon one party's insistence that the marriage is "irretrievably broken" due to "incompatibility" or "irreconcilable differences," and neither the other party nor the court can deny the requested divorce once these are shown.

- Other states impose a somewhat slower and more considered procedure under which the parties must "live separate and apart" for a specified period of time, and the court must find that the marriage in fact is irretrievably broken.

- Generally, **irretrievable breakdown** is defined as estrangement due to marital differences with no reasonable prospect of reconciliation. The standard for determining the existence of an irretrievable breakdown is broad, and the court, where permitted, should examine all evidence that bears on the viability of the marriage.

Defenses

Introduction

- Some affirmative defenses may be used to defeat a plaintiff's petition for dissolution. These defenses must be affirmatively pleaded by the defendant in order to be used at trial; otherwise, the conduct of the petitioner is not a bar to the action or a proper basis for the refusal of a judgment.

In Fault-Based Divorce Actions

DEFINITION ▶ **Collusion** is an agreement between the spouses, express or implied, whereby one of them wrongfully asserts that the other has committed a breach of marital duty in order to obtain a divorce. It implies an agreement whereby evidence is fabricated or suppressed in an attempt to deceive the court and obtain dissolution of the marriage in the absence of any legitimate legal grounds.

- **Connivance:** Connivance is conduct by the plaintiff facilitating the commission of a marital wrong, usually adultery, by the defendant. Unlike collusion, in the case of connivance, the marital wrong is actually committed.

- **Condonation:** Where one spouse knowingly forgives the other's marital wrong (usually adultery), by words or conduct, so that the marital relationship—i.e., cohabitation—is continued, such forgiveness may bar an action founded upon that marital wrong. Condonation is a question of fact which must be determined by an examination of all the evidence. Condonation can be either conditional or unconditional.

- **Recrimination:** Under the fault approach to divorce, there must be only one guilty party and one "innocent" spouse who is entitled to relief. Thus, where both spouses were guilty of fault grounds, the court would deny a divorce to either on the ground of recrimination. In many states today, if both spouses allege and prove fault grounds, the court may grant a divorce to each.

In No-Fault Divorce Actions

- In states that require a minimum period of separation as the basis for a no-fault divorce, the separation need not be consensual.

- It is also not a defense to a no-fault divorce in most states today that one spouse does not believe that the breakdown is irretrievable or the differences irreconcilable. No-fault divorce recognizes that the desire of one party to quit the marriage is sufficient, so a no-fault divorce may be granted without any attempt at reconciliation. Even if the difficulties might be curable and one spouse believes that the marriage can be saved, most states will not deny the other spouse a divorce.

- Where the states' no-fault regimes may differ most is in the treatment of marital fault or misconduct in making property division or alimony determinations.

THE DIVORCE DECREE

Contents of Decree

In General

- A decree granting a divorce (or other type of dissolution as well, in most states) may include orders determining and disposing of existing property rights between the parties, custody and visitation rights, child support, spousal maintenance, reasonable attorney's fees, costs and expenses, and any other related matters.

Statement of Reasons

- State statutes may specify where the order may set forth only general findings and where the order must state specific reasons for the court's decision. A court generally has a duty to make sufficient findings to inform the parties of the reasoning underlying the court's conclusions, and to allow for effective appellate review. However, a trial court has discretion in how much detail to provide.

- Some states require that, before entering an order of dissolution in a no-fault divorce, a court must make a specific finding that all reasonable efforts to effect a reconciliation have been made.

Settlement Agreements

Validity

- Like premarital and marital agreements, spousal agreements made during the divorce process are generally valid if voluntarily made and will be upheld in the absence of fraud, duress, concealment, or overreaching.

Merged into the Decree

- When the divorce is actually granted, the terms of such settlement agreements are typically incorporated into and made part of the decree, unless the agreement provides to the contrary, or unless the court finds the agreement should be set aside on grounds of fraud or duress. The court, before entry of judgment, has considerable latitude to reject or modify an agreement it finds unconscionable.

- Unless the parties agree otherwise, by default the agreement is deemed merged into the decree. The agreement is thereafter not enforceable as a contract obligation, but can be enforced only by remedies available for enforcement of judgments, including contempt proceedings.

- The terms of the agreement as merged into the judgment generally cannot be modified. However, provisions fixing child support and custody are always modifiable to protect children's welfare. The court also has an inherent power of modification regarding an alimony award in cases of changed circumstances, unless the parties' agreement provides that no alimony is payable or that alimony payments are nonmodifiable and such provisions are made part of the decree.

Where the Contract Survives the Decree

- The parties to a divorce action can and regularly do provide that the separation agreement will be incorporated into the decree but not merged into the decree. In such a case, contract obligations and remedies survive, and the terms may be enforced by either an action on the contract or through statutory remedies available, such as wage attachment or contempt proceedings.

Property Division

Generally

- The majority of states today follow an **equitable distribution** scheme to divide spousal property upon divorce.

- In divorces today, the financial interests of the parties are generally settled more substantially through property division at the time of divorce than by means of spousal support (alimony) payments.

Convergence of Community Property and Separate Property Systems at Divorce

- Although there are jurisdictional variations, most separate property states have adopted the community property system's dual classification approach of differentiating jointly owned property (called "community property" in community property states and "marital property" in separate property states) from property owned by a spouse individually (called "separate property").

- Note, however, that there are still important differences in the property regimes in effect at death and during an intact marriage. Most notably, the doctrine of equitable distribution is not applicable at death or during marriage in separate property states.

- The community property system views the marriage as a community in which each spouse is an equal partner. Generally, the spouses own undivided one-half interests in all community property during marriage and at death. At divorce, however, community property division is based on what is "equitable," with only a few of the community property states mandating an equal division of property.

- Specific rules govern the characterization of spousal property as separate or community, the transmutation of property from one classification to the other, and division of such property at divorce (or death of a spouse). Key rules from the community property regime are:

  (1) Property owned before marriage, acquired after dissolution of the marriage, or acquired by gift or inheritance to one spouse during the marriage, is that spouse's separate property. In contrast, property acquired during the marriage is presumed to be community (or marital) property to which both spouses have a claim.

  (2) Generally, earnings from the labor of either spouse or from the appreciation of community property are community property, whereas passive gains from separate property remain separate.

  (3) Commingling separate and community property may require the application of certain presumptions to determine ownership rights.

Equitable Distribution

Policy Considerations

- **Economic Justice Between the Parties:** Equitable distribution is flexible in that it allows the court to take into account numerous factors related to the financial situation of each spouse, rather than presuming a 50/50 split. Under modern law, fault has been eliminated from consideration in property distribution in many states, at least with respect to matters that are not related to the parties' finances (such as dissipation of assets, as discussed below). Neither the ALI Principles nor the UMDA allow marital fault to be considered.

- **Predictability of Results:** Whereas there are fairly clear rules governing the characterization of property, there is wide discretion allowed in its final division, leading to varying results, not only among different states but even within the same state.

Steps in Process

- Regardless of which system is used, there are three basic steps to property division:

  (1) identify the divisible property;

  (2) value it; and

  (3) divide it.

- **Identification and Classification of Assets and Debts:** A minority of states have an "all property" approach, also called the "**hotchpot**" or "kitchen sink" approach. In these states, all property owned by either spouse, however, and whenever acquired, is divisible between the parties. The court has authority to divide all the property, regardless of title and previous ownership.

■ However, a majority of states have adopted the **dual classification system** from the community property regime that differentiates between marital and nonmarital property. Separate property, once identified, is generally not divisible and must be assigned to the owner spouse. Marital property is divisible between the spouses.

■ **Valuation of Assets:** The time at which valuation is determined is generally as of the date of the parties' separation, but in some states is the date of the trial or hearing.

■ **Division of Assets:** In the last step, the court determines what would be an "equitable" distribution of all divisible property between the parties, considering a number of factors. In contrast, a few states mandate equal division.

Defining Marital Property

■ In both community property and common law (marital property) states, formal title does not determine ownership at divorce. Instead, states have widely adopted a presumption that property acquired during the marriage is marital property subject to division, with certain separate property exceptions, regardless of title.

■ The earnings of each spouse, and property acquired with those earnings or through the labor of a spouse, are presumptively marital or community property, in the absence of an enforceable agreement to the contrary.

■ **Increased Value of Separate Property:** The fact that a separate asset appreciates in value during the marriage does not, in itself, transform that asset into marital property. In most states, the increase during marriage of a separate asset will be separate if the increase was due to market forces, not the labor of either spouse. If the value of a separate asset is increased through marital funds or significant labor of one or both spouses, then the portion attributable to such labor is marital property. Courts may separate the increase into components, or alternatively, characterize the increase as all marital if the increase was primarily attributable to spousal labor (or all separate if primarily from passive forces).

Nonmarital Property

■ Marital property generally does not include property:

(1)   acquired by gift (except between spouses, in some states) or inheritance; or

(2)   excluded by valid agreement of the parties.

■ There is also a temporal aspect to the acquisition of nonmarital property, which includes property:

(1)   acquired prior to marriage or in exchange for property acquired prior to the marriage; or

(2)   acquired after the marriage effectively ends, which may be the date:

(a)   of the final separation of the parties, in a minority of states;

(b)   the divorce action was commenced; or

(c)   in the majority of states, when a final divorce decree is entered.

Mixed Character, Commingled, or Transmuted Property

■ Title does not generally determine ownership at divorce. However, in identifying marital versus separate property, it can be relevant (although not determinative). If spouses mix together separate and marital property, the question arises, what is the character of the asset? Taking separate property and combining it with marital property, or taking marital property and combining it with separate property, may imply a gift to the other estate. However, a spouse can trace the contribution to its source and prove its character as either separate or marital, notwithstanding the commingling.

- However, if commingling is so pervasive that it is no longer possible to separately identify the character of the contribution, resulting in a loss of identity of the contributed property, the contributed property takes on the classification of the estate that received the contribution. But, if marital and nonmarital properties are commingled into newly acquired property, the commingled property will be presumed marital property.

Dividing Property: Equitable Distribution

- In determining how the property should be divided, the court may "equitably" distribute it, generally meaning that there is no requirement that the distribution be "equal," although in some states there is a presumption that an equal distribution is an equitable distribution. In others, the court should consider certain factors in determining how the assets should be allocated to each spouse.

- Most community property states, with the exception of California, Louisiana, and New Mexico, apply equitable distribution principles, such that equal division of community property is not required.

- Factors that may generally be considered in determining what division would be "equitable," in addition to the length of the marriage and the standard of living enjoyed by the spouses during the marriage, relate primarily to the contributions, both monetary and nonmonetary of each party during the marriage, and the current financial circumstances of each party.

- Contributions of each spouse may include those made:

  (1) by one spouse to the education, training, or increased earning power of the other spouse;

  (2) to the acquisition, preservation, or appreciation of marital property, or conversely, to the depreciation or dissipation of assets and acquisition of debt; or

  (3) to the family's quality of life, such as services as a homemaker or child-care giver.

- Financial circumstances or need of each spouse at the time the division of property is to become effective, and in the future, may include:

  (1) age, health, vocational skills and employability, assets, liabilities, and needs;

  (2) sources of income, including medical, retirement, insurance, and other benefits;

  (3) the value of property set aside for each spouse, and the tax ramifications and expenses of the transfer or sale of particular assets, where relevant; and

  (4) opportunities for future acquisition of assets and income.

Division of Debts

- In many states, the court is also authorized to assign marital debts and liabilities to one or other of the spouses as equity demands. Debts are generally characterized using the same principles that govern the characterization of assets, such that debts incurred during marriage are marital debts, while those incurred before or after, are separate debts of the spouse who incurred them.

Final Order

- In fashioning an order that will effectuate the purposes of equitable distribution, courts are given broad equitable powers and may make an in-kind distribution, order the sale of property, or impose liens on property as security.

- An order for property division, unlike an alimony award, is not modifiable.

Classification and Division of Particular Types of Assets

Marital Residence

- Difficulties of allocation may arise if the house was purchased prior to marriage but marital earnings were used to pay off the mortgage and build equity in the house.

- If a spouse's separate funds are used to make improvements to the property, a gift to the "community" may be presumed, but this may be rebutted, and in some circumstances reimbursement may be required upon divorce.

- Appreciation of the property is apportioned in the same manner as the ownership of the house if solely due to market forces, but if appreciation is due to spousal labor, the increase is marital property to that extent.

Pensions and Other Retirement Accounts

- Pension and retirement benefits accumulated by either spouse during the marriage are subject to equitable distribution, whether the accounts are vested (the employee has a definitive and presently existing legal right to the asset) or nonvested (some contingency must occur such as working for the employer a certain number of years before legal entitlement attaches). These include deferred compensation agreements, profit sharing benefits, and military retirement benefits, to the extent allowed by federal law.

- Premarital contributions or post-separation increases or contributions to the plan are generally not deemed marital property. Upon divorce, the total retirement benefit owed to the employee-spouse is allocated into marital and nonmarital shares; only the marital share is subject to equitable distribution.

- Difficulties in calculation of the benefit to be divided may arise from a number of circumstances affecting defined benefit plans in particular. The value of the marital portion of the future benefit may be estimated as of the time of divorce for purposes of offsetting that value against other assets available for distribution to the other spouse. Under a deferred distribution method, the marital share will be divided between the spouses at the time the employee-spouse actually retires.

Stock Options

- Stock options granted to either spouse during the marriage, whether vested or non-vested and whether or not their value is ascertainable, are presumed to be marital property. If earned as employment compensation, their status as marital or nonmarital property depends on when acquired and whether the work for which the options are compensation was performed during the marriage.

- In making the allocation between the parties, the court may recognize that the value of the options may not be determinable at the time of the judgment of dissolution or declaration of invalidity. The court may consider, in addition to the usual factors in equitable distribution, all the circumstances underlying the grant of the stock options, including whether the grant was for past, present or future efforts, and the length of time from the grant of the option to the time the options are exercisable. The actual division of the options may not occur until a future date, and valuation may be difficult, given their market volatility.

Professional Degrees and Licenses

- Most states have held that a professional degree or license is not a property interest subject to equitable distribution.

- Even if a degree is not considered divisible marital property, however, it may be considered in the division of other marital property, as well as in an alimony or reimbursement award for a spouse who contributed to the support of the family while the degree-earning spouse was in school or training.

Professional Practice and Goodwill

- A professional practice or corporation, unlike a spouse's degree or license, is subject to disposition as a marital asset. The practice must be valued for its tangible assets and its goodwill, which represents the reputational value of the business.

- The majority of states distinguish between "personal" and "enterprise" goodwill. **Enterprise goodwill** is transferable with the business and thus, is not personal to a particular member. Enterprise goodwill should generally be included in the value of the practice and thus, may be divisible property because it is an asset of the business.

- On the other hand, **personal goodwill** is that generated solely by the reputation and professional expertise of the owner-spouse. To the extent that clients would follow the owner-spouse if he or she dissociated from the business or practice, that is personal goodwill – and is not marital property.

Personal Injury Claims

- The "analytic" approach—used by the majority of states—assesses what losses the damages compensate for and classifies the proceeds accordingly as either separate or marital property. To the extent the damages replace lost wages that would have been earned during marriage or medical expenses that were incurred during marriage, those damages are marital property. To the extent the damages replace future wages or pain and suffering or future medical expenses, those damages are the separate property of the injured spouse.

Lottery Winnings

- Lottery winnings of a spouse may be marital or separate property depending on the usual principles, such as the date of acquisition and whether community/marital earnings were used to purchase the ticket. Presumably, lottery winnings during the marriage are marital property.

Expectancies

- Contingent expectancies are subject to equitable distribution if they were acquired through spousal effort during the marriage.

Fraudulently Transferred Property

- Property owned by a party during the marriage, but fraudulently transferred in contemplation of the divorce, can also be included as a marital asset. A court will consider whether the transfer constitutes economic misconduct, and if so, it may award the harmed spouse a greater share of the remaining property.

Alimony / Spousal Maintenance

Introduction

RULE Alimony, referred to more commonly today as maintenance or spousal support, may be awarded to one of the spouses as part of a divorce decree. Alimony may be awarded to either spouse, after consideration of all relevant factors.

Types of Alimony

- **Periodic Alimony:** A periodic alimony order requires a certain amount of money to be paid at set intervals, usually monthly. The obligation will generally continue until the recipient dies, remarries, or the court modifies the order.

- **Lump Sum Alimony:** Under appropriate circumstances, the court may make an award of lump sum alimony. Lump sum alimony is distinguished from the normal alimony award in that it is for a fixed amount, rather than a periodic obligation with no aggregate limitations. Unlike a periodic alimony order, an award of lump sum alimony is a final order which may not be modified even if the lump sum is payable in installments.

- **Rehabilitative Alimony:** Rehabilitative alimony may be awarded to a spouse for a limited period of time. The purpose is support as necessary until the recipient spouse can become self-supporting by entering the work force.

Grounds

- **Purpose and Prerequisites:** The modern trend is to limit alimony awards in favor of encouraging the recipient spouse to become self-supporting within a reasonable time. Alimony is generally based on economic need and, in some circumstances, may be used to achieve fairness even if the claimant is not clearly in need. Some jurisdictions also employ a *quasi*-contract or unjust enrichment approach.

- Under the UMDA, an alimony order may be made only if the court finds that the spouse who is seeking alimony:

    (1) lacks sufficient property to provide for his reasonable needs; and

    (2) is unable to support himself through appropriate employment, or is the custodian of a child whose condition or circumstances make it appropriate that the custodian not be required to seek employment outside the home.

- **Factors:** Rules governing the factors to be considered in making an award of spousal maintenance vary from state to state, but they generally require the trial court to consider:

    (1) the parties' respective financial resources and needs;

    (2) the contributions each has made to the marital relationship, whether financially or by providing care within the home; and

    (3) the duration of the marriage.

- **Modification:** Under the UMDA, modification of spousal support is allowed only upon a showing of a substantial and continuing change in circumstances making the prior order "unconscionable." Most jurisdictions are not as stringent as the UMDA, but may place a heavy burden on the party requesting the modification, such as requiring a "substantial change in circumstances that rendered the original award unreasonable and unfair."

- **Termination:** Spousal maintenance generally terminates:

    (1) after a specified term;

    (2) on death of either spouse; or

    (3) automatically on remarriage or cohabitation. However, in cases of cohabitation instead of remarriage, alimony may be suspended rather than terminated, and reinstated when the cohabitation ends.

- **Enforcement:** State statutes generally provide that a court may enforce spousal support by wage garnishment and a variety of other means. Some states require income attachment orders in virtually every case.

Equitable Reimbursement

- Some states recognize a right of a spouse to be reimbursed under specified circumstances for contributions made during the marriage to the education, training, or increased earning capacity of the other spouse.

- This remedy, which is called **reimbursement alimony** in some states and **equitable reimbursement** in others, may be ordered in addition to any right to alimony or equitable distribution.

Child Support and Custody

Child Support

- In connection with the entry of a custody order, the court may require either parent to pay periodic sums for the support of his minor children during the period of their minority. A child support order is generally entered only against the non-custodial parent.

- Child support orders are issued after consideration of the state's child support guidelines, if any. These guidelines are generally a mathematical formula based on the income of the parents. There is a rebuttable presumption that the amount of child support, if computed consistent with the guidelines, is the proper amount of support to be ordered.

Child Custody

RULE ▶ While both parents of a minor are living and are competent and fit, they are jointly entitled to the custody of the person of the minor. The parents have equal powers, rights and duties concerning the minor. If one parent is dead and the surviving parent is competent and fit, the surviving parent is entitled to custody. If the parents live apart, the court may award the custody of the minor to either parent.

- **Presumption in Favor of Parents:** In any dispute as to the custody of minor children involving a parent and a non-parent, there is a presumption that it is in the best interests of the child to be in the custody of one of the parents.

- **Equality Between Parents:** As between the parents, custody is awarded on a sex-neutral basis today. In custody determinations between the father and mother of a minor child, the court must exercise its sound discretion to decide as to which parent, if either, the custody of such child should be committed. Regard is had to the best interests and welfare of the child and the fitness of the parent.

- **Best Interest of Child:** Under the UMDA, the best interest of the child is determined by examination of all relevant factors, including the following:

  (1)   the wishes of the child's parent or parents as to his custody;

  (2)   the wishes of the child as to his custodian;

  (3)   the interaction and interrelationship of the child with his parent or parents, his siblings, and any other person who may significantly affect the child's best interest;

  (4)   the child's adjustment to his home, school, and community; and

  (5)   the mental and physical health of all individuals involved.

- **Joint Custody:** Upon divorce, some states apply a presumption in favor of joint custody, whereas others do not award it unless the parents expressly agree. Joint custody does not necessarily mean equal parenting time. Shared physical custody means that the child will reside for set periods of time with each of the parents with each parent having full custodial rights.

- There are two aspects to custody: (1) the right to physical custody, and (2) the right to make important decisions relating to the child, such as those concerning health, religion, and education. **Joint custody** generally refers to shared physical custody (both parents have parenting time) and/or shared decisionmaking power (also called legal custody). Sharing either or both aspects qualifies as "joint" custody. A typical joint custody structure is where one parent has primary physical custody, the other has significant periods of physical custody, and both parents share decision-making power.

- **Marital Fault:** The fact that a parent was guilty of misconduct in connection with the divorce action will be relevant only insofar as the parent's moral fitness affects the child's welfare. Likewise, a parent's nonmarital relationships should not be relevant to a determination of child custody, unless they are shown to negatively affect the child.

- **Additional Factors:** The desires of a child of sufficient age and understanding are considered, but are not controlling. Many states require the judge to take the child's preference into account if he has reached a certain age (which varies by state). A policy against separating siblings may also be a factor in determining the best interests of the child. Domestic violence by one parent against the other is a factor to be considered, and is generally influential when shown to negatively affect the child.

- **Conditions to Award:** A court may attach reasonable conditions on the custodial rights of the parties to ensure that the child's best interests and welfare are protected. Similarly, a court may order a custodial parent not to remove a child from the state without prior court approval.

Visitation

- **By Non-Custodial Parent:** The non-custodial parent will generally be granted reasonable visitation rights, unless the court finds that visitation is detrimental to the best interests of the child.

- **By Third Persons:** In many states, a court could grant visitation rights upon divorce or annulment to grandparents, stepparents, or other adults who had established a substantial relationship with the child, if such an arrangement was deemed in the best interests of the child.

■ The statutory law on visitation rights by third persons has been reconsidered in light of a recent Supreme Court case, in which the court held that significant deference must be given to a legal parent's objection to visitation, but did not specify a standard. Several jurisdictions' grandparent visitation statutes have been found unconstitutional since then, but the current standard for grandparent visitation rights varies from state to state.

Standard for Modification: Child Support Orders

■ In most jurisdictions, modifications of child support orders may be made only upon a showing of a substantial and continuing change in circumstances making the prior order unreasonable. Under the UMDA, modification of a child support order is allowed "only upon a showing of changed circumstances so substantial and continuing as to make the terms unconscionable." Under any standard, however, the changes must be more or less permanent, rather than temporary.

■ Under the UMDA, a modification of support can be made retroactive only from the date of service of the motion to modify on the other party. Federal law requires the same result with respect to retroactive modification of child support orders.

Standard for Modification: Child Custody Orders

■ **Change of Circumstances Requirement:** The prevailing view is that a court may modify a custody order upon proof of a material and substantial change in circumstances such that a change in custody will be conducive to the best interests of the child. Even if there is a substantial change in circumstances, a court may not modify a custody order unless the change will serve the child's best interests. Most states require that the change in circumstances be unforeseen.

■ However, stability of the child's existing placement is a consideration that favors the existing custodial structure. Most states disfavor modification when sought shortly after a custody decree has been entered; the principle of *res judicata* and the belief that children's interests are served by stable custody arrangements both mitigate against frequent change.

■ **Parent's Cohabitation or Remarriage:** In some states, appellate courts have held that a custodial parent's post-decree nonmarital cohabitation represents a change of circumstances sufficient to warrant a modification hearing. But, even in states that authorize a hearing in these circumstances, modification is typically disallowed, unless the petitioner shows that the nonmarital cohabitation has an adverse impact on the children.

■ **Child's Custody Preference:** A child's custody preference is relevant to a custody determination, and alteration of a child's custody preference thus can constitute a substantial change of circumstance.

■ **Relocation:** Many courts have balanced the impact on visitation by the noncustodial parent against the benefits of the move to both the children and the custodial parent, with an overall trend toward leniency for the wishes and needs of the parent with whom the child has been primarily living.

Uniform Child Custody Jurisdiction and Enforcement Act

■ **Enactment and Purposes:** As a constitutional matter, a court taking jurisdiction of a custody matter need not, except as a matter of comity, give full faith and credit to the decree of a sister state because such a decree is almost always modifiable, and, therefore, not a final judgment. However, nearly all the states have adopted the Uniform Child Custody Jurisdiction and Enforcement Act ("UCCJEA"). The UCCJEA attempts to avoid relitigation of custody decisions of other states, to facilitate the enforcement of foreign custody decisions, and to deter abductions of children undertaken to obtain custody awards.

■ **Initial Jurisdiction:** Physical presence or personal jurisdiction over a party or a child is neither necessary nor sufficient for a state to make a child custody determination. A court has jurisdiction under the UCCJEA to make an initial child-custody determination only when:

(1) it is the home state of the child or had been within six months of the commencement of the proceeding, and, if the child is absent from the forum state, a parent continues to live in the forum state;

(2) another state does not have such home-state jurisdiction, or else the home-state court has declined to

exercise jurisdiction, the child and its parent(s) have a significant connection with the state other than mere physical presence, and substantial evidence is available in the state regarding the child's welfare;

    (3)   all other states having jurisdiction under either of the above provisions have declined to exercise jurisdiction on the ground that the state is the more appropriate forum to determine custody of the child; or

    (4)   no court of any other state would have jurisdiction under any of the above provisions.

- **Exclusive, Continuing Jurisdiction:** Once a state has made a valid child-custody determination. that state has exclusive jurisdiction over the determination. Such jurisdiction continues until:

    (1)   a court of the state determines that neither the child nor the child and one parent or person acting as parent have a significant connection with the state, and substantial evidence is no longer available in the state regarding the child's welfare; or

    (2)   a court of the state or of another state determines that the child, the child's parents, and any person acting as a parent do not presently reside in the state.

- **Jurisdiction to Modify Determination:** A court that has made an initial child-custody determination but does not have exclusive, continuing jurisdiction, may modify the determination only if it has jurisdiction to make an initial determination under the UCCJEA. A court may not modify a child-custody determination made by a court of another state unless the forum court has jurisdiction to make an initial determination and:

    (1)   a court of the other state determines it no longer has exclusive, continuing jurisdiction or that a court of the state would be a more convenient forum; or

    (2)   the forum court or a court of the other state determines that the child and the child's parents or any person acting as parent do not presently reside in the other state.

- **Temporary Emergency Jurisdiction:** A state has temporary emergency jurisdiction if the child is present in the state and:

    (1)   the child has been abandoned; or

    (2)   it is necessary in an emergency to protect the child because the child (or a sibling or parent of the child) is being subjected to or threatened with mistreatment or abuse.

- **Inconvenient Forum:** A state that has jurisdiction to make a child-custody determination may decline to exercise its jurisdiction at any time if it determines that it is an inconvenient forum under the circumstances, and that a court of another state is a more appropriate forum. The following factors should be considered:

    (1)   whether domestic violence has occurred and is likely to continue, and which state could best protect the parties and the child;

    (2)   the length of time the child has resided outside the state;

    (3)   the distance between the courts of the two states;

    (4)   financial circumstances of the parties;

    (5)   any agreement of the parties as to which state should assume jurisdiction;

    (6)   the nature and location of the evidence required to resolve the pending litigation;

    (7)   the ability of the court of each state to decide the issue expeditiously and the procedures necessary to present the evidence; and

    (8)   the familiarity of the courts in each state with the facts and issues in the pending litigation.

- **Jurisdiction Declined by Reason of Conduct:** If a court has jurisdiction because a person seeking to invoke its jurisdiction has engaged in unjustifiable conduct, the court should decline to exercise its jurisdiction, unless:

    (1)   the parents and any persons acting as parents have acquiesced in the exercise of jurisdiction;

    (2)   court of another state otherwise having jurisdiction determines that the state is a more appropriate forum; or

(3) no court of any other state would have jurisdiction.

- If a court declines to exercise jurisdiction on this ground, it may fashion a remedy to ensure the safety of the child and to prevent a repetition of the unjustifiable conduct, and it may assess fees and costs against the party who unjustifiably sought to invoke its jurisdiction.

Termination of Custody Order

- A custody order in a divorce proceeding is terminated by the death of the custodial parent, and the surviving parent is usually entitled to custody, unless the latter is determined to be unfit. A custody order also will terminate when a child attains the age of majority or otherwise becomes emancipated.

Enforcement of Custody or Visitation Orders

- A court may use its contempt power to enforce a custody or visitation award. Many states provide for specific civil sanctions for violation of a parenting plan or custody order; violation may also be a crime.

Enforcement of Child Support Orders

- All states have adopted the Uniform Interstate Family Support Act ("UIFSA"). This was to facilitate enforcement of support orders across state lines, making it easier to obtain jurisdiction over an obligor who moves. UIFSA establishes broad long-arm jurisdiction over non-residents in order to facilitate one-state proceedings whenever possible. When jurisdiction over a nonresident is obtained, the tribunal may obtain evidence, provide for discovery, and elicit testimony through use of the "information route" provided in the Act.

- Contrary to prior law, UIFSA takes the position that a responding state should enforce a child support obligation irrespective of another state's law. Tolerance for the laws of other States and nations, in order to facilitate child support enforcement, is a prime goal of the Act, which also contains provisions to help ease the transition to the new system.

- An order issued in one state may be registered for enforcement in another. It may also be registered for modification if:

  (1) the issuing state no longer has jurisdiction;

  (2) the petitioner is a non-resident of the forum state; and

  (3) the forum state has personal jurisdiction over the respondent.

- After a support order issued in another state has been registered in a second state, the responding court in the second state may modify the order only if a petitioner, who is a non-resident, seeks modification, and all the parties have filed written consents in the issuing tribunal for a court in the second state to modify the support order and assume continuing, exclusive jurisdiction over the order.

EFFECTS OF FINAL DIVORCE DECREE

RULE Once a divorce has been decreed, either party may generally marry again as if the party had never been married.

- Each divorced party loses the right to intestate inheritance and to take an elective share from the estate of the other party. Unless a will expressly provides otherwise, a divorce or annulment revokes any disposition or appointment of property made by the will to a former spouse and any provision naming the former spouse as executor or trustee. Property that is prevented from passing to the former spouse will pass as if the former spouse predeceased the testator.

Recognition of Foreign Divorce Decree

Only One Spouse Participated

- Where only one spouse participates in a divorce proceeding, the stay-at-home spouse has the right to attack the finding of the domicile of the procuring spouse because there has been no contested hearing on the issue of domicile in the rendering state.

Both Spouses Participated

- By participating in an out-of-state divorce, the spouse is barred by the **doctrine of collateral estoppel** from attacking the validity of the divorce, because the question of domicile has either actually been litigated or could have been litigated in the rendering state.

Divisible Divorce

- The Supreme Court has upheld the right of a state to continue a support order after an out-of-state divorce decree had purportedly terminated it by granting no alimony. An out-of-state court in an *ex parte* action has no *in personam* jurisdiction over the other spouse, and thus cannot order or alter economic incidents to a divorce.

Divorce Decree from Foreign Nation

- A state need not recognize the validity of foreign-country divorce decrees. However, states will generally recognize such decrees on the basis of comity if both spouses were represented and there was a hearing in the court of the foreign country.

Partnership

Partnership

General Partnership: an association of two or more persons to carry on as co-owners of a business or other undertaking for profit

Joint Venture: an association contemplating a single transaction or related series of transactions

Dissociation: the withdrawal of a partner from the partnership

Dissolution: the commencement of the winding up process

Winding Up: the process of settling partnership affairs

Termination: the point at which all the partnership affairs are wound up

Mandatory Dissolution: a partnership is dissolved and its business must be wound up upon the occurrence of a set of events set by statute

Permissive Dissolution: a partnership can be dissolved at any time by unanimous consent, regardless of any duration specified in the partnership agreement

Limited Liability Partnership: a partnership in which all the partners gain protection from liability for obligations of the partnership and protection from other partners' omissions, negligence, wrongful acts, misconduct, or malpractice, although they remain liable for their own negligence and the negligence of those they supervise

Limited Partnership: a partnership formed by two or more persons having one or more general partners and one or more limited partners

General Partner: a partner who manages the business and is personally liable without limitation for partnership obligations

Limited Partner: a partner who contributes capital and shares in profits, but takes no part in the control or management of the business, and whose liability is limited to his contributions

- Dissociation and Termination

- Formation and Proof of Association

- Other Forms of Partnership

- Partners and the Partnership Business

- Partnership Basics

- Generally, all partners in a general partnership are liable for debts of the partnership incurred by any partner in the course of partnership business.

- A partnership is the carrying on of a business as co-owners for profits, where those profits are shared.

- Unless otherwise agreed, each partner is entitled to be repaid his contributions and to share equally in the profits and surplus remaining after all liabilities are satisfied. Concomitantly, each partner must contribute toward the losses sustained by the partnership, according to his share in the profits.

- A dissociated partner can continue to bind the partnership after he dissociates unless a creditor knows he has dissociated and continues to give him a loan or sign a contract with him as a member of the partnership.

CREATION OF GENERAL PARTNERSHIPS

Introduction

- The Revised Uniform Partnership Act (RUPA) has been enacted in some form by almost all the states.

- Partnerships have the following characteristics:

  (1) unlimited liability for partners;

  (2) partners have the right to co-manage the partnership;

  (3) fiduciary duties exist between and among the partners and the partnership; and

  (4) partners share in profits.

In General

Terminology

DEFINITION ▶ A general partnership is an association of two or more persons to carry on as co-owners of a business for profit.

- The definition of **person** includes:

  (1) an individual;

  (2) a corporation;

  (3) a trust;

  (4) an estate;

  (5) a partnership; and

  (6) other associations.

- **Business** includes every trade, occupation, and profession.

Formation

- All that is required to create a partnership under the Revised Uniform Partnership Act ("RUPA") is "two or more persons who associate to carry on a business for profit." RUPA specifically states that intentionally does not matter.

- Partnership may be inferred from the conduct of the parties.

- No "agreement" or "consent" is required to form a partnership.

  (1) If individuals just act like partners, the law will treat them like partners, even if they had no idea that they were acting like partners and no intent to do so.

  (2) Where there is an official agreement or contract (which is not required), it may be oral.

- In the absence of any agreed terms, RUPA will fill in those partnership terms.

Partnership versus Joint Venture

- As a general rule, a **joint venture** is described as an association contemplating a single transaction or a related series of transactions, as compared to a **partnership**, which is generally said to be carrying on a business.

■ Although RUPA does not apply specifically to joint ventures, courts have applied the same rules of law.

Capacity

■ Any person who has the capacity to enter into a contract can enter into a partnership agreement.

■ A corporation can be a partner in any business enterprise that it would have the power to conduct by itself so long as the enterprise is appropriate under the corporation's articles and bylaws.

Tests of Partnership

■ The key test of whether a partnership has been formed is the intent of the parties to enter into a partnership relationship, no matter what it is called.

■ An express agreement is the best indication of intent.

■ If the partnership agreement was merely implied, other factors must be considered. The court may consider such evidence as the sharing of profits, the management practices of the entity, the amount and type of services rendered by the parties, and the record title to any real or personal property used by the entity.

Sharing of Profits

RULE ▶ A person's receipt of a share of the profits of a business is prima facie evidence that he is a partner in the business.

■ However, no such inference may be drawn if the profits were received in payment of the following:

(1) a debt by installments or otherwise;

(2) for services as an independent contractor, or wages to an employee;

(3) rent;

(4) an annuity or other retirement or health benefit to a beneficiary, representative, or designee of a deceased or retired partner;

(5) of interest or other charge on a loan, even if the amount of payment varies with the profits of the business; or

(6) for the sale of the goodwill of a business or other property by installments or otherwise.

■ It is not statutorily required that there be a sharing of losses to create a partnership. In the absence of a contrary agreement, however, the partners share losses in proportion to their share of the profits.

Sharing of Gross Returns

■ The sharing of gross returns does not in itself establish a partnership, whether or not the persons sharing the returns have a joint or common right or interest in any property from which the returns are derived.

Common Property

■ Joint tenancy, tenancy in common, tenancy by the entirety, joint property, common property, or part-ownership does not in itself establish a partnership, regardless of whether the owners share any profits made through use of the property.

Control

■ Partners, as co-owners of the business, must have the power of ultimate control.

■ If a person shares in the profits, but lacks any power to control, he is probably an agent, and is receiving his profit share merely as an incentive or a bonus, unless the agreement shows a contrary intent.

Partnership by Estoppel

- Even if a voluntary partnership does not exist, liability may be imposed on a person who has let it appear that he is in a partnership if a creditor is thereby misled.

- When a person, by words or conduct, represents himself to be a partner in an existing partnership, or with one or more persons who are not actual partners, he is liable to anyone who has extended credit in reliance on the representation of partnership.

- If the representation is made privately, it may be relied upon only by those to whom it was made. If the representation is made publicly, the "purported partner" is liable to anyone who has knowledge of it and has relied upon it.

Agency Created by Holding Out

- When a person has been represented to be a partner in an existing partnership, or with others who are not actual partners, he is an agent of those consenting to the representation, and he can bind them as if he were, in fact, a partner.

RELATIONSHIP BETWEEN PARTNERS AND THIRD PARTIES

Powers

In General

- Every partner is an agent of the partnership for the purpose of its business.

- The act of a partner for apparently carrying on in the ordinary course of business of the partnership binds the partnership, unless:

  (1) the partner has no authority to act in the matter; and

  (2) the person with whom he is dealing has knowledge that he has no such authority.

Authority

RULE A partner may have express authority to act by the terms of the partnership agreement, or by consent of the other partners.

RULE A partner may have apparent authority based on the nature and course of business of the partnership, or on the custom in similar partnerships in the same area.

- However, an act of a partner that is not apparently for carrying on in the ordinary course of business of the partnership does not bind the partnership unless authorized by the other partners.

Knowledge That Authority Is Lacking

- Partnership agreements may include specific restrictions on authority; if a partner acts in contravention of such a restriction, and the third party has knowledge of the restriction, the partnership will not be bound.

- A person has **knowledge** of a fact not only when he has actual knowledge thereof, but also when he has knowledge of such other facts in the circumstances showing bad faith.

Notice to Partner

In General

- Notice to any partner of any matter relating to partnership affairs constitutes notice to the partnership.

DEFINITION A person has notice of a fact when the notification:

- comes to the person's attention; or
- is duly delivered at the person's place of business, or at any other place held out by the person as a place for receiving communications.

Imputed Notice

- If a partner acting in a particular matter has acquired knowledge while a partner—or if his knowledge was otherwise acquired but is present in his mind when acting for the partnership—that knowledge is imputed to the partnership.

- If a partner not acting for the partnership in a particular matter has knowledge that he could and should have communicated to the acting partner, that knowledge also will be imputed to the partnership.

- An exception to this rule of imputation of notice or knowledge is made if a fraud on the partnership is committed by, or with the consent of, that partner.

Liability

Nature of Liability

- All partners are liable jointly and severally for all obligations of the partnership, whether arising under tort, contract, or otherwise.

- An action may be brought against any one or more of the partners, but a partner will not be bound by a judgment unless he has been served with notice. Therefore, unless one of the partners is no longer subject to jurisdiction, all of the partners must be joined in the action. However, a judgment may be satisfied against any one of the partners.

- RUPA also permits any partner to enter into a separate obligation to perform a partnership contract, in which case the partner's liability is several.

- At common law, all partners were required to be named in a lawsuit and served with process; however, in states that have enacted common law statutes, service on one partner is generally held sufficient.

Extent of Liability

- Even though a partnership obligation is joint, each partner is individually liable for the entire amount of the partnership's obligation.

- A partner is entitled to **indemnification** by the partnership for any payments he makes on its behalf.

- If a partner is forced to pay the entire debt, or more than his pro rata share, and the partnership is unable to indemnify him, he is entitled to **contribution** from his co-partners and may seek it through an **accounting** action.

RULE A dormant partner—one who is not active in managing partnership business and who is not known to the world as a partner—is nonetheless liable on partnership obligations.

RULE An incoming partner—one admitted as a partner into an existing partnership—is not personally liable for any partnership obligation incurred before the person's admission as a partner.

Partnership Liability for Acts of Partners

- A partnership is liable for loss or injury caused to a person, or for a penalty incurred, as a result of a wrongful act, omission, or other actionable conduct of a partner acting in the ordinary course of business of the partnership or with authority of the partnership.

- If, in the course of the partnership's business or while acting with authority of the partnership, a partner receives or causes the partnership to receive money or property of a person who is not a partner and the money is misapplied by a partner, the partnership is liable for the loss.

Retiring Partner

- Usually, a retiring partner remains liable on all obligations incurred before his retirement.

- A retiring partner can be discharged from liability by an agreement with the continuing partners and the partnership creditor.

RELATIONSHIP BETWEEN PARTNERS

Partnership Agreement

- Relations among the partners and between the partners and the partnership are governed by the partnership agreement. To the extent the partnership agreement does not otherwise provide, RUPA governs relations among the partners and between the partners and the partnership.

Contributions, Profits and Losses

Partners' Contributions and Shares

- Partners make contributions to the partnership in cash or otherwise (e.g., contribution of labor). Each partner is entitled to be repaid his contributions, whether made by way of capital or through advances to the partnership property, and to share equally in the profits and surplus remaining after all liabilities (including those to partners) are satisfied.

RULE ▶ Each partner must contribute toward the losses—whether of capital or otherwise—sustained by the partnership, according to his share in the profits.

- Partners may agree to share the profits other than equally, and would then share the losses in the same ratio, unless specifically agreed otherwise.

Rights of Partners

Right to Indemnity

- The partnership must indemnify every partner with regard to payments made and liabilities incurred by that partner in the ordinary course of the partnership's business or for the preservation of its business or property.

Right to Interest

- A payment made by a partner, incurred in the ordinary course of the partnership business or as an advance beyond the amount of capital he agreed to contribute, constitutes a loan that accrues interest from the date of the payment or advance.

Right to Compensation

- In general, a partner is not entitled to compensation for services performed for the partnership, except reasonable compensation for services rendered in winding up the partnership business.

- However, a partner's agreement may provide for salaries to be paid. Such an agreement should spell out the source of payments (i.e., from the partner's share of profits or from partnership income) and the work and time required in exchange.

Right to Accounting

- The accounting action is equitable in nature, and determines each partner's investment, the partnership's profits or losses, and the share of profits to which each partner is entitled.

- RUPA expands on UPA by permitting that, during any term of the partnership, a partner may maintain a legal or equitable action, including an action for an accounting.

- An accounting is not a prerequisite to the availability of other remedies.

Management and Control

- All partners have equal rights in the management and conduct of the partnership business. This may be changed by agreement; for example, votes might be assigned varying weights to correspond to capital contributions or shares in the profits.

- Any differences arising as to matters connected to the ordinary course of partnership business may be decided by a majority of the partners, but no act in contravention of any agreement between the partners may be accomplished properly without the consent of all the partners.

Property Rights of a Partner

- The property rights of a partner consist of:

    (1) his interest in the partnership (i.e., economic rights); and

    (2) his right to participate in management.

- A partner is not a co-owner of partnership property and has no interest in partnership property that can be transferred, either voluntarily or involuntarily.

- A partner's **transferable interest** includes his share of profits and losses of the partnership and his right to receive distributions (such interest is deemed personal property) and his economic or financial interest in the partnership.

- **Encumbrances:** A judgment creditor can subject the partner's transferable interest to a charging order. Upon application, a court can charge the debtor-partner's transferable interest to satisfy the judgment, and may then, or later, appoint a receiver of his share of the distributions due him from the partnership.

Fiduciary Duties

In General

RULE > As to partnership matters, partners have a fiduciary relationship to one another and owe the partnership and the other partners a duty of care and a duty of loyalty.

Duty of Care

- Each partner owes to the partnership a duty of care in the conduct and winding up of the partnership business.

- Such duty is limited to refraining from engaging in grossly negligent or reckless conduct, intentional misconduct, or a knowing violation of the law.

Duty of Loyalty

- **Good Faith:** A partner must discharge his duties to the partnership and the other partners exercising his rights consistent with the obligation of good faith and fair dealing.

- **Duty Not to Compete:** A partner must not compete with the partnership in the conduct of its business. If he does so, he must account to the partnership for his profits.

- **Business Opportunity:** A partner may not exploit a business opportunity of the partnership unless he has made full disclosure and received the approval of his other partners. If no conflict of interest or business opportunity is involved, a partner may engage in other enterprises, unless the partnership agreement specifies otherwise.

- **Duty to Disclose:** By statute, partners must render on demand true and full information concerning all things affecting the partnership to any partner, legal representative of any deceased partner, or partner under legal disability.

- **Duty to Account:** Under RUPA, every partner must account to the partnership for any benefit, and holds as trustee for the partnership any profit derived by him without the consent of the other partners from any transaction connected with the conduct and winding up of the partnership business or from any use by him of its property.

Duty to Keep Books and Right of Inspection

- The partnership books and records must be kept, subject to any agreement between the partners, at the chief executive office, and every partner shall, at all times, have access to and may inspect and copy any of the books and records.

New Members

- No person can become a member of a partnership without the consent of all partners.

- When a new member is admitted to the partnership by consent, the new partner's liability for obligations and torts arising before his joining is only his contribution to the partnership; the new partner is not personally liable for any such charges that arose prior to him joining the partnership.

Suits Between Partners

- A partner may maintain an equitable or legal action against another partner or the partnership to enforce the partner's rights under the partnership agreement, under RUPA, and any other rights otherwise protectable, whether or not arising under the partnership relationship.

PARTNERSHIP PROPERTY

Partnership Property

Property Originally Brought In

- All property originally brought into the partnership stock on account of the partnership is partnership property.

- Any property—cash, contributions in kind, goods, labor, or skill—brought into the business at its formation is the **capital** of the partnership.

Property Subsequently Acquired

- Unless a **contrary intention** appears, all property subsequently acquired by purchase or otherwise on account of the partnership is property of the partnership and not that of the partners individually.

Property Purchased With Partnership Funds

- Unless a contrary intention appears, property purchased with partnership assets is partnership property. Any receivables, judgments obtained, contracts, or profits are partnership property.

- Factors considered in establishing a **contrary intention** are:

  (1)   the terms of the partnership agreement or any other relevant express or implied agreement;

  (2)   the partnership's records;

  (3)   the payment of taxes, repair bills, or insurance premiums;

(4)   the conduct of the partners;

(5)   whether the property was used or improved by the business; and

(6)   how title to the property was held.

- As a corollary to this, it is presumed that property acquired in the name of one or more of the partners, without an indication of the person's status as a partner and without use of partnership funds, is separate property, even if used for partnership purposes.

Real Property

- Any estate in real property may be acquired in the partnership name. This is a departure from common law, which did not allow real estate to be held in a partnership name. However, RUPA does not require that title be taken in the partnership name (as long as it was purchased with partnership funds, it is presumed to be partnership property even if held in one partner's name).

Conveyance of Real Property

Title in Name of Partnership

- If title to real property is in the partnership name, any partner may convey title by a conveyance executed in the partnership name.

Title in Name of One or More Partners

- If title to real property is in the name of one or more of the partners, with an indication of their capacity as partners or of the existence of the partnership, but the record does not disclose the name of the partnership, the partners in whose name the title stands may convey title to the property.

Title in Name of Third Persons

- If title is in the name of one or more third persons (e.g., in trust for the partnership), without an indication (in the instrument transferring the property to the third person) of their capacity or of the existence of a partnership, the property may be transferred by an instrument of transfer executed by the persons in whose name the property is held.

DISSOCIATION, DISSOLUTION, AND WINDING UP

Dissociation

Terminology

DEFINITION Dissociation is the withdrawal of a partner from the partnership.

Events of Dissociation

- A partner is dissociated from a partnership upon the occurrence of any of the following:

(1)   the express intention partnership having notice of the partner's express intention to withdraw as a partner;

(2)   an event delineated in the partnership agreement as causing the partner's dissociation;

(3)   the partner's expulsion pursuant to the partnership agreement;

(4)   the partner's expulsion by a unanimous vote of the other partners for specific reasons;

(5)   a judicial determination, after application to the court by the partnership or another partner for specific reasons;

(6)   the partner's bankruptcy or other financial insolvency;

(7)   the partner's incapacity or death;

(8)   in the case of a partner that is a trust or trustee, the distribution of the trust's entire transferable interest in the partnership;

(9)   in the case of a partner that is an estate or representative of an estate, distribution of the entire transferable interest in the partnership; or

(10)   the termination of a partner who is not an individual, partnership, corporation, trust, or estate.

Power to Dissociate

- A partner has the power to dissociate at any time, rightfully or wrongfully, by expressly stating the intention to do so.

Wrongful Dissociation

- In the event of a willful dissociation, a partner's action is wrongful only if:

    (1)   it is in breach of an express provision of the partnership agreement; or

    (2)   in the case of a partnership for a definite term or particular undertaking, it occurs before the expiration of the term or the completion of the undertaking by virtue of:

        (a)   a partner's express will to withdraw, unless the withdrawal follows within 90 days after another partner's dissociation by death, bankruptcy or insolvency, incapacity, distribution by a trust or estate that is a partner of such trust or estate's entire transferable interest in the partnership, or termination of a partner who is not an individual, partnership, corporation, trust, or estate;

        (b)   the partner's expulsion following judicial determination;

        (c)   the partner's dissociation by becoming a debtor in bankruptcy; or

        (d)   in the case of a partner who is not an individual, trust, or estate, the partner is expelled or otherwise dissociated because the partnership willfully dissolved or terminated.

- A partner who wrongfully dissociates is liable to the partnership and the other partners for damages caused by the dissociation. This liability is in addition to any other obligation the partner has to the partnership or to the other partners.

Effect of Dissociation on Rights and Duties of Dissociating Partner

- Upon a partner's dissociation, that partner's:

    (1)   right to participate in the management and conduct of the partnership business terminates;

    (2)   duty of loyalty for future events terminates; and

    (3)   duty of loyalty and duty of care continue only with regard to matters that arose before the partner's dissociation.

- Under older versions of RUPA, the withdrawal of a partner resulted in dissolution of the partnership.

Dissociated Partner's Power to Bind Partnership

- For two years after a partner dissociates without resulting in a dissolution and winding up of the partnership business, the partnership is bound by an act of the dissociated partner that would have bound the partnership before dissociation only if, at the time of entering into the transaction, the other party:

    (1)   reasonably believed that the dissociated partner was then a partner; and

    (2)   is deemed not to have knowledge or notice of the dissociation.

■ If the partnership becomes liable for any obligation that the dissociated partner incurs after dissociation, then the dissociated partner will be liable to the partnership for such damages.

Dissolution and Winding Up

Terminology

■ **Dissolution** is the commencement of the winding up process.

■ **Winding up** is the process of settling partnership affairs.

■ **Termination** is the point at which all the partnership affairs are wound up.

Causes of Dissolution

Mandatory Dissolution

■ Dissolution is caused by:

   (1)   the express will of any partner in a partnership at will;

   (2)   termination of the definite term or particular undertaking specified in the partnership agreement;

   (3)   at least half of the remaining partners agree to wind up the partnership business within 90 days after a partner's dissociation by death, bankruptcy or insolvency, incapacity, distribution of all of a trust or estate in the partnership (where the partner is the trust or estate), or termination of a partner that is not an individual, partnership, corporation, trust, or estate; or

   (4)   an event which makes it unlawful for the business of the partnership to be carried on or for the members to carry it on.

Permissive Dissolution

■ A partnership can be dissolved at any time by unanimous consent, regardless of any duration specified in the partnership agreement.

■ A partnership can also be dissolved on application by a partner or a transferee of a partner's transferable interest, by a judicial determination stating the circumstances render dissolution equitable.

Continuance After Dissolution

■ A partnership continues after dissolution only for the purpose of winding up the business. The partnership is terminated when the winding up of its business is complete.

Effect of Dissolution on Authority of Partner

As to Third Parties

■ A partnership is bound by a partner's act after dissolution that:

   (1)   is appropriate for winding up the partnership business; or

   (2)   would have bound the partnership before dissolution, if the other party did not have notice of the dissolution.

■ RUPA allows a partner who has not wrongfully dissociated to file a statement of dissolution with the appropriate state agency stating the name of the partnership and that the partnership has dissolved and is winding up its business. A person not a partner is deemed to have notice of the dissolution and limitation on the partners' authority 90 days after the statement of dissolution has been filed.

As to Co-Partners

- After dissolution, a partner is liable to the other partners for his share of any partnership liability incurred following dissolution.

- A partner who knows of the dissolution, and incurs a partnership liability by an act that is not appropriate for winding up the partnership business, is liable to the partnership for any damage caused to the partnership arising from the liability.

Winding Up

Right to Wind Up

- Generally, all the partners who have not wrongfully dissociated (or the legal representative of the last surviving partner) may participate in winding up the partnership's affairs.

- Any partner, his legal representative, or his assignee, upon cause shown, may seek from a court judicial supervision of the winding up.

Powers and Duties in Winding Up

- A partner winding up a partnership may:

  (1) preserve the partnership business or property as a going concern for a reasonable time;

  (2) prosecute and defend actions and proceedings (whether civil, criminal, or administrative);

  (3) settle and close the partnership's business;

  (4) dispose of and transfer the partnership's property;

  (5) discharge the partnership's liabilities;

  (6) distribute the assets of the partnership;

  (7) settle disputes by mediation or arbitration; and

  (8) perform other necessary acts.

Distribution of Assets

Order of Distribution

- In winding up the business, the assets of the partnership must be paid in the following order:

  (1) first, those owing to creditors (including partners who are creditors, to the extent permitted by law); and

  (2) second, those owing to partners (in accordance with their distribution rights).

Settlement of Accounts

- Each partner is entitled to a settlement of all partnership accounts upon winding up the partnership business. Profits and losses that result from the liquidation of the partnership assets must be credited and charged to the partners' accounts, and the partnership must then make a distribution to each partner in an amount equal to the excess of the credits over the charges in such partner's account.

Contribution

- Liabilities are satisfied first out of partnership property; if this is insufficient, the partners must contribute the amount necessary to satisfy the liabilities.

LIMITED LIABILITY PARTNERSHIPS

Overview

- A **limited liability partnership** ("LLP") is a general partnership that is authorized by a state statute and complies therewith to adopt limited liability for its general partners.

- When a general partnership registers as an LLP, all the partners gain protection from liability for obligations of the partnership and of other partners, although they remain liable for their own negligence and the negligence of those they supervise.

Formation

- The name of a registered limited liability partnership must contain the words "Registered Limited Liability Partnership" or "Limited Liability Partnership," or the abbreviations "L.L.P.," "LLP," "R.L.L.P," or "RLLP."

- In order to become a limited liability partnership, a general partnership must file a registration with the Secretary of State executed by one or more partners. The filed statement provides notice that the partnership is a registered limited liability partnership.

Rights, Duties, and Obligations of Partners

- Partners in an LLP have the same fiduciary duties as partners in a general partnership.

Liabilities

- Partners in an LLP are not personally liable for the obligations of the LLP, whether arising from tort, contract, or otherwise, and are personally liable only for their own wrongful acts.

Distributions

- An LLP may not make a distribution if, after the distribution, it would not be able to pay its debts, or if the LLP's total assets would be less than the sum of its total liabilities and the amount the LLP would need if it were dissolved to satisfy superior rights of certain partners.

Dissolution

- Dissolution of an LLP occurs in the same manner as for general partnerships under RUPA.

LIMITED PARTNERSHIPS

In General

- There are several versions of the **Uniform Limited Partnership Act** ("ULPA"). Most states still follow the 1976 or 1985 Act. Approximately 13 states have adopted the 2001 version.

Creation of Limited Partnerships

DEFINITION A limited partnership is a partnership formed by two or more persons having one or more general partners and one or more limited partners.

DEFINITION A general partner manages the business and is personally liable without limitation for partnership obligations.

DEFINITION A limited partner contributes capital and share in profits, but takes no part in the control or management of the business; a limited partner's liability is limited to his or her contributions.

Formation

 RULE A limited partnership is formed by executing and filing with the Secretary of State a certificate of limited partnership, setting forth:

(1) the name of the limited partnership, which must contain the words "limited partnership" or the abbreviations "LP" or "L.P.";

(2) the address of the designated office, and the name and address of the initial agent for service;

(3) the name and address of each general partner;

(4) whether the limited partnership is a limited liability partnership; and

(5) any additional information otherwise required upon merger or conversion.

Limited Liability Limited Partnerships

- A limited liability limited partnership ("LLLP") is limited partnership whose certificate of limited partnership states that it is a limited liability limited partnership. In an LLLP, general partners, as well as limited partners, have limited liability.

- The name of an LLLP must contain the words "limited liability limited partnership" or the abbreviation "LLLP" or "L.L.L.P."

Doing Business

- A limited partnership may carry on any business that a general partnership is allowed to carry on—i.e., for any lawful purpose.

- A limited partnership must continuously maintain an office and a resident agent for the service of process in the state where it is organized.

- The limited partnership must maintain and make available for inspection and copying by any partner during business hours:

(1) a current list of the names and addresses of all partners;

(2) copies of the certificate of limited partnership and the partnership agreement with any amendments thereto; and

(3) copies of all income tax returns and financial statements for the immediately preceding three years.

- Except as provided in the partnership agreement, a partner may lend money to and transact other business with the limited partnership, and has the same rights as a general creditor in the case of an unsecured loan.

Contributions

- Under ULPA, a limited partner may contribute cash, property, services, or a promissory note. A partner's obligation to contribute is not excused by the partner's death, disability, or other inability to perform personally.

- If the partner fails to contribute property or services, he must pay the cash value of property or services at the option of the partnership, unless the partnership certificate provides otherwise. The obligation of a partner to make a contribution (or to return money or other property paid or distributed in violation of the Act) may be compromised only by consent of all partners. However, a creditor of a limited partnership that extends credit or otherwise acts in reliance on an obligation by a partner to make a contribution, without notice of any compromise by all partners, may enforce the original obligation.

Limited Partners—Liabilities and Limitations

Use of Limited Partner's Name

- The name of the limited partnership may contain the name of any partner.

Control of Business

- A limited partner is not personally liable for partnership obligations beyond his contribution solely by reason of being a limited partner, even if he participates in the management and control of the limited partnership.

- Under pre-2001 versions of ULPA, a limited partner could become personally liable for partnership obligations if he participated in the control of the business.

- The 1976, and later the 1985, versions of ULPA added a safe harbor list of activities that did not constitute participating in control and limited liability to those who reasonably believed the limited partner was a general partner.

Mistaken Status

- A person who erroneously, but in good faith, believes himself to be a limited partner is not liable as a general partner if, on learning of his mistake, he:

  (1) causes an amended certificate of limited partnership to be executed and filed; and

  (2) withdraws from future equity participation in the enterprise.

- He is liable as a general partner, however, to any third party who has transacted business with the enterprise prior to his withdrawal and filing of the amendment, if the third party believed in good faith that he was a general partner.

Limited Partners—Rights and Powers

Control of Limited Partnership

- A limited partner does not have the right or power to act for or bind the limited partnership.

Right to Information

- A limited partner has the right to inspect and copy partnership records and tax returns. A limited partner also has the right to obtain from the general partners from time to time upon reasonable demand:

  (1) true and full information as to the financial condition and state of the business of the partnership; and

  (2) such other information as is just and reasonable, if the limited partner seeks the information for a purpose reasonably related to the partner's interest as a limited partner.

New Limited Partners

- A person becomes a limited partner:

  (1) as provided in the partnership agreement;

  (2) as the result of a conversion or merger; or

  (3) with the consent of all the partners.

Fiduciary Duties

- A limited partner does not have any fiduciary duty to the limited partnership or to any partner solely because he is a limited partner.

- A limited partner must discharge the duties of the partnership and the other partners under the Act and under the partnership agreement, and exercise any rights consistent with the obligation of good faith and fair dealing. This obligation is not violated merely because the limited partner's conduct furthers his own interest.

General Partners

- A general partner in a limited partnership has most of the same rights and powers and is subject to the same restrictions and liabilities as a partner in a general partnership.

- A person becomes a general partner:

  (1) as provided in the partnership agreement;

  (2) by the consent of the limited partners following the dissociation of a limited partnership's last general partner in order to prevent dissolution of the partnership;

  (3) as a result of a conversion or merger; or

  (4) with the consent of all the partners.

- A person may be both a general partner and a limited partner simultaneously, with the rights, powers, and restrictions of a general partner, but, with respect to his contribution, the rights of a limited partner.

Transfer of Partnership Interests

In General

- A partnership interest is **personal property** and is generally transferable.

- A transfer does not dissolve a limited partnership, but a transferee is entitled only to receive the distributions to which his transferor would have been entitled.

- A transferor is not released from liability for any knowing false statement in the certificate, or from liability for promised contributions.

Executors, Administrators and Creditors

- The legal representative of a deceased or incompetent partner may exercise all of that partner's rights, including the power to make a transferee a limited partner.

- A judgment creditor of a partner can obtain a charging order against a partner's interest, and to that extent will be a transferee of the interest.

DISTRIBUTIONS

- Distributions of assets are allocated among the parties on the basis of the value of each partner's contribution. Regardless of the nature of his contribution, a partner has no right to receive his distribution in any form other than cash.

- A partner does not have a right to any distribution before the dissolution and winding up of the limited partnership unless the limited partnership decides to make an interim distribution.

- A partner has no right to receive a distribution upon dissociation.

Dissociation

Limited Partner

- A limited partner may withdraw at the time, or upon the happening of the events specified in writing in the partnership agreement, provided that a limited partner may not withdraw prior to dissolution and winding up of the limited partnership.

- Upon dissociation, the limited partner has no further rights in the limited partnership. However, dissociation as a limited partner does not discharge the person from any obligation to the limited partnership or to the other partners that incurred while a limited partner.

General Partner

- A general partner may withdraw by voluntary act at any time, rightfully or wrongfully by giving written notice to the other partners.

- A person ceases to be a general partner of a limited partnership upon the occurrence of any of the following events, most of which are the same as for the dissociation of a limited partner:

    (1)   the partner's voluntary withdrawal;

    (2)   an event agreed to in the partnership agreement;

    (3)   being removed in accordance with the partnership agreement;

    (4)   being removed by unanimous consent of the other partners;

    (5)   being removed by judicial order;

    (6)   death;

    (7)   distribution of the trust or estate's transferable interest (if the person is a trust or trustee, or an estate or representation of an estate);

    (8)   the termination of a partner that is not a natural person, trust, partnership, corporation, estate, or limited liability company; or

    (9)   the limited partnership's participation in conversion or merger.

Wrongful Dissociation

- A dissociation is wrongful if:

    (1)   it is in breach of an express provision of the partnership agreement; or

    (2)   it occurs before the termination of the limited partnership, and:

        (a)   the person withdraws as a general partner by express will;

        (b)   the person is expelled as a general partner by judicial determination;

        (c)   the person is dissociated as a general partner by becoming a debtor in bankruptcy; or

        (d)   in the case of a person who is not an individual, trust, or estate, the person is expelled or otherwise dissociated as a general partner because the limited partnership was willfully dissolved or terminated.

Effect of Dissociation

- Upon dissociation, the general partner's right to participate in management and conduct of the partnership's activities terminates, but obligations incurred while a general partner do not necessarily terminate.

Dissolution

Events of Dissolution

- A limited partnership is dissolved:

    (1)   upon the occurrence of the events specified in the certificate; or

    (2)   upon the written consent of all general partners and limited partners owning a majority of the rights to receive distributions as limited partners at the time the consent is to be effective.

- Dissolution will also occur automatically after the dissociation of a person as a general partner:

    (1) if there is at least one remaining general partner, consent to dissolve the limited partnership is given within 90 days after the dissociation by partners owning a majority of distribution rights at the time of consent; or

    (2) if there are no remaining general partners, 90 days after the dissociation (unless before the end of the 90-day period):

        (a) the limited partners owning a majority of distribution rights as limited partners consent to continue the activities of the limited partnership and admit at least one general partner; and

        (b) at least one person is admitted as a general partner.

Winding Up

- Upon dissolution, the general partners who have not wrongfully dissolved the partnership (or, if none, then the limited partners) may wind up partnership affairs.

Priority of Liabilities upon Dissolution

- In winding up a limited partnership's activities, the assets of the limited partnership, including contributions required upon winding up, must be applied in the following order:

    (1) first, the assets must be applied to satisfy obligations to creditors, including partners that are creditors; and

    (2) second, any surplus remaining must be paid in cash as a distribution.

- If the limited partnership's assets are insufficient to satisfy all of its obligations upon winding up, each person who was a general partner when the obligation was incurred and was not otherwise released from the obligation must contribute to the limited partnership in proportion to his right to receive distribution at the time the obligation was incurred.

- If a person does not contribute the amount required, the other general partners required to make a payment must contribute the additional amount needed in proportion to their right to receive distributions at the time the obligation was incurred.

Secured Transactions

Secured Transactions

DEFINITIONS

Security Interest: creditor's interest in collateral

Goods: type of collateral that includes all things that are movable at the time the security interest attaches

Fixtures: goods that become so related to particular real estate that an interest in those goods arises under real property law

Accessions: goods that are physically united with other goods in such a manner that the identity of the original goods is not lost

Commingled Goods: goods that are physically united with other goods in such a way that their identity is lost in a product or mass

Tangible Intangibles: intangibles that have been reduced to written form, such as negotiable instruments, documents of title, and chattel paper

Intangible Intangibles: intangible collateral including accounts, commercial tort claims, payment intangibles, and general intangibles

Security Agreement: an agreement that creates or provides for a security interest in certain collateral

Financing Statement: the document that is filed to give notice of the security interest

Attachment: the process by which a security interest is created

Purchase-Money Security Interest: a security interest that pertains to goods or software securing an obligation that a debtor incurs to purchase the goods as either all or part of the price of the collateral, or for value given to enable the debtor to acquire rights in, or the use of, the collateral, if the value is in fact so used

Perfection: the process by which the secured party gives notice to the entire world of its security interest

KEY TOPICS

- Attachment
- Collateral
- Default
- Perfection
- PMSI & Financing Statement
- Priorities
- Security Interest

IMPORTANT RULES OF LAW

- Perfection is the process by which the secured party gives notice to the entire world of its security interest. Perfection is necessary for priority purposes. A security interest is perfected if it has been attached and all of the requirements for perfection have been met.

- A security interest attaches when the following three requirements exist simultaneously: (1) the secured party gives value; (2) the debtor has rights in the collateral; and (3) the debtor has authenticated a security agreement that sufficiently describes the collateral.

- Unless otherwise agreed, a security agreement automatically gives the secured party a right to identifiable proceeds. Proceeds are whatever is received upon the sale, exchange or other disposition of collateral. Proceeds are identifiable if the secured party can trace the proceeds back to the original collateral.

INTRODUCTION

General Principles

DEFINITION A **security interest** arises when a party (the **debtor**) uses certain property as collateral to secure repayment of funds to another party (the **secured party**).

- By using the property as collateral, if the debtor defaults on repayment of the funds, the creditor may take possession of the collateral and apply the collateral to the balance owed.

DEFINITION The creditor's interest in the collateral is called a **security interest**.

Guarantor

DEFINITION A **guarantor** (or **surety**) is a person who promises to pay the obligation of the debtor only if the debtor defaults. A surety is liable only to the extent of the terms of the surety agreement.

DEFINITION A **guaranty** is a promise to answer for the debt, default, or miscarriage of another person.

DEFINITION A **continuing guaranty** is a guaranty relating to a future liability of the principal, under successive transactions, which either continues the guarantor's liability or from time to time renews it after it has been satisfied.

- A guaranty executed contemporaneously with the principal obligations does not require separate consideration; a guaranty not executed contemporaneously with the principal obligation does require separate and distinct consideration.

- If a surety makes a promise to perform at the same time that the creditor performs or promises to perform, the creditor's promise will serve as consideration for the surety's promise, because the creditor has incurred a detriment in exchange for the surety's promise.

- If a gratuitous surety does not make her promise until after the creditor has performed or made an absolute promise to perform, there is no consideration to support the surety's promise because of the preexisting legal duty rule (the creditor has not incurred any new detriment in exchange for the surety's).

APPLICATION OF ARTICLE 9 OF THE UNIFORM COMMERCIAL CODE

When Applicable

- The Code applies to:

    (1) any transaction, regardless of its form, that creates a security interest in personal property or fixtures by contract;

    (2) agricultural liens;

    (3) sales of accounts receivable, chattel paper, negotiable instruments, promissory notes, and payment intangibles;

    (4) consignments; and

    (5) certain lease-purchase agreements.

DEFINITION A **consignment** is a transaction in which a person delivers goods to a merchant for the purpose of sale; the merchant deals in goods of that kind; the aggregate value of each delivery is $1,000 or more; the goods are not consumer goods; and the transaction does not create a security interest that secures an obligation.

When Not Applicable

- UCC Article 9 is not applicable to:

  (1) landlord's liens;

  (2) a lien, other than an agricultural lien, given by statute or other rule of law for services or materials;

  (3) assignment of a claim for wages, salary, or other compensation of an employee;

  (4) a sale of accounts, chattel paper, payment intangibles, or promissory notes as part of a sale of the business out of which they arose;

  (5) assignment of accounts, chattel paper, payment intangibles, or promissory notes which is for the purpose of collection only;

  (6) assignment of a right to payment under a contract to an assignee that is also required to perform under the contract;

  (7) assignment of a single account, payment intangible, or promissory note to an assignee in full or partial satisfaction of a preexisting indebtedness;

  (8) a transfer of an interest in, or an assignment of, a claim under an insurance policy, other than with respect to a health insurance receivable owed to a provider;

  (9) assignment of a right represented by a judgment, other than one taken on a right to payment that was collateral;

  (10) a right of recoupment or set-off;

  (11) an interest in or lien on real property, including a lease or rents thereunder;

  (12) assignment of a claim arising in tort, other than a commercial tort claim;

  (13) assignment of a deposit account in a consumer transaction;

  (14) security interests governed by state or foreign law; or

  (15) security interests to the extent preempted by federal law.

TYPES OF COLLATERAL

TYPES OF COLLATERAL	
Category	Includes
Goods	• Consumer Goods • Inventory • Farm Products • Equipment
Tangible Intangibles	• Instruments • Documents • Chattel Paper
Intangible Intangibles	• Accounts • Commercial Tort Claims • General Intangibles
Investment Property	• Certificated and Uncertificated Securities • Securities Accounts • Commodity Contracts

Categories of Collateral

- The Code provides for certain broad types of collateral and then breaks each down into more specific categories. The collateral in any given secured transaction must fit into one, and only one, of these categories.

- Different rules governing enforcement, perfection of the security interest, and priorities often depend upon the category into which the collateral falls.

- The four categories are:

    (1) goods;

    (2) tangible intangibles;

    (3) intangible intangibles; and

    (4) investment property.

Goods

DEFINITION **Goods** include all things that are movable at the time the security interest attaches. This generally includes fixtures and computer programs embedded in goods, if the program is associated with the goods so that it is customarily considered part of the goods or if an owner of the goods has a right to use the program in connection with the goods.

EXCEPTION The term goods does not include accounts, chattel paper, commercial tort claims, deposit accounts, documents, general intangibles, instruments, investment property, letter-of-credit rights, letters of credit, money, a computer program embedded in goods that consist solely of the medium in which the program is embedded, or oil, gas, or other minerals before extraction.

- Goods are further broken down into several categories depending on in what capacity and how the debtor primarily uses them:

    (1) consumer goods;

    (2) inventory;

    (3) farm products; and

    (4) equipment.

DEFINITION **Consumer goods** are those "used or bought for use primarily for personal, family or household purposes."

DEFINITION **Inventory** is goods, other than farm products, that (1) are leased by a person as lessor; (2) are held for sale or lease or to be furnished under a contract of service; (3) are furnished under a contract of service; or (4) consist of raw materials, work in process, or materials used or consumed in business.

DEFINITION **Farm products** generally means "goods, other than standing timber, with respect to which the debtor is engaged in a farming operation," including crops, livestock, products of crops or livestock in their unmanufactured state, aquatic goods produced in aquacultural operations, and supplies used or produced in a farming operation.

DEFINITION **Equipment** is a catchall category, defined merely as goods "other than inventory, farm products, or consumer goods."

- In addition to placing the goods in one of the above categories, it is important to determine if any of the goods are, or will become, fixtures (parts of real estate) or accessions (identifiable parts of larger whole goods). These possibilities arise most often with consumer goods and equipment.

DEFINITION **Fixtures** are goods that become so related to particular real estate that an interest in those goods arises under real property law. A security interest in fixtures is generally subordinate to a conflicting interest in the related real estate by one other than the debtor.

DEFINITION **Accessions** are goods that are physically united with other goods in such a manner that the identity of the original goods is not lost. If a security interest is perfected when the collateral becomes an accession, the security interest remains perfected.

- Ordinary building materials (e.g., nails or wood), when incorporated into an improvement on land, are regarded by the Code as inseparable from the structure itself.

- A security interest may be created in an accession and continues in collateral which becomes an accession.

DEFINITION **Commingled goods** are goods that are physically united with other goods in such a way that their identity is lost in a product or mass. The term includes goods whose identity is lost through manufacturing or production (e.g., flour that has become part of baked goods) and through mere mixing with other goods from which they cannot be distinguished (e.g., ball bearings).

- A security interest does not exist in specific goods that have become commingled. However, a security interest may attach to a product or mass that results when goods become commingled.

- If a security interest in collateral is perfected before the collateral becomes commingled goods, the security interest that attaches to the commingled product or mass is perfected.

Tangible Intangibles

- Certain intangibles, such as contractual obligations to hold or deliver goods or to pay money, and ownership in goods or business entities, are commonly reduced to tangible or written form. The intangibles are transferred by transferring the writing.

- Tangible intangibles may be categorized as:

  (1) instruments;

  (2) documents; or

  (3) chattel paper.

DEFINITION **Instruments**, as defined in Article 9, means negotiable instruments, i.e., drafts and notes as defined in Article 3 or any writing that evidences a right to the payment of a monetary obligation but is not itself a security agreement or lease.

DEFINITION **Documents** are documents of title, which include warehouse receipts or orders for the delivery of goods.

DEFINITION **Chattel paper** means a record or records evidencing both a monetary obligation and a security interest in, or a lease of, specific goods.

Intangible Intangibles

- Many intangibles, such as monetary obligations or literary rights, while possibly evidenced by writings, are treated as intangibles. The writings take on no commercial significance of their own, i.e., they are not indispensable.

- Such intangibles include:

  (1) accounts;

  (2) commercial tort claims; and

  (3) general intangibles.

DEFINITION **Accounts** are rights to "payment of a monetary obligation, whether or not earned by performance," generally for property that has been transferred or otherwise disposed of, for services, or arising out of the use of a credit or charge card.

DEFINITION > A **commercial tort claim** is a claim arising in tort where the plaintiff is an organization, or where the plaintiff is an individual but the claim arose in the course of the plaintiff's business or profession and it does not include damages arising from personal injury or death.

DEFINITION > A **general intangible** is intangible collateral that fails to fit into any other category. It includes things (choses) in action, payment intangibles, and software. A **payment intangible** is a general intangible under which the account debtor's principal obligation is a monetary obligation.

Investment Property

DEFINITION > **Investment property** includes certificated and uncertificated securities, securities accounts, and entitlements, as defined in Article 8. It also includes commodity contracts and commodity accounts.

Proceeds

- Collateral subject to a security interest may also be in the form of proceeds of the disposition of other collateral.

- Proceeds include:

  (1) whatever is acquired upon the sale, lease, license, exchange, or other disposition of collateral;

  (2) whatever is collected on, or distributed on account of, collateral;

  (3) rights arising out of collateral;

  (4) to the extent of the value of collateral, claims arising out of the loss, nonconformity, or interference of rights in, or damage to, the collateral; or

  (5) to the extent of the value of collateral and to the extent payable to the debtor or the secured party, insurance on the collateral.

- There are two kinds of proceeds: cash proceeds (i.e., money, checks, deposit accounts and the like) and noncash proceeds, which includes all other proceeds.

THE SECURITY INTEREST

In General

- A security interest is created by a written security agreement or by the secured party's taking possession, delivery, or control of the collateral with the intent to secure a debt, plus attachment of the security interest to the collateral.

Security Agreement

DEFINITION > A **security agreement** is an agreement that creates or provides for a security interest in certain collateral.

- The security interest must be in writing and contain a granting clause, i.e., state that it is creating a security interest. It must also contain a description of the collateral and be authenticated by the debtor.

NOTE > The granting clause need not be formal and can be in a different document.

- Cases have uniformly held that a financing statement is not sufficient as a security agreement unless the financing statement itself, or some other writing, contains a "granting clause," indicating that the debtor intends to give a security interest to the secured party.

- A description is sufficient, whether or not it is specific, if it reasonably identifies what is described.

DEFINITION **Authentication** means either signing a written document or (to include electronic transmissions) executing or otherwise adopting a symbol, or encrypting or similarly processing a record in whole or in part, with the present intent of the authenticating person to identify the person and adopt or accept a record.

DEFINITION A **financing statement** is the document that is filed to give notice of the security interest—to perfect the security interest.

Possession

- A written security agreement is necessary for the creation of a security interest unless the secured party has possession of the collateral. Where the secured party has possession, all that is needed is an agreement, which can be oral, that the secured party is to have a security interest.

Control

- The security agreement may be evidenced by control if the collateral is deposit accounts, electronic chattel paper, investment property, or letter-of-credit rights, and the secured party has control of the collateral.

Validity

- A security agreement is generally effective between the parties, against purchasers of the collateral, and against creditors.

ATTACHMENT

Introduction

- **Attachment** is the process by which the security interest is created. A security interest is created by a contract between the debtor and the secured party. Once the security interest has attached, the secured party has all of the enforcement rights provided by Article 9, including the right to repossess the collateral upon the debtor's default.

Requirements

- The security interest attaches when the following elements exist simultaneously:

    (1) the secured party gives value;

    (2) the debtor has rights in the collateral or the power to transfer rights in the collateral to a secured party; and

    (3) the debtor has authenticated a security agreement that sufficiently describes the collateral.

NOTE A description of collateral is sufficient if it reasonably identifies what is described. However, a description by type is not sufficient if the collateral is consumer goods and the transaction is a consumer transaction. A more specific description is required in this case.

- A supergeneric description (e.g., "all the debtor's personal property") is not sufficient in a security agreement.

After-Acquired Collateral

DEFINITION **After-acquired collateral** is collateral that the debtor acquires or comes into ownership of after the security agreement has been signed.

- A security agreement may provide for an interest in after-acquired collateral.

- Inventory, by its nature, is constantly depleted and replenished. Therefore, a security agreement specifying an interest in inventory will create an interest in after-acquired collateral, notwithstanding the fact that there is no explicit after-acquired property clause. The same rule applies to accounts receivable.

- A security agreement cannot provide that it covers after-acquired consumer goods, unless the debtor acquires rights in the consumer goods within 10 days of the secured party giving value.

Future Advances

- A future advance clause generally indicates that the collateral secures future debt.

- A security agreement may also provide that collateral secures future advances. For instance, a security agreement may secure all advances under a revolving credit agreement, such that no additional security agreement is needed to secure the future advances.

Proceeds

- A security interest in collateral automatically extends to identifiable proceeds of the collateral.

PURCHASE-MONEY SECURITY INTEREST

In General

DEFINITION A security interest in goods is a **purchase-money security interest** (**PMSI**) if it pertains to goods that are purchase-money collateral.

DEFINITION **Purchase-money collateral** means goods or software securing a purchase-money obligation that a debtor incurs to purchase the goods.

- A debtor incurs a **purchase-money obligation** if the obligation is incurred:

  (1) as all or part of the price of the collateral (as when a seller finances the purchase); or

  (2) for value given to enable the debtor to acquire rights in, or the use of, the collateral, if the value is in fact so used (as when a third party, such as a bank, finances the purchase).

PMSI in Goods

- A security interest in goods is a PMSI:

  (1) to the extent the goods are given as collateral for an obligation the debtor incurred for the purchase of the goods and actually used to purchase the goods;

  (2) if the security interest is in inventory that is or was purchase-money collateral, also to the extent that the security interest secures a purchase-money obligation incurred with respect to other inventory in which the secured party holds or held a PMSI; and

  (3) also to the extent that the security interest secures a purchase-money obligation incurred with respect to software in which the secured party holds or held a PMSI.

PERFECTION

In General

DEFINITION **Perfection** is the process by which the secured party gives notice to the entire world of its security interest. Perfection is necessary for priority purposes.

- A security interest is perfected if it has attached and if all of the requirements for perfection have been met. If the requirements are met before attachment, then upon attachment, the security interest is perfected.

Law Governing Perfection and Priority

- Generally, the law governing perfection of a security interest is the law of the jurisdiction where the debtor is located.

- Where collateral is located in a jurisdiction, the local law of that jurisdiction will govern perfection, the effect of perfection or nonperfection, and the priority of a possessory security interest in that collateral.

Methods of Perfection

Filing

- Filing a financing statement in a public office is the most common way to perfect a security interest. Generally, filing can be done:

    (1)   in the secretary of state's office;

    (2)   in limited circumstances (when the collateral consists of fixtures), in the office of the county clerk (land records) in the county where the land to which the collateral is attached is located; or

    (3)   if the secured party is perfecting by filing a financing statement, the security interest is perfected only if the financing statement is filed in the correct office in the correct state.

- Filing is not effective for the following types of collateral:

    (1)   a deposit account, which may be perfected only by control;

    (2)   a letter-of-credit right, which may be perfected only by control; and

    (3)   money, which may be perfected only by possession.

Possession

- A secured party may also perfect a security interest by taking possession of the collateral. Taking possession of the collateral is possible only when the collateral is tangible. Perfection by possession only applies to the following types of collateral:

    (1)   negotiable documents;

    (2)   goods;

    (3)   instruments;

    (4)   money; or

    (5)   tangible chattel paper.

- Perfection by possession is not permitted for the following types of collateral:

    (1)   accounts;

    (2)   commercial tort claims;

    (3)   deposit accounts;

    (4)   investment property;

    (5)   letter-of-credit rights;

    (6)   letters of credit; and

    (7)   oil, gas, or other minerals before extraction.

- A security interest in money is perfected only by the secured party's taking possession. Such perfection is effective only when, and for as long as, the secured party has possession.

- A secured party who has taken possession of collateral must use reasonable care in its custody and preservation.

Control

- A security interest may also be perfected by taking control of the collateral. Taking control of the collateral applies only to:

  (1) investment securities;

  (2) letter-of-credit rights;

  (3) deposit accounts; and

  (4) electronic chattel paper.

Automatic Perfection

- If the security interest is a purchase-money security interest in consumer goods, perfection is automatic as soon as the security interest attaches and remains effective permanently (excluding motor vehicles and fixtures).

- The secured party need neither file nor have possession to have a perfected purchase-money security interest in consumer goods.

- Automatic perfection of a PMSI in consumer goods does not apply to property subject to a certificate of title statute (other than inventory) or fixtures, even if they are consumer goods.

Automatic Temporary Perfection

- A security interest attaches to any identifiable proceeds of collateral upon disposition of the collateral.

- A perfected security interest in proceeds is provided by the Code automatically when the security interest in the original collateral is perfected, unless the security agreement specifically provides that proceeds are not covered.

- This automatic perfection for proceeds continues for only 20 days after attachment (i.e., receipt of the proceeds by the debtor) unless:

  (1) a filed financing statement covers the original collateral, the proceeds are collateral in which a security interest may be perfected by filing in the office in which the financing statement has been filed, and the proceeds are not acquired with cash proceeds;

  (2) the proceeds are identifiable cash proceeds; or

  (3) the security interest in proceeds is otherwise perfected when the security interest attaches to the proceeds or within 20 days thereafter.

Purchase-Money Security Interests

- Perfection generally takes place at the moment of filing or of possession; however, the Code provides what is equivalent to a limited 20-day grace period where the security interest is a purchase-money security interest.

- If the financing statement is filed within 20 days after the debtor receives delivery of the collateral, perfection relates back to the date the security interest attached upon the debtor's receipt of the collateral.

Multiple Methods of Perfection

- If a security interest is perfected by one method and later perfected by another method without an intermediate period of being unperfected, the security interest is perfected continuously.

FINANCING STATEMENT

Notice Filing

- The Code adopts the system of **notice filing**, which essentially requires a filing that provides notice that a person may have a security interest in the collateral indicated. The security agreement itself need not be filed; instead, the financing statement is filed.

Necessary Information

- A financing statement must include:

  (1) the name of the debtor;

  (2) the name of the secured party or the secured party's representative; and

  (3) a description of the collateral covered by the financing statement.

- A financing statement sufficiently describes the collateral it covers if it provides:

  (1) a description of the collateral that reasonably identifies what is described; or

  (2) an indication that the financing statement covers all assets or all personal property.

> **NOTE** This rule differs from that for security agreements. A supergeneric collateral description in a financing statement is sufficient.

- If the financing statement includes collateral related to real property, such as minerals, timber-to-be-cut, or fixtures, the real property to which the collateral is related must also be described.

- The description must be sufficient to give constructive notice if used in a mortgage.

- A financing statement will perfect interests in after-acquired property and future advances as long as the indication of collateral in the statement is sufficiently broad to cover the after-acquired property and/or future advances, even if they are not mentioned specifically.

Authorization of Financing Statement

- A financing statement must be authorized by the debtor.

- A security agreement is authorization for the financing statement whether it says so or not.

Special Rules for Fixtures

- As noted above, **fixtures** are goods that are so related to real property that an interest in them passes under real estate law. Therefore, in order to be a fixture, the item must be:

  (1) attached to the real estate;

  (2) adapted to the use of the real estate; and

  (3) intended to be a permanent attachment to the real estate.

- A fixture filing must:

  (1) contain all of the information required in a financing statement by Section 9-502(a);

  (2) indicate that it covers fixtures;

  (3) indicate that it is to be filed in the real property records;

  (4) provide a description of the real property to which the fixture is related; and

(5) if the debtor does not have an interest of record in the real property, provide the name of the record owner.

Acceptance and Effectiveness of Financing Statement

- An ineffective financing statement does not perfect a security interest.

- A filing office must refuse to accept a financing statement, and therefore filing will not occur, if:

  (1) the record is not communicated by an authorized method;

  (2) the amount that is tendered is not equal to or greater than the sum of the applicable filing fee plus recording tax, if any, based on the representation of indebtedness required for the tax;

  (3) for an initial statement, the debtor's name is not provided;

  (4) for an amendment, the statement does not identify the initial financing statement or identifies an initial financing statement whose effectiveness has lapsed;

  (5) for real property, the statement does not provide a sufficient description of the real property;

  (6) there is a secured party of record, and the secured party's name or address is omitted;

  (7) the record does not contain, either on its face or in an accompanying sworn statement, the language required by section 67-4-409(b)(5)(C) with respect to the recording tax imposed by section 67-4-409(b), if any;

  (8) the debtor's address and status as an individual or organization are not provided; or

  (9) the financing statement indicates that the debtor is an organization and the statement does not provide the type or jurisdiction of the organization or an organizational identification number.

- A filing office may only refuse to accept a financing statement for one of the reasons set forth above.

Wrongful Rejection

- If a statement is filed with the filing fee, but the filing office refuses to accept it for a reason not enumerated above, the financing statement is still effective as a filing except as against a purchaser of the collateral that gives value in reasonable reliance upon the absence of the record from the files.

Errors or Omissions in Financing Statement

- A financing statement containing minor errors will still be effective if it substantially satisfies the requirements, unless the errors make the financing statement seriously misleading.

  (1) Failure to sufficiently provide the name of the debtor is seriously misleading.

  (2) However, if a search of the records of the filing office under the debtor's correct name, using the office's standard search logic, would disclose a financing statement that fails sufficiently to provide the name of the debtor, the financing statement is not seriously misleading.

Time of Filing

- A financing statement may be filed before a security agreement is made or a security interest otherwise attaches. This is important to priority.

Changes That Can Affect the Effectiveness of a Financing Statement

- A filed financing statement remains effective even if the collateral is sold, exchanged, leased, or otherwise disposed of, and in which a security interest continues, even if the secured party knows of or consents to the disposition.

- If the information in the financing statement becomes seriously misleading only after the financing statement is filed, the financing statement will remain effective unless the debtor changes its name or the original collateral is exchanged for proceeds.

- If a debtor changes his name, resulting in a financing statement that is seriously misleading, the financing statement will only be effective to perfect security interests in collateral acquired within four months of the name change, unless an amendment to the financing statement correcting this is filed within four months of the name change.

- A financing statement can also become ineffective if the debtor moves.

Period of Effectiveness of Filed Financing Statement

- A filed financing statement is effective for five years after the date of filing.

- If the financing statement expires without a continuation statement being filed, the financing statement will lapse. Upon lapse, the filing statement becomes ineffective and any security interest that was perfected by the filing statement becomes unperfected.

- A **continuation statement** must be filed within six months before the expiration of the five-year period.

- Continuation statements may be filed repeatedly to extend the effectiveness of the financing statement.

PRIORITIES

General Rule

- The general rule regarding priority under Article 9 is "first-in-time, first-in-right."

Unperfected Security Interest

- Among unperfected security interests, the first security interest to attach will prevail.

Perfected Over Unperfected

- A perfected security interest will prevail over an unperfected security interest.

Two Perfected Interests

- Between two perfected security interests, the security interest with the earliest time of filing or perfection, whichever is earlier, which has continued without interruption, will prevail.

Second-in-Time, First-in-Right

- A perfected PMSI in goods (and its identifiable proceeds) will prevail over a conflicting security interest if the PMSI is perfected when the debtor receives possession of the collateral or within 20 days thereafter.

- However, when the collateral is inventory, the purchase-money secured party has to take additional steps to acquire priority over the first-in-time secured party.

- The purchase-money secured party will have priority over a conflicting security interest in the same inventory, chattel paper or an instrument constituting proceeds of the inventory (and proceeds of the chattel paper), and identifiable cash proceeds of the inventory that are received on or before the delivery of the inventory to a buyer if:

    (1) the PMSI is perfected when the debtor receives possession of the inventory; and either

    (2) if the holder of the conflicting security interest filed a financing statement covering the same inventory before the PMSI was perfected by filing; or

(3) if temporarily perfected without filing or possession, before the beginning of the 20-day period, the purchase-money secured party sends an authenticated notification to the holder of the conflicting security interest, stating that it has or expects to obtain a PMSI in the inventory and describing the inventory; and the holder of the conflicting security interest receives the notification within five years before the debtor takes possession of the inventory.

Conflicting PMSIs

- If more than one security interest qualifies for PMSI priority in the same collateral, then:

  (1) a PMSI securing the price of the collateral (i.e., created in favor of the seller) prevails over a PMSI that secures a loan; and

  (2) in all other cases, the first-in-time, first-in-right rule applies.

Contests with Lien Creditors

- The first-in-time, first-in-right rule applies to priority contests between lien creditors and secured parties. Therefore, a secured party will have priority over a lien creditor if the secured party:

  (1) perfects before the lien creditor's interest arises; or

  (2) files a financing statement and evidences a security agreement (by authentication, possession, or control) before the lien creditor's interest arises.

- A **lien creditor** is:

  (1) a creditor that has acquired an interest in the property by attachment, levy, or the like;

  (2) an assignee for the benefit of creditors;

  (3) a trustee in bankruptcy; or

  (4) a receiver in equity.

Possessory Lien

- A **possessory lien** is an interest, other than a security interest or agricultural lien, that:

  (1) secures payment or performance of an obligation for services or materials furnished with respect to goods by a person in the ordinary course of business;

  (2) is created by statute or rule of law in favor of the person; and

  (3) its effectiveness depends on the person's possession of the goods.

- A possessory lien on goods has priority over a security interest in the goods unless the statute creating the lien provides otherwise.

Special Rule for PMSIs

- If the PMSI is perfected within 20 days after the debtor receives the collateral, the PMSI will take priority over an intervening lien creditor whose rights arise between the time the security interest attaches and the time of filing.

Accessions

- As noted above, an **accession** refers to goods that are physically united with other goods in such a manner that the identity of the original goods is not lost.

- A security interest created in collateral that becomes an accession will continue. If such a security interest is perfected when the collateral becomes an accession, it remains perfected.

- The priority of a security interest in an accession is determined in the same manner as in any other collateral, except that a security interest in an accession is subordinate to a security interest in the whole that is perfected by compliance with the requirements of a certificate of title statute (e.g., a motor vehicle).

Commingled Goods

- **Commingled goods** are goods that are physically united with other goods in such a manner that their identity is lost.

- A security interest does not exist *per se* in commingled goods, but attaches to the product that results when goods become commingled goods.

- If the security interest in collateral is perfected before the collateral becomes commingled, the interest attached to the product is also perfected.

- A security interest in collateral that is perfected before the collateral becomes commingled goods has priority over a security interest that is unperfected at the time the collateral becomes commingled goods.

- Multiple perfected security interests in commingled goods will rank equally in proportion to the value of the collateral at the time it became commingled goods.

Buyers versus Secured Parties

- Generally, a security interest survives a sale of the collateral.

Exceptions

- A security interest will not continue when the secured party authorizes the sale free of the security interest.

- Additionally, a security interest will not survive a sale if the buyer is:

  (1) a buyer in the ordinary course of business;

  (2) a buyer of consumer goods;

  (3) a buyer of chattel paper;

  (4) a buyer of an instrument; or

  (5) a buyer who takes delivery.

- A buyer in the ordinary course of business is a person who:

  (1) buys goods in good faith;

  (2) buys without knowledge that the sale violates the rights of another person in the goods; and

  (3) buys in the ordinary course from a person in the business of selling goods of that kind.

Consumer Goods Exception

- A buyer of consumer goods, where the sale qualifies as a consumer-to-consumer or garage sale exception, takes free of a security interest (even if perfected).

- This exception applies only when a person buys goods from a person who used or bought the goods for use primarily for personal, family, or household use:

  (1) without knowledge of the security interest;

  (2) for value;

  (3) primarily for the buyer's personal, family, or household purposes; and

  (4) before the filing of a financing statement covering the goods.

Future Advances

Competing Secured Parties

- Generally, a secured party takes subject to all advances secured by a competing security interest having priority under the first-in-time, first-in-right rule (under which the security interest with the earliest time of filing or perfection, whichever is earlier, which has continued without interruption, will prevail).

- However, when a security interest is perfected only automatically or temporarily, and the advance is not made pursuant to a commitment entered into while the security interest was perfected by another method, the advance will have priority from the date it is made.

Lienholders

- A secured party's previously perfected security interest in collateral and all future advances made pursuant to that interest have priority over a lienholder whose interest attaches after the initial security interest was perfected.

Proceeds

- The time of filing or perfection as to a security interest in collateral is also the time of filing or perfection as to a security interest in proceeds.

Special Rules for Fixtures

- When the collateral consists of a fixture, the creditor with a security interest in the fixture will want priority over the creditor who holds the mortgage on the real property to which the fixture is attached. Generally, the only way that such a creditor can obtain priority over the mortgagee is by filing a fixture filing.

- The general priority rule is first-in-time, first-in-right. Therefore, if the mortgage is recorded before the security interest in the fixture is perfected by a fixture filing, then the party holding the mortgage has priority.

ORDER OF PRIORITIES			
Interest	**Will Prevail Over**	**Will Not Prevail Over**	**Against Same Interest**
PMSI	• Perfected Security Interest • Lien Creditor • Unperfected Security Interest	• Buyer in Ordinary Course	• A PMSI securing price of the collateral prevails over a PMSI securing a loan • Otherwise, the first-in-time, first-in-right rule applies
Perfected Security Interest	• Unperfected Security Interest • Lien Creditor (if perfected first)	• Buyer in Ordinary Course • PMSI • Lien Creditor (if attached first)	• First to file or perfect will prevail
Lien Creditor	• Perfected Security Interest (if attached first) • Unperfected Security Interest (if attached before perfected)	• Buyer in Ordinary Course • PMSI • Perfected Security Interest (if perfected first)	• First to attach will prevail
Unperfected Security Interest		• Buyer in Ordinary Course • PMSI • Perfected Security Interest	• First to perfect will prevail
Buyer in Ordinary Course	• PMSI • Perfected Security Interest • Lien Creditor • Unperfected Security Interest		

DEFAULT

In General

- Generally, a **default** occurs whenever the debtor fails to tender an obligation when due. Thus, if a debtor fails to meet an installment payment, there is a default.

- The parties may agree that other acts (e.g., taking the collateral out of the state) constitute a default.

Rights upon Default

- Upon default, a secured party may reduce a claim to judgment, foreclose, or otherwise enforce the claim.

- The secured party's rights after default are cumulative and may be exercised simultaneously.

- A creditor must first seek payment from the debtor before approaching a guarantor.

- A secured party has the right to repossess tangible collateral if it can do so without a breach of the peace.

> **NOTE** Article 9 does not define breach of the peace. However, an act that is likely to lead to violence will be considered to breach the peace. An entry into a home to repossess collateral will always be considered a breach of the peace. A repossession made over any protest by the debtor constitutes a breach of peace even if no violence occurs. When a secured party breaches the peace, he loses the Code's authorization to repossess.

- A secured party who loses the authorization of the Code to repossess may be sued for conversion and is liable for actual damages and for punitive damages if there is evidence of reckless and wanton disregard of another's rights.

- If the secured party cannot obtain the collateral without a breach of the peace, the secured party will be required to bring an action for replevin. A court will issue a writ of replevin, under which the sheriff can seize the property for the secured party.

Payment to Secured Party

- If the collateral consists of accounts receivable, instruments, or chattel paper, the secured party may, upon the debtor's default, notify the person obligated on the collateral to make payment to the secured party.

- The notification must:

  (1) be authenticated by the secured party or the debtor; and

  (2) reasonably identify the rights assigned.

Debtor's Right to Redeem

- The debtor has a right to redeem the collateral by tendering to the secured party the amount of the obligation, including interest, together with reasonable expenses and attorney's fees caused by the default (unless the debtor has agreed otherwise in writing after default).

- However, redemption must be effected before:

  (1) the collateral has been collected;

  (2) the secured party has disposed of the collateral or has entered into a contract for its disposition; or

  (3) the secured party has accepted the collateral in full or partial satisfaction of the obligation.

Waiver

- A debtor may waive his right to redeem the collateral by an agreement entered into, and authenticated after, the default. The agreement of waiver may not be made in advance of the default or at the inception of the secured transaction.

> EXCEPTION A debtor may not waive the right to redeem in a consumer goods transaction.

Disposition after Default

- After default and repossession, a secured party may sell, license, or otherwise dispose of any or all of the collateral in its present condition, or following any commercially reasonable preparation or processing.

- All aspects of disposition must be commercially reasonable, including the method, time, place, and other terms. Disposal may occur by public or private sale.

Whether Sale Is Commercially Reasonable

- A sale is considered commercially reasonable if it is made:

    (1) in the usual manner on any recognized market;

    (2) at the price current in any recognized market at the time of the sale; or

    (3) otherwise in conformity with reasonable commercial practices among dealers in the type of property that was sold.

- The fact that a greater amount could have been obtained by a sale, collection, enforcement, or acceptance at a different time or in a different method from that selected by the secured party is not, in and of itself, sufficient to preclude the secured party from establishing that the sale or other conduct was commercially reasonable.

Notification

- Before disposing of collateral, the secured party must send to the debtor and any secondary obligor a reasonable authenticated notification of disposition.

- This requirement does not apply to collateral that is perishable, that may decline quickly in value, or that is of a type customarily sold on a recognized market.

- Notice is an element of commercial reasonableness. Therefore, if no notice is sent, or if the notice is not sent within a reasonable time before disposition, the sale may be considered commercially unreasonable.

Effect of Sale

- A sale of collateral generally transfers to a transferee for value all of the debtor's rights in the collateral and discharges the security interest and any subordinate security interests or liens.

- This is true as long as the transferee acts in good faith, even if the secured party fails to comply with the rules governing sales and dispositions.

- A transferee who acts in bad faith takes subject to the debtor's rights in the collateral and the security interests in the collateral.

Proceeds of Collection, Enforcement, or Disposition

- The cash proceeds of collection, enforcement, or disposition shall be applied as follows:

    (1) the reasonable expenses of collection and enforcement, or retaking, holding, preparing for disposition, processing, and disposing of the collateral, and reasonable legal fees and expenses incurred by the secured party;

NOTE ▶ Costs of sale are always paid first.

    (2)   the satisfaction of obligations secured by the security interest under which the collection, enforcement, or disposition is made; and

    (3)   the satisfaction of obligations secured by any subordinate security interest in, or other subordinate lien on the collateral, if the secured party has received an authenticated demand before disposal.

- The secured party must pay to the debtor any surplus, or the debtor shall be liable for any deficiency following sale, unless the underlying transaction is a sale of accounts, chattel paper, payment intangibles, or promissory notes.

Deficiency

- If the collateral does not bring enough at sale or collection to pay all outstanding obligations, the secured party is entitled to a judgment for the deficiency (except where the underlying transaction is a sale of accounts, chattel paper, payment intangibles, or promissory notes).

DEFINITION ▶ The **deficiency** is the difference between the amount owed on the debt and the proceeds received at sale.

Debtor's Remedies

- A debtor may seek any lost surplus caused by the secured party's violation of Article 9, even if the debtor's deficiency is eliminated or reduced.

Trusts

Trusts

DEFINITIONS

Trust: fiduciary relationship where a trustee holds legal title to property subject to an equitable obligation to protect or use the property for the beneficiary's benefit, who holds equitable title

Settlor: property owner who creates the trust by transferring assets to a trustee with manifest intent to create a trust relationship

Trustee: legal owner of trust property, who holds it for the benefit of the beneficiaries

Beneficiaries: equitable owners of the trust property who have the right to enforce the terms of the trust and can hold trustees personally liable for breach of their duties

Express *Inter Vivos* Trust: created by the expressed intention of the owner of some property which takes effect during the settlor's life

Testamentary Trust: created by a valid will or other document where the settlor's death is a condition precedent to the creation of any interest under the trust

Discretionary Trust: payment to the beneficiary (even for a stated purpose) is to be made, if at all, at the trustee's absolute discretion

Support Provision: trustee is directed to provide only so much income and/or principal of the trust assets as is necessary for the beneficiary's support and for no other purpose

Spendthrift Provision: a provision that precludes a beneficiary from voluntarily transferring his interest in the trust and creditors from reaching that interest

Prudent Investor Rule: trustee shall invest and manage trust assets as a prudent investor would, by considering the purposes, terms, distribution requirements, and other circumstances of the trust, while exercising reasonable care, skill, and caution

KEY TOPICS

- **Alienability of Trust Interests**
- **Creation and Types of Trusts**
- **Express Trusts**
- **Implied Trusts**
- **Modification, Revocation, and Termination of Trusts**
- **Trustees**
- **Trust Provisions**

IMPORTANT RULES OF LAW

- A Totten trust is a bank account held with a named beneficiary who will receive the contents of the account on the owner's death.

- The trustee of a constructive trust has only one duty—to convey the property to the beneficiary.

- Intent to create a trust requires more than just permissive instructions. It requires the settlor to give instructions that must be followed.

- A trustee owes a duty not to commingle trust assets or benefit from the trust assets.

- A constructive trust is an equitable remedy whereby property that has been obtained by improper means of which the defendant has title, and is traceable to the harm, is conveyed from the defendant to the victim.

INTRODUCTION

In General

DEFINITION ▶ A **trust** is a fiduciary relationship where one party holds legal title to property for the benefit of another.

■ Trusts are created when someone (the grantor, settlor, donor, or testator) transfers legal title to property to a trustee, who administers the trust in accordance with the settlor's wishes for the benefit of the beneficiaries.

Sources of Law

■ In 2000, the National Conference of Commissioners on Uniform State Laws approved a **Uniform Trust Code** ("UTC") to provide a comprehensive codification of trust law for those states that have not addressed these issues comprehensively.

■ The **Restatement (Third) of Trusts** is an important interpretive aid and gap-filler to supplement the uniform codes.

Types of Trusts

RULE ▶ There are two types of trusts:

- **express trusts**, which arise from the intention of the property owner; and
- **implied trusts**, which are equitable remedies and arise by operation of law in certain circumstances.

■ There are two types of express trusts:

(1) private express trusts, which comprise most of the trusts established by individuals; and

(2) charitable trusts, which resemble private express trusts but have some significant, distinguishing characteristics.

■ There are two types of implied trusts:

(1) **resulting trusts**, which place property in the hands of rightful owners when circumstances require it, even though there has not been any wrongdoing on anyone's part; and

(2) **constructive trusts**, which deprive a wrongdoer from retaining improperly obtained property. Constructive trusts are usually erected to remedy fraud or unjust enrichment.

CREATING EXPRESS TRUSTS

Parties to a Trust

Parties

■ Every trust has three parties, though these parties need not be three different people:

(1) The property owner who creates the trust is called the **settlor**, **grantor**, or **testator**. The settlor creates the trust by transferring assets to a trustee with manifest intent to create a trust relationship.

(2) The **trustee** is the legal owner of trust property, who holds it for the benefit of the beneficiaries. Legal title to, and responsibility for, the management of the trust property resides in the trustee.

(3) **Beneficiaries** are the equitable owners of the trust property.

Settlor

■ A trust created during the settlor's lifetime is called an ***inter vivos* trust**. A trust created in a settlor's will is called a **testamentary trust**.

- The settlor of an *inter vivos* trust can also serve as trustee and may be one of the trust's beneficiaries. When the settlor also serves as trustee, the trust is created by **declaration of trust**. The declaration can be oral unless the trust assets include real property, in which case the Statute of Frauds requires that it be written.

- The settlor must deliver title to the trust assets to the trustee. When the settlor names a third-party trustee, trust assets must be actually transferred to the trustee. A mere recital of transfer in a written instrument is insufficient.

Trustee

RULE A trustee can also be the settlor and may be a beneficiary. Central to a trustee's position, however, is that he owes duties to someone other than himself.

- There must always be a beneficiary in existence who can enforce the trust against the trustee. The sole trustee may be one of several beneficiaries, but the trustee may not be the sole beneficiary; rather, there must be at least one additional beneficiary.

- A trust must have a trustee, but failure to designate or appoint a qualified trustee will not necessarily cause the trust to fail. Generally, the court will appoint a trustee if no trustee is designated, or if the designated trustee:

    (1) is incompetent;

    (2) fails to survive the settlor; or

    (3) otherwise fails to qualify.

- **Capacity:** A trustee must have the mental capacity to administer the trust. She cannot be a minor or a mentally incompetent person. Under modern law, corporations are allowed to be trustees. Many states, however, have statutes prohibiting corporations from engaging in trust activities, unless the corporate entity is incorporated under the laws of the particular jurisdiction.

- **Duties of a Trustee:** A trustee must be given some active duties to direct him with respect to the trust property in order for the trust to be valid. If the trustee does not have active duties, the trust is considered "passive" or "dry," and title to the trust assets will pass directly to the beneficiaries.

- The trustee is a fiduciary and duties of the trustee vary by trust. Duties commonly assigned by statute or legally implied include the obligations:

    (1) to preserve property;

    (2) to make trust property productive;

    (3) to invest prudently;

    (4) to administer the trust pursuant to the settlor's directions;

    (5) to keep accurate accounts;

    (6) to segregate trust assets; and

    (7) to exercise fairness with respect to all beneficiaries, regardless of the nature of their interests.

- **Co-Trustees:** Co-trustees who are unable to reach a unanimous decision may act by majority decision. If a vacancy occurs in a co-trusteeship, the remaining co-trustees may act for the trust. A trustee who does not join in an action of another trustee is not liable for the action.

- A trustee may be removed involuntarily from his position in accordance with the terms of the trust, or for cause by a proper court.

Beneficiaries

- A beneficiary is a person that:

    (1) has a present or future beneficial interest in a trust, vested or contingent; or

(2)   in a capacity other than that of trustee, holds a power of appointment over trust property.

■ Beneficiaries have the right to enforce the terms of the trust. Beneficiaries can hold trustees personally liable for breach of their duties. Beneficiaries can recover wrongfully transferred property from gratuitous transferees.

■ A beneficiary must have the ability to enforce terms of the trust. Minors and other legally incompetent beneficiaries can sue to enforce a trust through a guardian *ad litem*.

General Effects of Trust Creation

■ Once a trust has been created, the settlor no longer owns the assets because they have been transferred into the trust. The beneficiaries are the beneficial owners of the trust assets, but cannot ordinarily affect or alter the dispositive or administrative provisions of the trust.

■ The trustee has legal title to the assets and is obligated to adhere to the terms of the trust with respect to the preservation, enhancement, and distribution of the trust property to the beneficiaries.

Elements Necessary to Create a Trust

Required Elements

■ A valid trust requires:

(1)   that a settlor, with the requisite capacity, expresses a present intent to create a trust (i.e., to create the trust now, not some time in the future);

(2)   delivery of specific trust property;

(3)   an ascertainable beneficiary;

(4)   active duties imposed on the trustee;

(5)   a proper trust purpose; and

(6)   a trustee.

Intent to Create a Trust

RULE ▶ The settlor's intention is determined from the language used, his relationship with the parties involved, and any other appropriate circumstances. No particular words (e.g., "trust") or actions are necessary to manifest the settlor's intention to create a trust. Oral declarations of trust are allowed under the Restatement.

■ Where the settlor "suggests" or expresses only a "hope" ("precatory" language) that the property being transferred be used for the benefit of another, the requisite intent to create a trust is usually deemed to be lacking.

■ If the settlor purports to create a trust, but designates certain prerequisites (e.g., delivery of the trust property, description of the beneficiaries, etc.) to be completed in the future, no "present" trust intent exists. However, if the settlor re-manifests the intent when the missing element is furnished, the trust is effective as of the later date.

■ A transfer "in trust" with no specification of the trust's terms will not create a trust.

Delivery

■ A trust cannot exist without property (the **trust *res*, *corpus*, or principal**) that is the subject of the trust relationship. Once created, the trustee owes fiduciary obligations to the beneficiaries with respect to the specified trust assets.

■ The trust *res* must be capable of being identified.

- A settlor may use several methods to place title to the trust *res* in the trustee, including the following:

    (1) the settlor can make an *inter vivos* transfer of title to the trustee sometimes called a deed of trust;

    (2) the settlor can orally or in writing declare himself the trustee over particular property standing in his name (a declaration of trust);

    (3) the settlor can, in a valid will, direct the executor to distribute property to a trustee (i.e., a testamentary trust); or

    (4) a settlor can enter into an enforceable contract with another person who thereby becomes obligated to transfer property to a trustee for the purpose of establishing a trust.

- In general, any identifiable property right that is transferable and capable of ownership may constitute a trust *res*. Property interests that can serve as a trust *res* include:

    (1) vested possessory interests;

    (2) contingent, non-possessory, future interests;

    (3) contract rights; and

    (4) equitable interests in another trust.

- As a general matter, the following interests may not be used as the *res* of a trust:

    (1) the mere expectancy that a person has in the prospective estate at death of a living person as his heir or under a will;

    (2) expectations of future earnings that are unsupported by an enforceable contract; and

    (3) debts or obligations owed by the trustees.

Ascertainable Beneficiary

- Except with respect to charitable trusts, a trust must have definite or ascertainable beneficiaries whose interests will vest or fail within a period of time dictated by the Rule Against Perpetuities.

- Any natural or artificial person may be a beneficiary, as long as he or she can legally own property. The trust beneficiaries must be:

    (1) presently ascertainable (i.e., either specifically named or capable of being determined without undue difficulty); or

    (2) ascertainable at a future time (within the Rule Against Perpetuities) when their interests are to vest.

- The members of a class usually are determined at the time when their interests are to vest, rather than when the trust was created. The beneficiaries of a trust may be a designated class of persons if:

    (1) the class is sufficiently definite; and

    (2) all of its members are ascertainable within the period of time prescribed by the Rule Against Perpetuities.

- There must be some reasonably objective basis for determining the members of the class.

Proper Trust Purpose

- Trusts may be created for virtually any purpose, except for one that:

    (1) is illegal;

    (2) violates rules relating to perpetuities; or

    (3) is contrary to public policy.

- A trust provision that encourages a beneficiary to refrain from marrying or to obtain a divorce is invalid (except that restraints upon remarriage by the settlor's spouse are ordinarily upheld). A trust condition that terminates a beneficiary's interest if he subsequently becomes divorced is usually valid.

- Whenever possible, courts attempt to merely delete an objectionable provision and retain the balance of the trust. However, where this result would frustrate the settlor's overall purposes, the entire trust is invalidated.

Creation of Express *Inter Vivos* Trusts

Transfer of Property

- Legal title to the trust *res* must be transferred to the trustee of the trust. Where the trust *res* is real property, transfer is effectuated by:

  (1) execution of a deed conveying title to the trustee; and

  (2) delivery of that document to the trustee (or his agent).

- Where the trust *res* is personal property, transfer may be made by:

  (1) physical delivery;

  (2) symbolic delivery; or

  (3) constructive delivery (i.e., executing a deed or gift or instrument of title in favor of the trustee, and delivering that document to the trustee or his agent).

- The settlor may also manifest an intent to create a trust by:

  (1) declaring himself trustee; and

  (2) earmarking particular assets as the trust *res*.

Statute of Frauds

- *Inter vivos* transfers of personal property to a trust are generally not subject to the Statute of Frauds. A few jurisdictions, however, have extended the Statute of Frauds writing requirement to trusts of personal property.

- Where an *inter vivos* conveyance of an interest in real property is made, the requirements of the Statute of Frauds must be met, or the trust is not enforceable against the trustee. The Statute of Frauds requires that a trust of real property be evidenced by a writing that is signed by the party to be charged (i.e., the party who, at the time of the transfer, had the power to create a trust upon that property).

- Failure to comply with the Statute of Frauds does not preclude voluntary performance of the trust by a willing trustee; notwithstanding the Statute of Frauds, an oral trust involving real property may be performed by the trustee.

- When the trustee permits the alleged beneficiary to be in possession of the land, and the beneficiary makes substantial improvements to the property or otherwise relies upon the trust to his substantial detriment, lack of compliance with the Statute of Frauds can be overcome under the equitable part performance doctrine.

- Where a trustee's own actions clearly and objectively indicate a trust relationship, despite title standing in his name (personally), a trustee may be equitably estopped from denying the existence of the trust.

Testamentary Trusts

Creation

DEFINITION A **testamentary trust** is created by the testator's will. Its essential terms are described in or incorporated by reference into a valid will. The "present intent" element is satisfied, because a will "speaks as of the testator's death" and the settlor intended that the trust take effect at that time.

Secret Trust

- A **secret trust** situation arises where property is devised to another without reference in the will to the fact that the devisee promised the settlor-decedent, or (expressly or impliedly) agreed, to hold the property received under the will in trust for another.

- A secret trust also arises where a decedent refrains from making a will based upon promises by his intestate heirs to hold the estate in trust for specific beneficiaries at his death.

- If the devisees/trustees refuse to perform the secret trust, extrinsic evidence is admissible to prove its existence.

Semisecret Trust

DEFINITION ▶ Where a testator indicates in his will that property is being devised to a trustee "in trust," but fails to identify the beneficiaries, a **semisecret trust** results. In a majority of jurisdictions, semisecret trusts are void. The trustee holds the property in a resulting trust for the settlor's estate.

- In a minority of jurisdictions, assuming the terms of the trust can be proven, a constructive trust can be imposed upon the property for the benefit of the beneficiaries if the trustee refuses to perform the trust.

"Pour-Over" Provisions

- Wills frequently contain **"pour over" provisions** that direct the transfer of the decedent's property into a trust established either by the testator during his lifetime or by another person.

- In order to pour assets into such a trust under the traditional rules of wills, a court must find that one of two doctrines applies:

  (1) In jurisdictions that have adopted the **incorporation by reference** doctrine, pour over provisions are valid if in existence when a will is executed and may be incorporated by reference if the will manifests this intention and describes the writing sufficiently to permit its identification, with further technical requirements sometimes imposed by the law of a given jurisdiction.

  (2) Pour over provisions may also be valid under the **facts of independent significance** doctrine if the trust has assets in it prior to the testator's death. Under this doctrine, the pour over assets will go to the trust in its current version at the time the will takes effect.

- Frustration with doctrinal obstacles to pour over gifts led every state to adopt the **Uniform Testamentary Additions to Trusts Act** (UTATA), first promulgated in 1960 and significantly amended in 1991. UTATA makes it possible to craft valid pour over wills in a much wider variety of circumstances.

- Under UTATA, a will can devise assets to a trust that is established during the testator's lifetime or established at her death by the devise itself, as long as the terms of the trust are set forth in a written instrument, other than a will, executed before, concurrently with, or after execution of the will.

Trusts Arising by Contract

- A person can create a trust by entering into an enforceable contact with someone who, by virtue of the agreement, is obligated to:

  (1) become a trustee of certain property that he owns; or

  (2) transfer title to property to another person as trustee.

- If the promisor fails to perform his obligations, the promisee or beneficiaries can often compel specific performance.

Totten Trusts

- When a person opens a bank account in his own name, as trustee for other parties, it is often unclear as to whether he intends to create a trust relationship pertaining to the deposited funds and subject himself to the fiduciary duties of a trustee.

- If he executes a trust instrument pertaining to the deposit or otherwise indicates he is creating a formal trust, an *inter vivos* trust arises. If, however, the depositor's intention was merely tentative, in most jurisdictions the arrangement is viewed as a "Totten" trust.

DEFINITION A **Totten trust** is a hybrid creation of the courts that melds both will and trust characteristics. Totten trusts are created like trusts and do not have to comply with the formalities of a will. However, Totten trusts are similar to wills in that:

  - they are revocable by the depositor at any time;
  - the beneficiary has no interest in the account until the depositor dies;
  - the beneficiary must survive the depositor to receive the account;
  - the depositor owes no fiduciary duties to the beneficiary; and
  - the deposit is subject to the claims of the depositor's creditors.

- The withdrawal or transfer of all funds from the Totten trust account will act as a complete and permanent revocation of the trust.

Supplemental Needs Trust

DEFINITION A **supplemental needs trust** is a specially designed trust that permits a person with severe disability to collect limited income from a trust without sacrificing eligibility for Medicaid or other forms of governmental assistance.

Honorary Trusts

DEFINITION An **honorary trust** is one that does not qualify as a charitable trust, but lacks definite beneficiaries.

- A trust may be created to provide for the care of an animal alive during the settlor's lifetime. The trust terminates upon the death of the animal or, if the trust was created to provide for the care of more than one animal alive during the settlor's lifetime, upon the death of the last surviving animal. If enforceable in a particular jurisdiction, such trusts may also be used to provide for the care of a grave site.

Limits on Trust Duration

General Rule

- As a general proposition, private trusts cannot last forever. The **Rule Against Perpetuities** ("RAP") serves as the primary limit on the duration of trusts and states that "no interest is good unless it must vest, if at all, not later than 21 years after some life in being at the creation of the interest."

- "No interest is good" means that any contingent interest that does not conform to the rule is void *ab initio*. All vested interests are valid under the rule, even if subject to partial or total divestment.

- "Must vest" means that the contingent interest must become a vested interest (or fail) within the period of the rule. The time for vesting is generally calculated from the time the creating instrument takes effect. In the case of a will, it is the date of the testator's death. In the case of an irrevocable trust, it is the date the trust is created. In the case of a revocable trust, it is the date of the testator's death.

- "If at all" means that if the contingent interest is absolutely certain either to "vest" or "fail" entirely within the period of the rule, it is valid.

- "Not later than 21 years after some life in being" includes within the period lives in being, provided they are not so numerous as to prevent practical determination of the time when the last one dies, plus 21 years, plus such actual periods of gestation as come within the proper purpose of the rule. Any person in being at the time the interest is created can serve as a "measuring life."

- "At the creation of the interest" means that, in the ordinary case, the period of the rule begins when the creating instrument (e.g., trust or will) takes effect.

APPLICATION OF THE RULE AGAINST PERPETUITIES	
Interests Subject to RAP	Interests Not Subject to RAP
Contingent remainders	Present possessory interests
Executory interests	Reversions
Options to purchase land not incident to a lease	Vested remainders (whether or not subject to partial or complete divestment)
Powers of appointment	Possibilities of reverter
Class gifts	Powers of termination
Rights of first refusal	Charitable trusts
	Resulting trusts
	Constructive trusts

Modification and Interpretation of the Rule

- Most jurisdictions have modified the common law Rule Against Perpetuities in some way. One reform adopted by some states has been the "wait-and-see," or "second look" doctrine for contingent future interests. Under this doctrine, the court's determination of whether the rule has been violated depends upon what actually happened rather than what might have happened.

- In jurisdictions with *cy pres* statutes, courts look to the grantor's intent and attempt to meet the grantor's wishes as closely as possible by altering the grant slightly to fit the Rule.

- Where the settlor's intent as to the identity of the beneficiaries of a trust is subject to more than one meaning, an interpretation that avoids application of the RAP is ordinarily preferred.

THE TRUSTEE'S POWERS AND RESPONSIBILITIES

Sources of the Trustee's Powers

- A trustee's powers are:

  (1) derived from the trust instrument (either expressly or by implication); and

  (2) granted by statute or implied in law as necessary or appropriate to accomplish the trust's purposes.

- In addition to exercising those powers that are specifically delegated to the trustee in the trust instrument, the trustee is also authorized to undertake acts that are, by implication, necessary or convenient to accomplish the trust's purposes.

- Unless expressly precluded by the trust instrument, a trustee has the power, *inter alia,* to:

  (1) settle or abandon trust claims;

  (2) exercise all rights and powers of a competent, unmarried individual with respect to individually owned property;

(3) borrow money;

(4) sell or lease trust assets;

(5) to apportion the trust income; and

(6) incur reasonable expenses, including the purchase of insurance, that are necessary to maintain trust property.

■ The trustee has no implied power to invade trust principal for a beneficiary who has merely the right to receive income from the trust.

■ A trustee's actions pertaining to matters within his discretion are not subject to attack, unless he has abused his discretion in undertaking the conduct in question.

■ The trustee's exercise of discretion is ordinarily reviewed under an objective standard (i.e., he must act reasonably under the circumstances). Where the trustee is given "sole" or "absolute" discretion under the trust instrument, his actions are reviewed under a good-faith standard (i.e., they are not improper unless undertaken in bad faith).

Duty of Loyalty and Good Faith

General Rule

RULE ▶ A trustee owes a duty of utmost loyalty and good faith to the beneficiaries in carrying out her obligations under the trust.

■ A trustee is:

(1) prohibited from self-dealing, in any manner (even in good faith) with trust assets; and

(2) ordinarily precluded from obtaining any personal benefit other than the agreed-upon or statutory fees as a consequence of his position.

■ Examples of prohibited self-dealing include the trustee, or persons under his control:

(1) buying assets from, or selling assets to the trust (even if the sales are for fair market value or occur at a public auction); or

(2) borrowing money from, or loaning money, to the trust.

■ The trustee cannot obtain any personal benefit from a third party with respect to dealings involving the trust estate. Thus, for example, obtaining a personal commission, bonus, finder's fee, or other benefit for placing trust business with others is strictly prohibited.

Other Implications of Duty

■ The trustee is precluded from permitting himself to be in an apparent conflict of interest with respect to the trust and third parties.

■ The trustee is ordinarily expected to segregate trust assets from his own assets, and earmark or otherwise identify trust property.

■ The trust instrument may expressly permit specified acts of self-dealing. For example, the trustee may be authorized to lend money to, or purchase assets from, the trust. Even in these instances, however, the trustee must act in good faith and with the "utmost fairness" in transactions involving trust property.

■ Any profits earned by the trustee as a result of self-interested transactions belong solely to the trust. Conversely, any losses become debts to the beneficiaries.

Affirmative Duties with Respect to Trust Assets

General Rule

- A trustee has an affirmative duty to preserve and enhance trust property.

- This duty includes considering the best interests of all life beneficiaries and remaindermen (i.e., the trustee must consider both the investment's ability to produce a reasonable rate of income and the safety of the principal).

- The Uniform Principal and Income Act specifies the distribution of receipts between trust principal and income.

  (1) Rents and cash dividends received allocated to trust income, and then are distributed to trust's income beneficiary.

  (2) Sales proceeds and stock dividends are allocated to principal of trust.

  (3) The default rules may be preempted by the terms of the trust. There are different implications depending on how clear the testator is: E.g. "allocate all capital gains to the income account" versus "T is authorized to exercise its discretion in matters of principal-and-income accounting." So receipts (rents, dividends) may be allocated differently depending on the terms of the trust and the specific state statute involved, if any.

- In administering a trust, the trustee may incur only costs that are reasonable in relation to the trust property, the purposes of the trust, and the skills of the trustee.

- The duty of care incumbent upon a trustee includes the affirmative obligation to take reasonable steps to protect and preserve the trust estate (i.e., obtain necessary insurance, satisfy trust obligations as they become due, maintain trust assets to prevent untimely deterioration and ensure that no one is injured on the premises, defend the trust when subjected to legal attack by creditors of the settlor, prevent trust property from being stolen or otherwise appropriated, etc.).

Standard of Care

- The trustee's actions must be examined under an objective standard of care. He must exercise that degree of care, skill, and prudence with respect to trust assets as would a reasonably prudent businessperson with respect to his own affairs and property.

- Where a trustee possesses superior business expertise or is a professional fiduciary (e.g., a trust company or bank), a higher standard is applied. He will be held to the care, skill, and prudence of an individual or entity possessing those capabilities.

- The trustee is obliged to attempt to utilize trust property in a productive manner; subject, at all times, to the obligation to be prudent (i.e., invest only in a conservative manner). Thus, land should be leased and personal property utilized, if possible, to produce income for the trust. Where cash is a trust asset, it should be invested, consistent with the trust's overall liquidity needs.

Prudent Investor Rule

- Almost all jurisdictions follow the **prudent investor rule**. The vast majority of states have enacted legislation codifying the prudent investor principles, most by enacting the Uniform Prudent Investor Act. The remaining states have comparable, modernized statutes. Under this doctrine, a trustee is permitted to invest trust assets as would a prudent investor, considering both the interests of life beneficiaries and remaindermen. Under this standard, the trustee must also seek to diversify the investments, so that all of the trust's "eggs are not placed in one basket."

- The following types of investments are generally appropriate for trust assets:

  (1) government and highly rated corporate bonds;

  (2) first-trust deed mortgages (assuming they are adequately secured); and

  (3) blue-chip common and preferred stock.

- Impermissible investments often include unsecured loans, "penny" stocks and commodities futures.

Accounting and Advice

- The trustee has the duty to maintain a clear, accurate accounting with respect to all transactions that he enters into on behalf of the trust.

- In deciding whether to undertake, or refrain from undertaking, action for or on behalf of the trust, the trustee may seek the advice of professionals.

- A trustee may not ordinarily delegate discretionary functions. A trustee may (and if he lacks the necessary background to make a reasonably competent decision, must) delegate investment functions, provided he uses reasonable care, skill, and caution in:

  (1) selecting the investment agent;

  (2) establishing the scope and terms of the delegation, consistent with the purposes and terms of the trust; and

  (3) periodically reviewing the agent's actions in order to monitor the agent's performance and compliance with the terms of the delegation.

Trustee's Liability

General Rule

- A trustee stands in a fiduciary relationship with respect to the beneficiaries of his trust. Thus, when duties owed to the beneficiaries have been breached, any questions of liability are typically resolved against the trustee.

- Only the beneficiaries (or their guardians *ad litem*) can commence an action against the trustee for breach of the duties that are owed to them. The settlor, except where he is also a beneficiary, ceases to have any interest in the trust once delivery of the trust *res* has occurred.

Remedies Available

- Where a trustee breaches his duty of loyalty, the beneficiaries have several potential actions and remedies. To remedy a breach of trust that has occurred or may occur, the court may:

  (1) compel the trustee to perform the trustee's duties;

  (2) enjoin the trustee from committing a breach of trust;

  (3) compel the trustee to redress a breach of trust by paying money, restoring property, or other means;

  (4) order a trustee to account;

  (5) appoint a special fiduciary to take possession of the trust property and administer the trust;

  (6) suspend the trustee;

  (7) remove the trustee;

  (8) reduce or deny compensation to the trustee;

  (9) void an act of the trustee, impose a lien or a constructive trust on trust property, or trace trust property wrongfully disposed of and recover the property or its proceeds; or

  (10) order any other appropriate relief.

- Where the trustee has utilized trust funds for his own purposes, the court may:

  (1) compel the trustee to convey to the trust any property that he obtained with those funds; or

  (2) recover any profits made by the trustee with those monies.

- Where property removed from the trust has been dissipated or can no longer be identified, the trustee is liable for:

    (1) its value; and

    (2) any interest that could have been earned on those funds.

Loss of Value

- Absent a breach of trust, a trustee is not liable to a beneficiary for a loss or depreciation in the value of trust property or for not having made a profit. The trustee is liable, however, to the beneficiaries for any damages or losses resulting from:

    (1) improper investments; or

    (2) his failure to take reasonable steps to make trust assets productive.

Liability for Acts of Former Trustee

- A trustee ordinarily has no liability for breaches of duty by the trustee whom he succeeds, except where the successor-trustee:

    (1) knew, or should have become aware of the prior trustee's breach and failed to undertake appropriate action to minimize its effects or to pursue the appropriate remedies on behalf of the beneficiaries; or

    (2) was negligent in failing to obtain a complete accounting and delivery of trust property from the preceding trustee.

Exculpatory Clauses

- An **exculpatory clause** is a provision in the trust instrument that relieves the trustee of liability for potentially wrongful acts (e.g., "the trustee shall not be liable for negligence or errors of judgment with respect to his activities involving the trust estate").

- When the trustee's conduct falls within the purview of this clause, he is ordinarily relieved of liability, as long as they are within the scope of the instrument's authorization. Thus, the trustee incurs no liability in these circumstances (unless his acts would violate the state's public policy).

- An exculpatory clause is ineffective to the extent that it purports to relieve the trustee of liability for acts of bad faith and intentional misconduct, recklessness, or gross negligence. Permitting its application in these situations is viewed as violating public policy.

- Exculpatory clauses are narrowly construed by the courts.

Estoppel

- Where a beneficiary has full knowledge of the material facts and expressly approves of the complained-of action by the trustee, he may:

    (1) be deemed to have waived the trustee's breach; or

    (2) be estopped from asserting an action.

Removal and Resignation of Trustees

- The settlor, a cotrustee, or a beneficiary may request the court to remove a trustee, or a trustee may be removed by the court on its own initiative. A court may remove a trustee if:

    (1) the trustee has committed a serious breach of trust;

    (2) lack of cooperation among co-trustees substantially impairs the administration of the trust;

    (3) because of unfitness, unwillingness, or persistent failure of the trustee to administer the trust effectively, the court determines that removal of the trustee best serves the interests of the beneficiaries; or

(4) there has been a substantial change of circumstances or removal is requested by all of the qualified beneficiaries, the court finds that removal of the trustee best serves the interests of all of the beneficiaries and is not inconsistent with a material purpose of the trust, and a suitable cotrustee or successor trustee is available.

■ Once a trustee has accepted the appointment to his position, he can resign at any time by giving notice to the co-trustee(s), if any, or to the successor trustee, or to all of the income-beneficiaries.

■ When a co-trustee resigns, the remaining trustee shall continue to act with all of the rights, powers, and duties of a trustee. If one or more co-trustees remain in office, a vacancy in a trusteeship need not be filled. A vacancy in a trusteeship must be filled if the trust has no remaining trustee.

Trustee's Liability to Third Parties

■ Although the trustee is performing trust duties, he may incur personal liability to those with whom he interacts on behalf of the trust. In certain situations, the trustee can obtain indemnification from the trust to the extent of his personal liability. For example, a trustee is entitled to be indemnified by the trust where:

(1) the tort was a normal incident to an activity in which the trustee was properly engaged on behalf of the trust;

(2) the tort is based on strict liability; or

(3) liability is based upon *respondeat superior* principles, and the trustee did not make an improper delegation of discretionary functions to the agent or violate his duty to exercise reasonable care in the selection and supervision of the agent.

■ Except as otherwise provided in the contract, a trustee is not personally liable on a contract properly entered into in the trustee's fiduciary capacity in the course of administering the trust if the trustee in the contract disclosed the fiduciary capacity. The trustee has an implied right of reimbursement and indemnification against the trust where the contract was for the benefit of the trust and within his authority.

ALIENABILITY OF TRUST BENEFICIARIES' INTERESTS AND CREDITORS' RIGHTS

Beneficiaries' Interests

In General

■ In the absence of a restrictive provision to the contrary, a trust beneficiary may freely assign (gratuitously or for consideration) his right to receive income or principal from a trust. Where the trust estate is composed of an interest in land (including leasehold interests), the Statute of Frauds is applicable.

■ Except where expressly required by the trust instrument, notice to the trustee is not necessary for an assignment by the beneficiary to be effective. However, the trustee ordinarily has no liability to an assignee for refusing to honor a purported assignment if:

(1) there is no writing evidencing the assignment; and

(2) the beneficiary contends that no assignment has been made.

■ Unless the trust agreement provides for a gift over in case of the beneficiary's death (i.e., the beneficiary only has a life estate), a beneficiary's interest in a trust can be devised by will or pass pursuant to intestacy principles.

■ Where a beneficiary makes multiple assignments of his interest in a trust, the **first in time, first in right rule** will usually apply. Where an earlier transferee neglects to inform the trustee of the assignment and a subsequent assignee pays consideration to the assigning beneficiary for the assignment after inquiring of the trustee as to the existence of any previous assignments and receiving a negative response, the latter assignee is often given priority.

Restrictions on Assignment

- In the absence of a restrictive provision in the trust instrument to the contrary, creditors can ordinarily attach and foreclose upon a beneficiary's interest in a trust. Where a beneficiary's interest in a trust is restricted by a valid discretionary, support, or spendthrift provision, she cannot assign that interest.

Support Provision

- A **support provision** is one in which the trustee is directed to provide only so much income and/or principal of the trust as is necessary for the latter's support and for no other purpose. A typical support provision is "for the beneficiary's health, education, maintenance, and support." A support provision is not merely an expression of the settlor's motive for creating the trust, but actually limits the beneficiary's interest to amounts necessary for her support.

Discretionary Trust

DEFINITION ➤ A **discretionary trust** interest is one in which payment to the beneficiary (even for a stated purpose) is to be made, if at all, at the trustee's absolute discretion.

- Where a discretionary provision exists independent of a support clause, the beneficiary can assign his interest in the trust. However, an assignee's right is of no marketable value unless and until the trustee determines that a distribution to the beneficiary is to be made.

- In jurisdictions without mandatory spendthrift statutes, creditors may attach a beneficiary's interest in a discretionary trust. However, that interest has no marketable value until the trustee determines that a contribution to the beneficiary should be made and a creditor cannot compel a trustee of a discretionary trust to pay him.

- In some states, the creditor can obtain a "cutoff" order, which directs the trustee to pay the creditor before paying the beneficiary. Such an order has the effect of depriving the beneficiary of trust income, though it does not necessarily ensure that the creditor is ever paid.

Spendthrift Provision

- A **spendthrift provision** is one that precludes:

  (1) a beneficiary from voluntarily transferring his interest in the trust; and

  (2) creditors from reaching that interest. No specific language is necessary to accomplish this result.

- Whether the settlor intended to create a spendthrift trust is a factual issue, determined from all of the circumstances. In some states, a spendthrift provision is implied into all income interests unless affirmatively rejected in the trust instrument.

- Where, despite a valid spendthrift provision, the beneficiary attempts to voluntarily assign her interest, the trustee may (if she chooses to do so) comply with the transferee's demand, unless the beneficiary has expressly notified the trustee to disregard the assignment.

- Where the spendthrift provision prevents alienation by the beneficiary and attachment by creditors, creditors cannot ordinarily reach the beneficiary's interest directly. Once there has been a distribution, however, from the spendthrift trust to the beneficiary, creditors have the right to reach that distribution.

- Spendthrift provisions that limit only the beneficiary's right of alienation are valid. In this situation, creditors of the beneficiary are not prevented from reaching his interest in the trust.

Limitations upon the Enforceability of Spendthrift, Support, and Discretionary Trusts

- In certain situations, creditors of a beneficiary can reach the beneficiary's interest in a trust despite a valid support, discretionary, or spendthrift clause.

- Once the trustee has actually made a distribution to the beneficiary, the beneficiary's creditors can attach that property through the same means that are applicable to any debt or owned assets.

- The UTC provides that even if a trust contains a spendthrift provision, a creditor of a beneficiary may reach a mandatory distribution of income or principal if the trustee has not made the distribution to the beneficiary within a reasonable time after the designated distribution date.

- Outside of a few states and offshore locations, a settlor is not permitted to insulate his own property from creditors by means of spendthrift, support, or discretionary provisions. Where a person creates a trust, or furnishes consideration to another person to establish a trust in which he is a beneficiary, his creditors can reach the maximum portion of the trust that could have been distributed to him despite a valid support, discretionary or spendthrift provision.

- In most states, a beneficiary's interest in a trust is subject to the claims of spouses, ex-spouses, and his children for alimony or support, notwithstanding a spendthrift clause.

- In most jurisdictions, persons or entities that furnish necessities of life (i.e., food, clothing, emergency medical attention, etc.) to a beneficiary are entitled to reimbursement from the trust despite a valid support or spendthrift clause.

- The Restatement (Third) of Trusts provides that a beneficiary's interest, even though protected by a spendthrift provision, is subject to the claims of creditors who "preserve the beneficial interest" of that beneficiary. For example, an attorney who, on behalf of the beneficiary of a spendthrift trust, performs services that protect or preserve the trust interest of that otherwise impecunious beneficiary, is able to collect his fees from the beneficiary's interest in the trust.

- A trust can be invaded by the United States or a state governmental entity to satisfy tax claims against a beneficiary.

- In some jurisdictions, creditors are permitted to reach that part of income not needed for the beneficiary's support or exceeding a certain fixed amount (e.g., $10,000).

- In some jurisdictions, creditors can reach some percentage of the income from a spendthrift trust.

- In some jurisdictions, tort creditors can reach spendthrift trust income.

Rights of the Settlor's Creditors

- Any beneficial interest (e.g., a life estate or reversion) retained by the settlor in a trust is subject to the claims of his creditors.

- Where the settlor creates a trust in favor of others, as a consequence of which he is, or will be rendered, insolvent, or for the purpose of hindering or defrauding his creditors, the creditors can reach the trust *res* to satisfy their claims against the settlor.

- In most jurisdictions, the fact that an *inter vivos* trust is revocable by the settlor does not permit his creditors to attach the trust's assets to satisfy their claims against him (unless the trust also constitutes a fraudulent conveyance). Nevertheless, if the settlor is placed into bankruptcy, the court may exercise his power of revocation.

MODIFICATION OR TERMINATION OF TRUSTS

Termination by Settlor

- Unless the terms of a trust expressly provide that the trust is irrevocable, the settlor may revoke or amend the trust created after the effective date of the code. A settlor may terminate an irrevocable trust only with consent of all the beneficiaries.

- Under common law, irrevocability of trust is presumed unless the right of revocation is reserved. Under the UTC, the settlor may revoke or amend a trust unless the terms of the trust expressly provide that it is irrevocable.

- A revocable *inter vivos* trust may be revoked by the settlor:

    (1) by substantially complying with the method specified in a trust instrument; or

    (2) if no method is specified, by:

        (a) executing a later will or codicil that expressly refers to the trust or specifically devises property that would otherwise have passed according to the terms of the trust; or

        (b) any other method manifesting clear and convincing evidence of the settlor's intent.

- If the terms of the trust reserve to the settlor a power to revoke or amend the trust exclusively by a particular procedure, the settlor can exercise the power only by substantial compliance with the method prescribed. If the terms of the trust do not make that method exclusive, the settlor's power can be exercised either in the specified manner or in any way that provides clear and convincing evidence of the settlor's intention to do so.

Termination of a Trust by Merger

RULE If a sole trustee becomes the only beneficiary (i.e., becomes the holder of all of the beneficial interests of the trust), the trust ceases to exist and he (personally) becomes the owner of the trust assets.

Termination by Operation of Law

- A trust is terminated by operation of law where:

    (1) accomplishment of the material purposes of the trust have become illegal, impossible, or impractical;

    (2) the trust *res* has been consumed, destroyed, or lost; or

    (3) the trust's purposes have been fully accomplished.

Administrative Deviations

- Where exact compliance with the administrative provisions of the trust would, as a result of unforeseen circumstances, frustrate or substantially impair a material purpose sought to be accomplished by the trust, the court, on petition of the trustee, may allow deviation from those administrative provisions, as necessary to accomplish the settlor's purposes.

- The administrative deviance doctrine may not, however, be used to change the beneficial interests in the trust.

Termination by Beneficiaries After Settlor's Death

- The rule of Claflin v. Claflin is that after the settlor's death, the trust will not be terminated before the period specified by the settlor has expired and the purposes of the trust have been accomplished, even though all of the beneficiaries approve of such termination. If the trust is a spendthrift or discretionary trust, courts are likely to find that the settlor's purpose of protecting the beneficiary continues, and the trust cannot be terminated by consent.

- However, where no material purpose of the settlor remains, the court may allow termination upon request of the beneficiaries, if all have vested interests, are before the court to grant approval, and are of legal age and not under guardianship.

- If the trust creates the possibility of interests in unborn beneficiaries, the trust may be impossible to terminate unless a statute permits the appointment of a guardian *ad litem* for an unconceived child.

- **With Consent of the Trustee:** While the trustee alone has no power to terminate the trust unless such power was expressly granted, the trustee and beneficiaries acting together can effect a termination without court order by a conveyance of legal title from the trustee to the beneficiaries, or other conveyance which merges legal and equitable title and automatically terminates the trust.

- However, if, by the terms of the trust or by statute, a valid restraint is imposed upon the transfer by the beneficiary of his interest, a conveyance of his interest by the beneficiary to the trustee is ineffective to terminate the trust.

Natural Expiration

- Where the trust was to be in operation for a specified number of years or until the occurrence of a prescribed event, and that period of time has elapsed or the incident has occurred, the trust ordinarily terminates in accordance with the instrument's terms.

Modern Trends

- The Restatement (Third) of Trusts and the Uniform Trust Code both urge that courts have greater authority to grant requests for modification or termination of trusts. In addition, courts have shown increasing willingness to permit modification or termination in order to achieve tax advantages for beneficiaries.

TRUSTS ARISING BY OPERATION OF LAW: IMPLIED TRUSTS

Resulting Trusts

- There are two circumstances in which resulting trusts arise:

    (1) when an express trust makes an incomplete disposition of assets or fails after property has been conveyed to the trustee; and

    (2) purchase money trusts.

- Where an express trust partially or completely fails, or is terminated by operation of law, and there is no alternative disposition for the trust's assets, a resulting trust ordinarily arises. Typical situations are where:

    (1) the trust has no beneficiaries (e.g., none were ever named, they have died, they cannot be located or identified, or they disclaim their trust interests);

    (2) no provision has been made for a portion of the trust *res*;

    (3) where a trust designated for a specific purpose is invalid, insufficient, or excessive;

    (4) the trust purpose was never described or is unclear; or

    (5) carrying out the material purposes of the trust has become impractical or illegal.

- Some jurisdictions have abolished the purchase money resulting trust by statute. Purchase money resulting trusts also arise where:

    (1) one or more persons provide all or part of the purchase money for property; and

    (2) title is taken in the name of another, or in the names of the payors in shares different from the proportions in which the purchase money was provided.

- As a general matter, the trustee of a resulting trust has the same duties and obligations as other trustees. Primary among his responsibilities, however, are to:

    (1) convey the trust *res* back to the settlor (or her estate) or payor (where a purchase money trust is involved); and

    (2) account for any income traceable to the trust from the time that it arose.

Constructive Trusts

DEFINITION A **constructive trust** is an equitable remedy, whereby a trust is erected on the holder of specific property to redress wrongdoing or prevent unjust enrichment. It is typically imposed when property has been wrongfully obtained (e.g., acquired by fraud or undue influence) or the beneficiary has killed the decedent (if a "slayer statute" does not apply).

- The purpose of a constructive trust is to oblige the holder of property to divest himself of it and transfer it to the person entitled to that asset. The Statute of Frauds does not apply to resulting or constructive trusts.

CHARITABLE TRUSTS

Distinguishing Characteristics

Introduction

DEFINITION **Charitable trusts** have certain characteristics that distinguish them from express, private trusts. Four significant aspects of a charitable trust are its charitable purpose, indefinite beneficiaries, exemption from the RAP, and use of the *cy pres* doctrine.

Charitable Purpose

- The trust must have a charitable purpose. The major categories of charitable purposes are:

    (1) the relief of poverty;

    (2) the advancement of education;

    (3) the advancement of religion;

    (4) the promotion of health;

    (5) the performance of governmental and municipal purposes (e.g., maintenance of parks, etc.); and

    (6) other purposes beneficial to the community.

- A charitable purpose can be broad as long as the trustee is constrained to use the trust exclusively for that objective. The objective of a charitable trust must be to benefit the public, but the subjective motive of the settlor for establishing the trust may be selfish in nature.

- The terms of a charitable trust must facilitate the valid charitable purpose.

- A settlor cannot restrict benefits of a charitable trust to a small group of people like friends or relatives, even if the benefits are payable only for otherwise charitable purposes like education or health.

Indefinite Beneficiaries

- The beneficiaries must be indefinite. The fact that there are a limited number of persons actually receiving funds does not cause a charitable trust to fail if the recipients are to be chosen from a sufficiently large and indefinite group.

- **Enforcement by Beneficiaries:** Potential beneficiaries of a charitable trust have no standing to sue for enforcement of its terms unless they comprise a small group of beneficiaries with a special interest in the trust. The attorney general in most states, as representative of the community, has the authority and duty to sue to enforce charitable trusts operating in their state. The settlor can also sue to enforce a charitable trust that she created.

Perpetual Existence

- Charitable trusts may have a perpetual existence (i.e., the Rule Against Perpetuities has limited application to charitable trusts).

- Although a charitable trust may be of perpetual duration, where the charitable trust is preceded by a non-charitable estate, the charitable interest must vest within the period of time prescribed by the RAP.

DEFINITION ▷ A **mixed trust** has both charitable and private purposes. The characteristics of charitable and private trusts are mutually exclusive in that:

- a charitable trust must have indefinite beneficiaries; and
- a private trust must have ascertainable beneficiaries.

- A trust that has both charitable and private purposes will fail unless the private and public purposes can be segregated (either proportionally or at different points in time) into separate trusts.

Cy Pres Doctrine

- If the settlor's exact charitable purpose cannot be carried out, the court may direct the application of the trust property to another charitable purpose that approximates the settlor's intention. This is called the **cy pres** doctrine, which permits courts to draw on their general equitable powers over trusts, and is necessary to meet contingencies that arise over time.

- *Cy pres* may be applied where:

  (1) the settlor's specific charitable purpose with respect to a valid charitable trust becomes impossible, impracticable, or illegal to carry out; and

  (2) the settlor had, in addition to this specific charitable purpose, a general charitable intent (i.e., the settlor's specific charitable purpose was not intended to be exclusive).

- Generally, the court will infer from the making of a charitable trust that the settlor had a general charitable intent. However, where the trust instrument makes clear that the settlor would have preferred the trust to terminate rather than to be used in another manner, the *cy pres* doctrine cannot be utilized.

- If the settlor has provided for a "gift over" in the event that the charitable purpose cannot be accomplished, this is ordinarily viewed as an indication that the settlor lacked a general charitable intent.

- Language in a trust instrument that the trust *res* is to be used "only" for the stated charitable purpose is not dispositive on the question of whether the settlor had a general charitable intent.

- The *cy pres* doctrine can be used only to modify an already valid, existing charitable trust. This doctrine cannot be used to turn a private trust into a charitable trust or to reform an invalid trust.

- *Cy pres* is not applicable when the trust instrument specifies an alternative charitable beneficiary.

Termination

- If a charitable trust cannot be performed as intended and the requirements for *cy pres* are not met, the trust terminates and a resulting trust in favor of the settlor's estate arises.

FUTURE INTERESTS

Powers of Appointment

Introduction

- A **power of appointment** is a power created by the **donor** of property which enables another individual (the **donee** of the power) to designate transferees of the property and the shares they are to receive. The donor may limit the donee's power by specifying in what manner or upon what conditions the power may be exercised. A power of attorney qualifies as a power of appointment.

■ Powers of appointment are classified in several ways, including on the basis of the manner in which they may be exercised (by *inter vivos* deed, by will, or by either deed or will), and the permissible objects (appointees) specified.

■ Where the donee of the power may appoint to anyone, including the donee or the donee's estate, the donee is said to have a **general power**. A general power exercisable by *inter vivos* deed is considered the equivalent of outright ownership of the property. The power to convey only by will is, of course, somewhat more restrictive.

■ Under a **special power**, the donee is limited by the donor's selection of the ultimate takers. Thus, the donor may give the power to appoint certain property to "such one or more of my children as the donee may believe are in need," or "to such of my descendants as the donee may select," or "to such of the following charities as the donee may believe most deserving."

Exercise of Power, Generally

■ Powers of appointment may be classified not only as general or special, but by the time at which the power may be exercised. A power exercisable only by will is a **testamentary** power. A power which may be exercised at any time by deed is a presently exercisable (or *inter vivos*) power.

■ The power must be exercised in the manner specified by the donor. In the absence of restrictions by the donor, the donee effectively exercises the power whenever the donee's intent to exercise the power is evident.

■ The donee may not delegate to others a power of appointment, but may circumvent this restriction by exercising the general power to create a partial estate (e.g., a life estate) and creating in a new donee a power of appointment to take effect when the partial estate has terminated.

Exercise by Residuary Clause in Donee's Will

■ Testamentary power of appointment gives the appointee, in his will, power to designate who receives what share of trust assets, and can be limited to a group selected by the donor of power.

■ A power of appointment which permits the donee of the power to exercise that power in the donee's will may be exercised by a general devise of all the donee's property.

■ Absent a specific reference requirement, a power of appointment is exercised if the general residuary clause is coupled with a **blanket exercise clause**. A blanket exercise clause exercises a power of appointment if it contains language that encompasses all property over which a testator has a power of appointment.

Exercise in Favor of Fiduciary

■ Unless specifically allowed by the will, trust document, or other writing appointing a fiduciary, the fiduciary may not exercise a power of appointment in favor of himself, his estate, creditors, or creditors of the his estate.

Exercise of Special Powers

■ The donee of a special power must exercise it in compliance with the expressed intention of the donor. If the instrument creating the special power enables the donee to distribute the subject matter to any one or more of the designated objects (appointees), the power is called **exclusive**.

■ If the donee is required to distribute at least part of the subject matter to each object, it is a **nonexclusive** power. With a nonexclusive power, the donee determines the amount that each object, or appointee, will receive, but the donee may not refuse to distribute some part of the subject matter to each object. An extremely small share could be challenged by the object as an "illusory" exercise of the donee's power.

- The donee of a special power of appointment can only exercise in favor of objects designated by the donor of power, excluding the donee, donee's creditors, and donee's estate as permissible objects.

Release of Power

- A donee may **release**, or destroy, a power of appointment in most circumstances. This differs from failure to exercise a power in that a donee who releases a power takes action to effect the release.

- A release of the power, which is normally made by written *inter vivos* instrument, is distinguishable from a disclaimer, or renunciation, where the proposed donee refuses to accept the power.

Creditors' Rights

- Creditors of the donee may seek to reach the assets of the power of appointment. Creditors will be unsuccessful in attempting to reach the subject matter of special power, because the donee serves in a capacity analogous to that of a trustee.

- If the donee exercises the general power of appointment, creditors will be able to reach the assets. The result is the same as if a person creates a protective trust for the settlor's own benefit.

Rule Against Perpetuities Applied to Powers of Appointment

- All special powers of appointment and general testamentary powers are subject to the Rule Against Perpetuities.

- A special power of appointment and a general testamentary power, since they both relate back to the time of the creation of the power, are void if the power is capable of being exercised beyond the period of perpetuities.

Wills

WILLS

Wills

Intestate: person who dies without a will dies intestate

Testate: one who dies leaving a will dies testate

Testamentary Capacity: to have the requisite mental state, the testator must understand that the document being signed is a will, know the nature and extent of the property subject to distribution, and know the natural objects of the testator's bounty

Holographic Will: a will entirely in the testator's handwriting and requires no attesting witnesses; South Carolina does not recognize holographic wills

Codicil: a codicil is an addition to, or an alteration of, a will

Joint Will: a joint will is a document executed by two or more testators that is intended to serve as the will of each and every person who signed it

Mutual Will: mutual wills are separate wills executed by two or more persons with reciprocal provisions for the distribution of assets

Specific Bequest: a specific devise or bequest disposes of an identified item of property owned by the testator

Demonstrative Bequest: a demonstrative bequest is a gift (usually of an amount of money) payable primarily from a specified source and, if that is inadequate, then from the general assets of the estate

General Bequest: a general bequest is one payable out of the general assets of the estate, rather than one requiring distribution of or payment from particular assets

Probate: the procedure in which the court decides the validity of the instrument before the court and ascertains whether it is the last will of the deceased

- **Distribution**
- **Family Protections**
- **Intestacy**
- **Revocation & Revival**
- **Testamentary Disposition**
- **Will Construction**
- **Will Contests & Probate Proceedings**
- **Will Substitutes**

- Where a valid codicil to a will is executed, the codicil is considered to republish the will as of the date of its execution.

- A spouse who has been disinherited (or who inherits very little) can take an elective share instead of the amount that he or she takes under the will.

- When spouses die at the same time, each of their estates are treated as if the beneficiary spouse predeceased the other spouse. This rule is applied when the time of death cannot be determined, or under the Uniform Probate Code, if the spouse dies within 120 hours of the testator.

INTRODUCTION

Governing Law

- The law governing wills and intestate succession developed from the common law and has largely been codified in the statutes of the 50 states, the District of Columbia, and the territories.

- Where the law has not been codified in statute, those states have typically adopted the **Uniform Probate Code** ("UPC") in whole or in part.

Definitions

Decedent

- A deceased person is known in the law of estates as a **decedent**.

Estate, Real Property, Personal Property

- A decedent's **estate** is the real and personal property the decedent leaves at death.

- A decedent's **personal property** passes according to the law of the decedent's domicile at the time of his death.

- A decedent's **real property** passes according to the law of the state where it is located.

Intestate, Testate

- A person who dies without a will dies **intestate**. One who dies leaving a will dies **testate**.

Probate

- The process of distributing intestate property is often referred to as **estate administration**; the process of proving a will is technically referred to as **probate**. Nowadays, however, the terms are used somewhat interchangeably.

Issue

- **Issue** means all lineal descendants from an ancestor in any degree (children, grandchildren, etc.).

Heirs

- **Heirs** mean persons, including the surviving spouse, who are entitled under the statutes of intestate succession to the property of a decedent.

Devise, Devisee

- A **devise** means a testamentary disposition of real or personal property.

- A **devisee** is any person designated in a will to receive a devise.

INTESTATE DISTRIBUTION

In General

- A person who dies without a will dies intestate; his estate is an intestate estate.

- Property of the estate that, for some reason, does not pass under a will passes according to the intestacy laws, which are called "the laws of descent and distribution."

- **Testacy proceeding** means a proceeding to establish a will or determine intestacy.

- Intestacy is total if the person who dies either does not make a will or makes a will that is totally invalid.

- Intestacy is partial when the testator makes a will, but part of the property in the estate does not pass under the will.

If Spouse Survives

Only Spouse Survives

- The entire estate goes to the surviving spouse if:

    (1) no descendant or parent of the decedent survives the decedent; or

    (2) all of the decedent's surviving descendants are also descendants of the surviving spouse and there is no other descendant of the surviving spouse who survives the decedent.

Spouse and Parent(s) Survives

- If there is no surviving descendant of the decedent, but he is survived by a parent or parents, the first $300,000 plus three-fourths of the balance of the intestate estate goes to the surviving spouse. The remainder of the property goes to the surviving parent, or if both parents survive, in equal shares to each.

Spouse and Issue Survive

- If there are surviving descendants of the decedent, all of whom are issue of the surviving spouse, and the surviving spouse has one or more surviving descendants who are not descendants of the decedent, the first $225,000 plus one-half of the balance of the intestate estate goes to the surviving spouse. The remaining portion of the estate is divided among the descendants.

Spouse and Issue Not of Surviving Spouse Survive

- If there are surviving descendants of the decedent, one or more of whom are not issue of the surviving spouse, the first $150,000 plus one-half of the intestate estate goes to the surviving spouse. The remaining portion of the estate is divided among the descendants.

No Surviving or Entitled Spouse: Order of Distribution

First To Decedent's Descendants

- If decedent's spouse is not entitled to a share in the estate, or does not survive him, or if the decedent is unmarried, then his descendants take in equal shares.

- If a decedent's intestate estate passes **by representation** or per capita to the decedent's descendants, the estate is divided into as many equal shares as there are surviving descendants in the generation nearest to the decedent, and deceased descendants in the same generation who left surviving descendants, if any.

To Surviving Parents

- If the decedent is not survived by his spouse nor his descendants, then the surviving parents take in equal shares.

To Descendants of Parents

- If the decedent is not survived by his spouse, his descendants, nor his parents, then the descendants of the decedent's parents or either of them take by representation.

To Grandparents and their Descendants

- If the decedent is not survived by his spouse, his descendants, his parents, nor descendants of his parents, then surviving grandparents (or descendants of grandparents) take:

  (1) half to the decedent's paternal grandparents equally if both survive; to the surviving paternal grandparent if only one survives; or to the descendants of the decedent's paternal grandparents if both are deceased, the descendants taking by representation; and

  (2) half to the decedent's maternal grandparents equally if both survive; to the surviving maternal grandparent if only one survives; or to the descendants of the decedent's maternal grandparents if both are deceased, the descendants taking by representation.

- If there is no surviving descendant, parent, or descendant of a parent, but the decedent is survived by one or more grandparents or descendants of grandparents on the paternal but not the maternal side, or on the maternal but not the paternal side, to the decedent's relatives on the side with one or more surviving members.

To Deceased Spouse's Relatives

- If there is no taker by a descendant of the grandparents, but the decedent has:

  (1) one deceased spouse who has one or more descendants who survive the decedent, the estate passes to that spouse's descendants by representation; or

  (2) more than one deceased spouse who has one or more descendants who survive the decedent, an equal share of the estate passes to each set of descendants by representation.

Escheat

- If there is no spouse or other person entitled to inherit under the statute, the property escheats (passes) to the state.

Children

Adopted Children

- The UPC follows a **transplantation theory** with regard to adopted children. An adopted child loses any relationship with his natural parents and is treated as the natural-born child of the adoptive parents. An adopted child has full rights to inherit from and through his adoptive parents (and their relatives), they in turn are able to inherit from and through the adopted child.

- If the adoptee dies intestate, his property is distributed among those persons who would have been kindred if he had actually been born to the adopting parents.

Stepchildren

- Stepchildren have no inheritance rights unless they are adopted, or unless they can prove adoption by estoppel. **Adoption by estoppel** can be shown if there is an attempt to adopt that does not occur because of a technical defect, or if the stepparent contracts with the natural parents to adopt the child but for some reason does not.

Children Born Out of Wedlock

- A child born out of wedlock is considered the child of his mother and her kindred for purposes of intestate inheritance.

- A child born out of wedlock is considered to be the child of his father when the identity of the father is determined in any one of the following ways:

  (1) the parents marry each other;

(2) during the lifetime of the child, the father openly holds out the child to be his and receives the child into his home, or openly holds the child out to be his and provides support for the child; or

(3) there is clear and convincing evidence that the man was the father of the child; this may include a prior court determination of paternity.

Advancements

- Property given *inter vivos* to an heir by an intestate may be treated as an **advancement** against the estate only if:

  (1) declared in a contemporaneous writing by the decedent or acknowledged in writing by the heir as an advancement; or

  (2) the decedent's contemporaneous writing or the heir's written acknowledgement indicate that the gift is to be taken into account in computing the division and distribution of the decedent's intestate estate.

- The property advanced is valued as of the earlier of the time the heir came into possession or enjoyment of the property, or the time of the decedent's death.

WILLS

Capacity to Make a Will

RULE ▶ To be valid, a will must be executed by a competent individual, 18 years of age or older, with the requisite testamentary intent, in accordance with prescribed statutory formalities.

- In order to possess the requisite mental capacity to make a will, the testator must possess both:

  (1) testamentary intent; and

  (2) testamentary capacity.

Formal Requirements of Wills

Execution

RULE ▶ A valid will must generally be:

- in writing, signed by the testator or in the testator's name by another person in the testator's presence and at the testator's direction; and
- witnessed by two individuals.

Witnesses

- The witnesses must be competent to observe and comprehend the act. Mental incompetency, whether from mental deficiency, extreme intoxication, or the influence of drugs, remains a ground of disqualification as a witness.

- Generally, the age of a witness is not specified in the statute. A minor is a valid witness, unless the minor was not old enough to observe, remember, and relate the facts occurring at the execution ceremony.

- The UPC does not require the witnesses to sign in the presence of the testator or in the presence of each other. It requires the witnesses to "witness" the testator's act of signing the will or acknowledging the signature or the will.

- A will can also be acknowledged by the testator before a notary public or other authorized individual.

SPECIAL WILLS, CODICILS, AND WILL PROVISIONS

Types of Wills

Holographic Wills

DEFINITION ▶ A **holographic will** is a will in the handwriting of the testator, signed by the testator but unattested by witnesses.

■ The will may be sufficiently proven by the testimony of two witnesses who are familiar with the testator's handwriting.

Conditional Wills

■ In a **conditional will,** a testator may choose to make a particular gift, or a will, conditional on the occurrence or non-occurrence of a specific event. The condition or contingency must be clear on the face of the will and must comply with the formal requirements for a will. Most states require that the condition be an event independent from the making of the will.

■ Conditional wills are permitted in most states by statute or common law.

■ However, due to the fact that invalid conditions result in some or all of the property to pass by intestacy, courts generally do not favor conditional wills and narrowly construe conditional language. In fact, most courts, when faced with a questionable provision, will hold that it is not a condition, but rather merely a statement of the testator's motive for making a will.

Codicils

DEFINITION ▶ A **codicil** is an addition to, or alteration of, a will and must be executed with the same formalities as a will.

■ A reference to a will includes all codicils.

■ A validly executed codicil cures any defects in the execution of the original will.

Foreign Wills

■ A will is validly executed if it complies with:

(1) statutory provisions (relating to form and execution of the will);

(2) the law of the place and at the time the will was executed; or

(3) the law of the place where the testator was domiciled or had a place of abode or was a national, either at the time of execution or the time of death.

Classification of Testamentary Distributions

■ A **specific gift** or devise is a gift by will of a specifically identified article or other real or personal property.

■ A **general gift** is a transfer from the general assets of the decedent's estate.

■ A **demonstrative gift** or devise is a general gift that specifies the fund or property from which the transfer is to be made.

LIMITATIONS ON TESTAMENTARY DISPOSITIONS

Spouse's Elective Share

In General

- State laws regulating the distribution of a decedent's property generally put restrictions on the decedent's ability to reduce his spouse's share in his estate below a statutorily specified minimum percentage.

- A surviving spouse has the right to decline to take under the will or pursuant to the intestacy statute, and instead may choose to take an **elective share** amount equal to 50 percent of the value of the marital-property portion of the augmented estate.

Procedure for Election

- The surviving spouse must file a claim for an elective share in writing in the court in the county of the decedent's domicile, and mail or deliver a copy to the personal representative, if any.

- The claim must be filed within nine months after the date of decedent's death, or within six months after the probate of the will, whichever is later.

- The estate consists of the sum of all property (real or personal) that constitutes:

  (1) decedent's net probate estate;

  (2) the decedent's non-probate transfers to persons other than the surviving spouse;

  (3) the decedent's non-probate transfers to the surviving spouse; and

  (4) the value of the surviving spouse's net assets at the decedent's death, plus the surviving spouse's non-probate transfers to others.

- Under the UPC, the amount of the surviving spouse's elective share is calculated by applying a specified percentage to the augmented estate. The percentage increases with the length of marriage until it reaches a maximum of 50 percent (for marriages 15 years or longer).

Children Not Mentioned in the Will

Omitted Heirs: Children Living at Time of Execution of Will

- Generally, under the UPC, a testator can disinherit a child intentionally. There is no forced or elective share for children as there is for a spouse.

- **Omitted heirs** are children of the testator, living at the time of the execution of the testator's last will, who are neither mentioned nor provided for in the will and would have inherited from the testator had he/she died intestate.

- The UPC allows disinheritance of these heirs by the testator, but disinheritance must be by express language or necessary implication of the will.

Children Born After Execution of the Will: Statutory Protection

- If a testator's will fails to provide for a child born or adopted after the execution of the will, unless it appears from the will that the failure was intentional, the UPC protects such child from unintentional disinheritance.

- The omitted after-born or after-adopted child receives a share in the net probate estate that depends on whether or not the testator had children living when the will was executed and, if so, whether the will made a devise to any of the then-living children.

- **No Child Living When the Will was Executed:** An omitted after-born or after-adopted child receives an intestate share, unless the will devised all or substantially all of the estate to the other parent, who survives the testator and is entitled to take under the will. In satisfying the child's intestate share, devises abate as provided under the ordinary rules of abatement for the payment of claims.

- **One or More Children Living, Devise Made to One or More of the Then-Living Children:** An omitted after-born or after-adopted child is entitled to share in the portion of the testator's estate devised to the testator's then-living children as if the child had been given an equal share of that portion of the estate.

- **One or More Children Living When the Will was Executed and No Devise Made:** The UPC does not grant a share to an after-born or after-adopted child.

Family Allowance

- The surviving spouse and minor children whom the decedent was obligated to support are entitled to a reasonable allowance in money out of the estate for their maintenance during the period of administration. It may be paid as a lump sum or in periodic installments.

- The family allowance is intended to provide the family with enough money to pay their expenses during the probate period.

Restrictions on Charitable Dispositions

- Any rule that a charitable devise is invalid if it exceeds a certain proportion of the testator's estate or if it is contained in a will that was executed within a certain time before the testator's death is abolished.

- All of the **mortmain** statutes, however, have been repealed. There is now no restriction on charitable dispositions.

INTERPRETATION OF WILLS

Incorporation by Reference

> **RULE** The UPC recognizes the common law doctrine of **incorporation by reference**, which permits the inclusion by reference of unattested documents as part of a will if:

- the writing was in existence at the time of execution of the will; and
- the language of the will manifests this intent, and describes the writing sufficiently to permit its identification.

- However, a paper not referred to in the will is not incorporated, even if it was in existence at the execution of the will. A devise not in the will also cannot be made effective by a reference.

Facts of Independent Significance

- Under the doctrine of **facts of independent significance**, a will may dispose of property by reference to acts and events that have significance apart from their effect upon the dispositions made by the will, whether they occur before or after the execution of the will, or before or after the testator's death.

- These acts and events may include the execution or revocation of another individual's will.

STATUTORY PROVISIONS COVERING SPECIAL CIRCUMSTANCES

Slayer Act

 RULE Any person who participates, either as a principal, co-conspirator, or an accessory before the fact, in the willful and unlawful killing of any other person may not acquire any property or receive any benefit as a result of the death of the decedent.

- The slayer rule does not apply if the killing was reckless, accidental, or negligent.

- The slayer will be deemed to have died immediately before the decedent, and therefore, receives nothing from the estate regardless of whether the decedent died testate or intestate.

Refusal to Support; Desertion

- Although some statutes bar a surviving spouse for desertion or adultery, the UPC requires some definitive legal act in order to bar the surviving spouse. Normally, this is divorce. Thus, desertion or adultery would not be sufficient.

Simultaneous Death

- A simultaneous death occurs when two or more persons, one of whom is the beneficiary of the other, die under circumstances where there is insufficient evidence to determine which party survived the other (e.g., a common disaster such as a plane crash).

- An individual who fails to survive the decedent cannot take as an heir or a devisee.

 RULE Under the UPC, a person who cannot be established by clear and convincing evidence to have survived the decedent by 120 hours is deemed to have predeceased the decedent.

CHANGES IN PROPERTY AND BENEFICIARIES AFTER EXECUTION OF THE WILL

Ademption

Ademption by Extinction

DEFINITION A testamentary gift is **adeemed by extinction**—that is, it fails—when property specifically bequeathed or devised is not in the testator's estate at his death.

- The ademption may occur by an intentional act on the part of the testator (e.g., a sale or gift), or by an involuntary circumstance (e.g., fire or theft). The doctrine of ademption by extinction applies only to specific bequests or devises.

- Under the common law, ademption occurs even if the property has been exchanged for other property. Under the UPC, if the testator acquired a replacement for the specifically devised property, the devisee receives the replacement property.

Ademption by Satisfaction

DEFINITION An **ademption by satisfaction** is similar to the idea of an advancement; it occurs when a testator makes an *inter vivos* gift of property to a beneficiary of a general or residuary disposition with the intent that the provision of the will be thereby satisfied.

- Property a testator gave in his lifetime to a person is treated as a satisfaction of a devise only if:

    (1) the will provides for deduction of the gift;

(2) the testator declared in a contemporaneous writing that the gift is in satisfaction of the devise or that its value is to be deducted from the value of the devise; or

(3) the devisee acknowledged in writing that the gift is in satisfaction of the devise or that its value is to be deducted from the value of the devise.

- For purposes of partial satisfaction, property is valued as of the time the devisee came into possession or enjoyment of the property or at the testator's death, whichever occurs first. If the devisee fails to survive the testator, the gift is treated as a full or partial satisfaction of the devise, as appropriate, unless the testator's contemporaneous writing provides otherwise.

Encumbered Property: No-Exoneration Rule

- At common law, a person to whom the testator specifically devised real estate was entitled to have any mortgage or lien outstanding on the property paid off out of the other assets of the estate, leaving his devise unencumbered. The UPC abolishes the common law rule.

- Under the UPC, the beneficiary of a devise or bequest under a will is entitled only to the interest of the testator in the property; that is, he takes the property subject to any lien or mortgage outstanding at the testator's death. There is no exoneration. A **specific devise** passes subject to any mortgage interest existing at the date of death, without right of exoneration, regardless of a general directive in the will to pay debts.

- This no-exoneration rule applies to both real and personal property, and it applies whether the security interest was created by the testator or by a previous owner.

Abatement

- If the assets of the testator's estate are insufficient, after payment of all claims against the estate, to satisfy all the bequests or devises, the beneficiaries' shares will **abate** (i.e., be reduced).

RULE ▶ Absent contrary directions in the will, the shares of distributees abate, without any preference or priority as between real and personal property, in the following order:

- property not disposed of by the will;
- residuary devises;
- general devises; and then
- specific (demonstrative) devises.

Class Gifts

In General

- A **class gift** exists when the testator makes a gift to a number of persons as a group, and the group may either increase or decrease in number.

- The share of each member depends on the ultimate number in the class.

Closing of Class—Maximum Membership

- Generally, the courts employ the **rule of convenience**—a person must be born before the period of distribution in order to share in a class gift.

- If the gift is an immediate gift, the class closes at the death of the testator. If the gift is postponed, ordinarily there will be no inconvenience involved in allowing the class to remain open until the time set for distribution. Therefore, the closing is not at the testator's death but at the distribution date.

Lapse

In General

- Under the common law, a **lapse** occurs when a disposition fails because the beneficiary predeceases the testator. Lapse can generally be avoided by class gifts or by naming an alternative beneficiary.

- Lapsed dispositions pass to the residuary estate, or, if there is no residuary provision, they pass by intestacy.

Anti-Lapse Statute

- The common law lapse doctrine applies, except where prevented by the anti-lapse statute.

- In the absence of a contrary intent expressed in the will, a gift to a beneficiary who fails to survive the testator will not lapse when the devisee is a grandparent, a descendant of a grandparent, or a stepchild of either the testator or the donor of a power of appointment exercised by the testator's will.

- **Not a Class Gift and Deceased Leaves Surviving Issue:** A substitute gift is created in the devisee's surviving descendants. They take by representation the property to which the devisee would have been entitled had the devisee survived the testator.

- **Class Gift:** If the devise is in the form of a class gift, other than a devise to "issue," "descendants," "heirs of the body," "heirs," "next to kin," "relatives," or "family," or a class described by language of similar import, a substitute gift is created in the surviving descendants of any deceased devisee.

- **In Any Other Case:** if the devise that is not part of the residuary estate fails or is void because the beneficiary fails to survive the testator, it is contrary to law, it is otherwise incapable of taking effect, it was revoked by the testator, it is not disposed of, or it is released or disclaimed by the beneficiary, the devise will be included in the residuary clause contained in the will.

REVOCATION AND REVIVAL OF WILLS

Methods of Revocation

RULE ▶ Under the UPC, wills may be revoked by:

- performing a revocatory act (burning, tearing, cancelling or destroying) all or any part of the will with the intent to revoke the will by the testator or another at the testator's direction and in his presence;
- executing a subsequent will that revokes the previous will or part expressly or by inconsistency; or
- operation of law.

Dependent Relative Revocation

- Frequently, a testator revokes an old will with the intention that a newly executed will shall replace it. If the new will is not made or is invalid, some jurisdictions will admit the revoked will to probate on the theory that the testator did not intend the revocation to occur unless the new will's provisions should take effect; that is, that the revocation occurred through a mistake of law or fact by the testator.

RULE ▶ The **doctrine of dependent relative revocation** is the law of second best, i.e., its application does not produce the result the testator actually intended, but is designed to come as close as possible to that intent.

- Dependent relative revocation has been applied only where there is:

  (1) a defective execution of a subsequent will or codicil; or

  (2) an intrinsic defect in a subsequent will or codicil.

- The doctrine is not favored and is rarely applied by courts. If it is applied by the courts, it is used as a rule of testamentary construction, in aid of ascertaining the testator's intent.

Revival of Revoked Wills

- The UPC provides that if, after the making of a will, the testator executes a later will that expressly or impliedly revokes the earlier will, the revocation of that later will does not revive the earlier will. The previous will is revived only if it is evident from the circumstances of the revocation of the subsequent will or from the testator's contemporary or subsequent declarations that the testator intended the previous will to take effect as executed.

- Alternatively, revival can be accomplished if, after the revocation of the later will, the earlier will is re-executed.

CONTRACTS TO MAKE A WILL

Contract to Make a Will or Die Intestate

- The UPC will uphold as valid a contract to dispose of by will all or part of a person's property, whether real or personal. The contract must exhibit the general contractual requisites of consideration, contractual intent, and definiteness of terms.

- A contract to make a will or devise, or not to revoke a will or devise, or to die intestate, may be established only by:

  (1) provisions of the decedent's will stating material provisions of the contract;

  (2) an express reference in the decedent's will to a contract and extrinsic evidence proving the terms of the contract; or

  (3) a writing signed by the decedent evidencing the contract.

Real Estate

- The Statute of Frauds requires that an agreement to will real estate be in writing. The statute can be satisfied, however, if the promisee relies on an oral promise or contract to leave him certain real estate by will, if the will or another writing is connected with and supports the oral contract.

Joint and Mutual Wills

DEFINITION A **joint will** is a document executed by two or more testators that is intended to serve as the will of each and every person who signed it. A **mutual will** is a separate will executed by two or more persons, with reciprocal provisions for the distribution of assets.

- In some states, the execution of a joint will gives rise to a presumption that the parties had contracted not to revoke the will except by consent of both.

- Under the UPC, however, the execution of a joint will or mutual will does not create a presumption of a contract not to revoke the will. Thus, both joint and mutual wills are revocable by either party.

PROBATE OF WILLS

In General

- Probate is the process by which a will is established as the valid last will of a decedent.

- A formal testacy proceeding is litigation to determine whether a decedent left a valid will. Venue for the proceeding is:

  (1) in the county where the decedent had his domicile at the time of his death; or

(2) if the decedent was not domiciled in the state, in any county where property of the decedent was located at the time of his death.

Proof of Wills

Burden of Proof

- The burden of proving that a will was duly executed is always on the person offering the will for probate. **Contestants** of a will have the burden of establishing lack of testamentary intent or capacity, undue influence, fraud, duress, mistake, or revocation.

- Proof of a will requires that it be established that the signature appearing on the will is the testator's. There is no requirement that the testator's signature be at the end of the will. Thus, if the testator writes his name in the body of the will and intends it to be his signature, the statute is satisfied.

- If the will is witnessed, but not notarized or self-proved, the testimony of at least one of the attesting witnesses is required to establish proper execution if the witness is within the state, competent, and able to testify. Proper execution may be established by other evidence, including an affidavit of an attesting witness. An attestation clause that is signed by the attesting witnesses raises a rebuttable presumption that the events recited in the clause occurred.

- If the will is notarized, but not self-proved, there is a rebuttable presumption that the will satisfies the requirements for execution upon filing the will.

Self-Proving Affidavit

- Most probate proceedings are uncontested. To avoid the inconvenience of calling witnesses and to simplify proof of wills in such cases, affidavits of witnesses may be filed in uncontested cases in lieu of their testimony.

- The affidavits can be executed together with the will; they set forth facts sufficient to establish due execution of the will and the capacity of the testator.

Proof of Lost Wills

- If a will is traced to the testator's possession and cannot be found after death, the law presumes that the testator destroyed the will with intent to revoke it. This presumption may be overcome by the proponents of a lost will.

- If a will cannot be located after death but the trier of fact finds that it was not revoked, the will is entitled to probate if its due execution and contents can be proved.

- If the original will is neither in the possession of the court nor accompanies the petition for formal probate of the will, and no authenticated copy of a will probated in another jurisdiction accompanies the petition, the petition must state the contents of the will and indicate that it is lost, destroyed, or otherwise unavailable. Commonly in such cases, the will is proved by evidence of a law office or other copy, or from the drafter's notes and recollection. If its full contents cannot be proved, the will is entitled to probate to the extent that its contents can be proved.

WILL CONTESTS

In General

- In a will contest, a person interested in the distribution of the estate objects to the admission of the will to probate on the ground that the will is invalid for some reason.

- If the contesting party is successful in preventing the will from being admitted and there is no other will in effect, the estate will be distributed as if the creator of the will died intestate.

RULE ▶ The grounds for contest of a properly executed will are:

- lack of testamentary capacity;
- undue influence;
- mistake; and
- fraud.

Undue Influence

- The doctrine of **undue influence** protects against overreaching by a wrongdoer seeking to take unfair advantage of a donor who is susceptible to such wrongdoing on account of the donor's age, inexperience, dependence, physical or mental weakness, or other factors.

- Circumstantial evidence is sufficient to raise an inference of undue influence if the contestant proves that:

    (1)   the donor was susceptible to undue influence;

    (2)   the alleged wrongdoer had an opportunity to exert undue influence;

    (3)   the alleged wrongdoer had a disposition to exert undue influence; and

    (4)   there was a result appearing to be the effect of the undue influence.

- A presumption of undue influence arises if the alleged wrongdoer was in a confidential relationship with the donor and there were suspicious circumstances surrounding the preparation, formulation, or execution of the will.

Mistake

- Mistake may be distinguished from fraud by the lack of intent to deceive the testator. Mistake may arise from an innocent or negligent misrepresentation regarding a material fact, or from a misunderstanding on the part of the testator.

DEFINITION ▶ **Mistake in the inducement** is a mistake as to facts outside the will that induced the testator to dispose of his property in a certain manner. Generally, provisions of a will cannot be set aside for mistakes in the inducement.

DEFINITION ▶ **Mistake in the factum** relates to a mistake in the will itself. The general rule is that the court will not reform a will for mistake in the factum (e.g., an erroneous identification of a beneficiary). However, if the mistake goes to the testator's testamentary capacity, the will may be held invalid.

- The burden of proof of a mistake in a will is on the party alleging the mistake.

Fraud

- **Fraud in the inducement** is established upon proof that a beneficiary made a knowingly false representation to the testator for the purpose of inducing the testator to draw a will in his favor, and that the testator made a different will than he would have made in the absence of the representation.

- **Fraud in the execution** is fraud as to the very nature of an instrument or its contents.

- In both fraud in the inducement and fraud in the execution, the will, or the fraudulently induced part of it, will be denied probate. If fraud is alleged with respect to only a part of the will, the court may reject that part and admit the rest to probate. The legacy that is void due to fraud then falls into the residue, or, if there is no residuary clause, passes by intestacy. If the entire will is tainted, all the property will pass by intestacy.

- The burden of proving fraud is on the party alleging fraud. To invalidate a will, a party must show that the contested will was the fruit of the fraud.

Ambiguity

In General

- An **ambiguity** in a donative document is an uncertainty in meaning that is revealed by the text or by extrinsic evidence other than direct evidence of intention contradicting the plain meaning of the text.

- Ambiguities are resolved by construing the text of the will in accordance with the donor's intention, to the extent that the donor's intention is established by a preponderance of the evidence. Because the primary objective of construction is to give effect to the donor's intention, extrinsic evidence relevant to the donor's intention may be considered along with the text of the document in seeking to determine the donor's intention.

Patent Ambiguities

- **Patent ambiguities** appear on the face of the instrument.

Latent Ambiguities

DEFINITION **Latent ambiguities** arise when language of the will, otherwise clear, is applied to the thing given or the person benefited under the will, and some extrinsic fact necessitates interpretation or choice among two or more possible meanings.

- Where the ambiguity is latent, extrinsic evidence is admissible to resolve the ambiguity.

Interpretation

- In the interpretation of a will, however, the testator's oral statement of his intentions is inadmissible to prove his intentions because the testamentary wishes of a testator must be in writing.

- Once an ambiguity, patent or latent, is established, both direct and circumstantial evidence of the donor's intention may be considered in resolving the ambiguity in accordance with the donor's intention.

Standing to Contest

RULE An **interested person** may contest a will. Case law generally holds that an interested person is one who has a pecuniary interest that is directly and adversely affected by a judgment of the validity of the will. The person contesting the will must stand to gain financially.

- Persons who cannot take under the intestacy statute if the will is declared invalid have no standing to contest the will, unless they can show another will under which they would take or a contract to make a will in their favor.

- Generally, no informal probate or formal testacy proceeding may be commenced more than three years after the decedent's death. However, a proceeding to contest an informally probated will and to secure appointment of the person with legal priority for appointment in the event the contest is successful, may be commenced within the later of 12 months from the informal probate or three years from the decedent's death.

In Terrorem Clauses (No-Contest Clauses)

- Generally, an *in terrorem clause* in a will attempts to disqualify anyone contesting the will from taking under it.

- Most states hold that the clause is ineffectual if the person affected had reasonable cause to contest the will.

- Under the UPC, a provision in a will purporting to penalize an interested person for contesting the will or instituting other proceedings relating to the estate is unenforceable if probable cause exists for instituting such proceedings.

- An *in terrorem* clause will be enforceable if the will contest is unsuccessful and no probable cause existed.

Provisions Restraining Marriage or Religion

- Will provisions attempting to condition a bequest on a beneficiary's future behavior are often said to be attempted instances of **dead-hand control**. Courts will refuse to enforce these if they are found to be overly intrusive or disruptive to living persons contrary to public policy.

- If a testator's purpose in imposing a condition to a legacy is to induce a future separation or divorce of a married couple, the condition will be void as against public policy and the legacy will take effect. However, if the will merely provides for the contingency of divorce and does not express an intent to bring it about, then the provision may be held valid.

- A condition requiring adherence to a specific religion is void as against public policy.

Universal Succession

- The Uniform Probate Code permits the heirs of an intestate or residuary devisees of a testator to accept the estate assets without administration by assuming responsibility for discharging those obligations that normally would be discharged by the personal representative. An application to become universal successors by the heirs of an intestate or the residuary devisees under a will must be signed and verified by each applicant.

- Universal succession is favored because it helps to avoid will contests.

NON-TESTAMENTARY TRANSFERS

Gifts

Inter Vivos Gifts

- To make a valid **gift *inter vivos***, there must be donative intent, delivery, and acceptance by the donee.

Gifts *Causa Mortis*

DEFINITION ▶ A **gift *causa mortis*** is an *inter vivos* gift made with the understanding that the donee takes possession upon delivery but does not acquire title unless the donor dies of a feared imminent threat of death.

- Gifts *causa mortis* require delivery and that the donor dies from an imminently feared death. The imminent fear must relate to some dangerous impending matter, not just a normal fear of death.

Joint Tenancy

In General

- Surviving joint tenants become the full owners of the joint tenancy property because the deceased tenant's interest is deemed to disappear upon his or her death.

- When a grantor transfers property into joint tenancy with another person, there is a presumption that the grantor has made a gift to that person.

Joint Bank Accounts

- Unlike traditional joint tenancies, joint bank accounts are governed by the agreement the tenants make with the bank. Unless otherwise provided, joint account tenants have the right to withdraw the full amount of the funds on deposit without seeking permission from or accounting to the other tenant(s).

Convenience Accounts

- **Convenience accounts** usually are joint accounts in which all of the funds have been supplied by one tenant with the other tenant being put on the account to access funds on behalf of the contributing tenant.

- Convenience accounts do not give survivorship rights to the non-contributing tenant because there was no present donative intent to make a gift at the time the account was established.

- Because convenience accounts are usually joint accounts, the person (normally the deceased tenant's heir, will beneficiary, or a representative thereof) claiming a convenience account must overcome the presumption of gift raised by the creation of a joint tenancy.

Payable on Death (P.O.D.) Accounts

DEFINITION A **P.O.D. (payable on death) account** is a bank account in which a person remains the owner during his life with complete control over the funds on deposit, and the funds in the account pass directly to a named beneficiary or beneficiaries at the owner's death.

- The beneficiary does not have any right, title, or interest in the account until the owner dies. The owner has the unfettered right to cancel the account, withdraw all or part of the funds, or change its beneficiary until the owner dies.

- **Pay-on-death registrations** can be established for brokerage accounts. These are called TOD (transfer-on-death) security registrations. The rules for TOD security registrations are the same as those for pay-on-death bank accounts.

Power of Attorney

- A **power of attorney** is a relationship wherein the principal appoints an agent to act on his behalf. The power gives the agent the authority to deal with the principal's property and execute business transactions on behalf of the principal during the latter's life.

- A **springing power of attorney** will become effective upon the principal's loss of mental capacity or otherwise becoming disabled.

- The agency can be either durable or non-durable. **Non-durable** means that the agency terminates upon the principal's incompetence. **Durable** powers continue even during the principal's incapacity.

- A power of attorney terminates upon the death of the principal.

Simulated Practice Exam

Morning Session

In re Rowan

INSTRUCTIONS

1. You will be instructed when to begin and when to stop this test. Do not break the seal on this booklet until you are told to begin. This test is designed to evaluate your ability to handle a select number of legal authorities in the context of a factual problem involving a client.

2. The problem is set in the fictitious state of Franklin, in the fictitious Fifteenth Circuit of the United States. Columbia and Olympia are also fictitious states in the Fifteenth Circuit. In Franklin, the trial court of general jurisdiction is the District Court, the intermediate appellate court is the Court of Appeal, and the highest court is the Supreme Court.

3. You will have two kinds of materials with which to work: a File and a Library. The first document in the File is a memorandum containing the instructions for the task you are to complete. The other documents in the File contain factual information about your case and may include some facts that are not relevant.

4. The Library contains the legal authorities needed to complete the task and may also include some authorities that are not relevant. Any cases may be real, modified, or written solely for the purpose of this examination. If the cases appear familiar to you, do not assume that they are precisely the same as you have read before. Read them thoroughly, as if they all were new to you. You should assume that the cases were decided in the jurisdictions and on the dates shown. In citing cases from the Library, you may use abbreviations and omit page references.

5. Your response must be written in the answer book provided. If you are using a laptop computer to answer the questions, your jurisdiction will provide you with specific instructions. In answering this performance test, you should concentrate on the materials in the File and Library. What you have learned in law school and elsewhere provides the general background for analyzing the problem; the File and Library provide the specific materials with which you must work.

6. Although there are no restrictions on how you apportion your time, you should allocate approximately half your time to reading and digesting the materials and to organizing your answer before you begin writing it. You may make notes anywhere in the test materials; blank pages are provided at the end of the booklet. You may not tear pages from the question booklet.

7. This performance test will be graded on your responsiveness to the instructions regarding the task you are to complete, which are given to you in the first memorandum in the File, and on the content, thoroughness, and organization of your response.

IN RE ROWAN

FILE

LIBRARY

FILE

In re Rowan

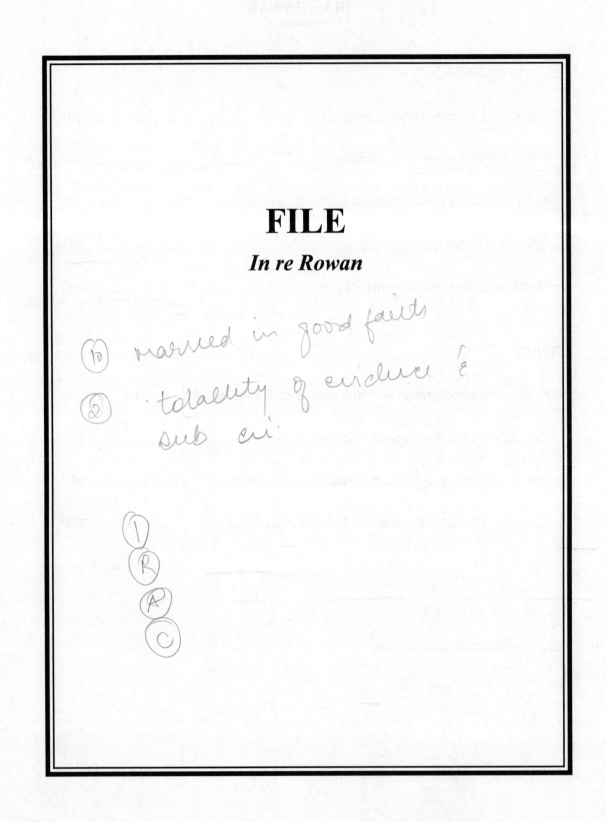

① married in good faith

② totality of evidence &
sub evi

Ⓘ
Ⓡ
Ⓐ
Ⓒ

Law Offices of Jamie Quarles
112 Charles St.
Franklin City, Franklin 33797

TO: Examinee
FROM: Jamie Quarles
DATE: February 25, 2014
RE: *Matter of William Rowan*

We represent William Rowan, a British citizen, who has lived in this country as a conditional permanent resident because of his marriage to Sarah Cole, a U.S. citizen. Mr. Rowan now seeks to remove the condition on his lawful permanent residency.

Normally, a married couple would apply together to remove the conditional status, before the end of the two years of the noncitizen's conditional residency. However, ten months ago, in April 2013, Ms. Cole and Mr. Rowan separated, and they eventually divorced. Ms. Cole actively opposes Mr. Rowan's continued residency in this country.

However, Ms. Cole's opposition does not end Mr. Rowan's chances. As the attached legal sources indicate, he can still file Form I-751 Petition to Remove Conditions on Residence, but in the petition he must ask for a waiver of the requirement that he file the petition jointly with his wife.

Acting pro se, Rowan timely filed such a Form I-751 petition. The immigration officer conducted an interview with him. Ms. Cole provided the officer with a sworn affidavit stating her belief that Rowan married her solely to obtain residency. The officer denied Rowan's petition.

Rowan then sought our representation to appeal the denial of his petition. We now have a hearing scheduled in Immigration Court to review the validity of that denial. Before the hearing, we will submit to the court the information described in the attached investigator's memo, which was not presented to the immigration officer. We do not expect Cole to testify, because she has moved out of state.

Please draft our brief to the Immigration Judge. The brief will need to argue that Mr. Rowan married Ms. Cole in good faith. Specifically, it should argue that the immigration officer's decision was not supported by substantial evidence in the record before him and that the totality of the evidence supports granting Rowan's petition.

I have attached our guidelines for drafting briefs. Draft only the legal argument portion of the brief; I will draft the caption and statement of facts.

Law Offices of Jamie Quarles
112 Charles St.
Franklin City, Franklin 33797

TO: Attorneys
FROM: Jamie Quarles
DATE: March 29, 2011
RE: Format for Persuasive Briefs

These guidelines apply to persuasive briefs filed in trial courts and administrative proceedings.

I. Caption
[omitted]

II. Statement of Facts (if applicable)
[omitted]

III. Legal Argument

Your legal argument should be brief and to the point. Assume that the judge will have little time to read and absorb your argument. Make your points clearly and succinctly, citing relevant authority for each legal proposition. Keep in mind that courts are not persuaded by exaggerated, unsupported arguments.

Use headings to separate the sections of your argument. In your headings, do not state abstract conclusions, but integrate factual detail into legal propositions to make them more persuasive. An ineffective heading states only: "The petitioner's request for asylum should be granted." An effective heading states: "The petitioner has shown a well-founded fear of persecution by reason of gender if removed to her home country."

Do not restate the facts as a whole at the beginning of your legal argument. Instead, integrate the facts into your legal argument in a way that makes the strongest case for our client. The body of your argument should analyze applicable legal authority and persuasively argue how both the facts and the law support our client's position. Supporting authority should be emphasized, but contrary authority should also be cited, addressed in the argument, and explained or distinguished.

Finally, anticipate and accommodate any weaknesses in your case in the body of your argument. If possible, structure your argument in such a way as to highlight your argument's strengths and minimize its weaknesses. If necessary, make concessions, but only on points that do not concede essential elements of your claim or defense.

Law Offices of Jamie Quarles

112 Charles St.
Franklin City, Franklin 33797

TO: File
FROM: Jamie Quarles
DATE: November 25, 2013
RE: Interview with William Rowan

I met with William Rowan today. Rowan is a British citizen and moved to the United States and to Franklin about two and a half years ago, having just married Sarah Cole. They separated in April 2013; their divorce became final about 10 days ago. In late April, after the separation, Rowan, acting pro se, petitioned to retain his permanent residency status. After that petition was denied by the immigration officer, Rowan called our office.

Rowan met Cole in Britain a little over three years ago. He had been working toward a graduate degree in library science for several years. He had begun looking for professional positions and had come to the realization that he would have better job opportunities in the United States. He had two siblings already living in the United States.

He met Cole when she was doing graduate work in cultural anthropology at the university where he was finishing his own academic training as a librarian. He says that it was love at first sight for him. He asked her out, but she refused several times before she agreed. After several weeks of courtship, he said that he felt that she shared his feelings. They moved in together about four weeks after their first meeting and lived together for the balance of her time in Britain.

Soon after they moved in together, Rowan proposed marriage to Cole. She agreed, and they married on December 27, 2010, in London, England. Cole subsequently suggested that they move to the United States together, to which he readily agreed. In fact, without telling Cole, Rowan had contacted the university library in Franklin City, just to see if there were job opportunities. That contact produced a promising lead, but no offer. He and Cole moved to Franklin City at the end of her fellowship in May of 2011.

Rowan soon obtained a job with the Franklin State University library. He and Cole jointly leased an apartment and shared living expenses. At one point, they moved into a larger space, signing a two-year lease. When Cole needed to purchase a new car, Rowan (who at that point had the more stable salary) co-signed the loan documents. Both had health insurance

2 JTax

through the university, and each had the other named as the next of kin. They filed two joint tax returns (for 2011 and 2012), but they divorced before they could file another.

Their social life was limited; if they socialized at all, it was with his friends. Rowan consistently introduced Cole as his wife to his friends, and he was referred to by them as "that old married man." As far as Rowan could tell, Cole's colleagues at work did not appear to know that Cole was even married.

Cole's academic discipline required routine absences for field work, conferences, and colloquia. Rowan resented these absences and rarely contacted Cole when she was gone. He estimates that, out of the approximately two and a half years of cohabitation during the marriage, they lived apart for an aggregate total of seven months.

In March of 2013, Cole announced that she had received an offer for a prestigious assistant professorship at Olympia State University. She told Rowan that she intended to take the job and wanted him to move with her, unless he could give her a good reason to stay. She also had an offer from Franklin State University, but she told him that the department was not as prestigious as the Olympia department. He made as strong a case as he could that she should stay, arguing that he could not find another job in Olympia comparable to the one that he had in Franklin.

Cole chose to take the job in Olympia, and she moved there less than a month later. Rowan realized that he would always be following her, and that she would not listen to his concerns or needs. He told her that he would not move. She was furious. She told him that in that case, she would file for a divorce. She also told him that she would fight his effort to stay in the United States. Their divorce was finalized on November 15, 2013, in Franklin.

Rowan worries that without Cole's support, he will not be able to keep his job in Franklin or stay in the United States. He does not want to return to the United Kingdom and wants to maintain permanent residency here.

In re Form I-751, Petition of William Rowan to Remove Conditions on Residence

Affidavit of Sarah Cole

Upon first being duly sworn, I, Sarah Cole, residing in the County of Titan, Olympia, do say:

1.   I am submitting this affidavit in opposition to William Rowan's Form I-751 Petition to Remove Conditions on Residence.

2.   I am a United States citizen. I married William Rowan in London, England, on December 27, 2010. This was the first marriage for each of us. We met while I was on a fellowship in that city. He was finishing up his own graduate studies. He told me that he had been actively looking for a position in the United States for several years. He pursued me and after about four weeks convinced me to move in with him. Shortly after this, William proposed marriage and I accepted.

3.   We decided that we would move to the United States. I now believe that he never seriously considered the option of remaining in Britain. I later learned that William had made contacts with the university library in Franklin City, Franklin, long before he proposed.

4.   Before entering the United States in May 2011, we obtained the necessary approvals for William to enter the country as a conditional resident. We moved to Franklin City so that I could resume my studies.

5.   During our marriage, William expressed little interest in my work but expressed great dissatisfaction with the hours that I was working and the time that I spent traveling. My graduate work had brought me great success, including the chance at an assistant professorship at Olympia State University, whose cultural anthropology department is nationally ranked. But William resisted any idea of moving and complained about the effect a move would have on our marriage and his career.

6.   Eventually, I took the job in Olympia and moved in April 2013. While I knew that William did not like the move, I had asked him to look into library positions in Olympia, and he had done so. I fully expected him to follow me within a few months. I was shocked and angered when, instead, he called me on April 23, 2013, and informed me that he would stay in Franklin.

7.   I filed for divorce, which is uncontested. It is my belief that William does not really care about the divorce. I believe now that he saw our marriage primarily as a means to get

U.S. residency. I do think that his affection for me was real. But his job planning, his choice of friends, and his resistance to my career goals indicate a lack of commitment to our relationship. In addition, he has carefully evaded any long-term commitments, including children, property ownership, and similar obligations.

Signed and sworn this 2nd day of July, 2013.

Sarah Cole

Sarah Cole

Signed before me this 2nd day of July, 2013.

Jane Mirren

Jane Mirren
Notary Public, State of Olympia

Law Offices of Jamie Quarles
112 Charles St.
Franklin City, Franklin 33797

TO: File
FROM: Victor Lamm, investigator
DATE: February 20, 2014
RE: Preparation for Rowan Form I-751 Petition

This memorandum summarizes the results of my investigation, witness preparation, and document acquisition in advance of the immigration hearing for William Rowan.

Witnesses:

— George Miller: friend and coworker of William Rowan. Has spent time with Rowan and Cole as a couple (over 20 social occasions) and has visited their two primary residences and has observed them together. Will testify that they self-identified as husband and wife and that he has heard them discussing leasing of residential property, purchasing cars, borrowing money for car purchase, and buying real estate, all together and as part of the marriage.

— Anna Sperling: friend and coworker of William Rowan. Has spent time with both Rowan and Cole, both together and separately. Will testify to statements by Cole that she (Cole) felt gratitude toward Rowan for moving to the United States without a job, and that Cole was convinced that Rowan "did it for love."

Documents (Rowan to authenticate):

— Lease on house at 11245 Old Sachem Road, Franklin City, Franklin, with a two-year term running until January 31, 2014. Signed by both Cole and Rowan.

— Promissory note for $20,000 initially, designating Cole as debtor and Rowan as co-signer, in connection with a new car purchase.

— Printouts of joint bank account in name of Rowan and Cole, February 1, 2012, through May 31, 2013.

— Joint income tax returns for 2011 and 2012.

— Certified copy of the judgment of divorce.

LIBRARY

In re Rowan

EXCERPT FROM IMMIGRATION AND NATIONALITY ACT OF 1952

TITLE 8 U.S.C., Aliens and Nationality

8 U.S.C. § 1186a. Conditional permanent resident status for certain alien spouses and sons and daughters

(a) In general

(1) Conditional basis for status: Notwithstanding any other provision of this chapter, an alien spouse . . . shall be considered, at the time of obtaining the status of an alien lawfully admitted for permanent residence, to have obtained such status on a conditional basis subject to the provisions of this section.

. . .

(c) Requirements of timely petition and interview for removal of condition

(1) In general: In order for the conditional basis established under subsection (a) of this section for an alien spouse or an alien son or daughter to be removed—

(A) the alien spouse and the petitioning spouse (if not deceased) jointly must submit to the Secretary of Homeland Security a petition which requests the removal of such conditional basis . . . .

. . .

(4) Hardship waiver: The Secretary . . . may remove the conditional basis of the permanent resident status for an alien who fails to meet the requirements of paragraph (1) if the alien demonstrates that—

. . .

(B) the qualifying marriage was entered into in good faith by the alien spouse, but the qualifying marriage has been terminated (other than through the death of the spouse) and the alien was not at fault in failing to meet the requirements of paragraph (1).

EXCERPT FROM CODE OF FEDERAL REGULATIONS

TITLE 8. Aliens and Nationality

8 C.F.R. § 216.5 Waiver of requirement to file joint petition to remove conditions by alien spouse

(a) General.

(1) A conditional resident alien who is unable to meet the requirements . . . for a joint petition for removal of the conditional basis of his or her permanent resident status may file a Petition to Remove the Conditions on Residence, if the alien requests a waiver, was not at fault in failing to meet the filing requirement, and the conditional resident alien is able to establish that:

. . .

(ii) The marriage upon which his or her status was based was entered into in good faith by the conditional resident alien, but the marriage was terminated other than by death . . .

. . .

(e) Adjudication of waiver application—

. . .

(2) Application for waiver based upon the alien's claim that the marriage was entered into in good faith. In considering whether an alien entered into a qualifying marriage in good faith, the director shall consider evidence relating to the amount of commitment by both parties to the marital relationship. Such evidence may include—

(i) Documentation relating to the degree to which the financial assets and liabilities of the parties were combined;

(ii) Documentation concerning the length of time during which the parties cohabited after the marriage and after the alien obtained permanent residence;

(iii) Birth certificates of children born to the marriage; and

(iv) Other evidence deemed pertinent by the director.

. . .

Hua v. Napolitano
United States Court of Appeals (15th Cir. 2011)

Under the Immigration and Nationality Act, an alien who marries a United States citizen is entitled to petition for permanent residency on a conditional basis. *See* 8 U.S.C. § 1186a(a)(1). Ordinarily, within the time limits provided by statute, the couple jointly petitions for removal of the condition, stating that the marriage has not ended and was not entered into for the purpose of procuring the alien spouse's admission as an immigrant. 8 U.S.C. § 1186a(c)(1)(A).

If the couple has divorced within two years of the conditional admission, however, the alien spouse may still apply to the Secretary of Homeland Security to remove the conditional nature of her admission by granting a "hardship waiver." 8 U.S.C. § 1186a(c)(4). The Secretary may remove the conditional status upon a finding, *inter alia*, that the marriage was entered into in good faith by the alien spouse. 8 U.S.C. § 1186a(c)(4)(B).

On September 15, 2003, petitioner Agnes Hua, a Chinese citizen, married a United States citizen of Chinese descent and secured conditional admission as a permanent United States resident. The couple later divorced, and Hua applied for a hardship waiver. But the Secretary, acting through a U.S. Citizenship and Immigration Services (USCIS) immigration officer, then an immigration judge, and the Board of Immigration Appeals (BIA), denied Hua's petition. Hua appeals the denial of the petition.

Hua has the burden of proving that she intended to establish a life with her spouse at the time she married him. If she meets this burden, her marriage is legitimate, even if securing an immigration benefit was one of the factors that led her to marry. Hua made a very strong showing that she married with the requisite intent to establish a life with her husband. Hua's evidence, expressly credited by the immigration judge and never questioned by the BIA, established the following:

(1) She and her future husband engaged in a nearly two-year courtship prior to marrying.

(2) She and her future husband were in frequent telephone contact whenever they lived apart, as proven by telephone records.

(3) Her future husband traveled to China in December 2002 for three weeks to meet her family, and she paid a 10-day visit to him in the United States in March 2003 to meet his family.

(4) She returned to the United States in June 2003 (on a visitor's visa which permitted her to remain in the country through late September 2003) to decide whether she would remain in the United States or whether her future husband would move with her to China.

(5) The two married in a civil ceremony on September 15, 2003, and returned to China for two weeks to hold a more formal reception (a reception that was never held).

(6) The two lived together at his parents' house from the time of her arrival in the United States in June 2003 until he asked her to move out on April 22, 2004.

Hua also proved that, during the marriage, she and her husband jointly enrolled in a health insurance policy, filed tax returns, opened bank accounts, entered into automobile financing agreements, and secured a credit card. *See* 8 C.F.R. § 216.5(e)(2)(i).

Nevertheless, the BIA cited four facts in support of its conclusion that Hua had failed to carry her burden: (1) her application to secure conditional permanent residency was submitted within two weeks of the marriage; (2) Hua and her husband married one week prior to the expiration of the visitor's visa by which she came to the United States in June 2003; (3) Hua's husband maintained an intimate relationship with another woman during the marriage; and (4) Hua moved out of the marital residence shortly after obtaining conditional residency. Hua's husband's extramarital affair led to cancellation of the reception in China and to her departure from the marital home.

We do not see how Hua's prompt submission of a conditional residency application after her marriage tends to show that Hua did not marry in good faith. As we already have stated, the visitor's visa by which Hua entered the country expired just after the marriage, so Hua had to do something to remain here lawfully.

As to the affair maintained by Hua's husband, that might offer an indication of Hua's marital intentions if Hua knew of the relationship at the time she married. However, the uncontradicted evidence establishes that Hua learned of the affair only after the marriage.

The timing of the marriage and separation appear at first glance more problematic. Ordinarily, one who marries one week prior to the expiration of her visitor's visa and then moves out of the marital home shortly after the conditional residency interview might reasonably be thought to have married solely for an immigration benefit.

But well-settled law requires us to assess the entirety of the record. A long courtship preceded this marriage. Moreover, Hua's husband, and not Hua, initiated the separation after Hua publicly shamed him by retaining counsel and detailing his affair at her conditional residency interview.

We conclude that the Secretary's decision lacks substantial evidence on the record as a whole, and thus that petitioner Hua has satisfied the "good faith" marriage requirement for eligibility under 8 U.S.C.

§ 1186a(c)(4)(B). Remanded for proceedings consistent with this opinion.

Connor v. Chertoff

United States Court of Appeals (15th Cir. 2007)

Ian Connor, an Irish national, petitions for review of a decision of the Board of Immigration Appeals (BIA), which denied him a statutory waiver of the joint filing requirement for removal of the conditional basis of his permanent resident status on the ground that he entered into his marriage to U.S. citizen Anne Moore in bad faith. 8 U.S.C. § 1186a(c)(4)(B).

Connor met Moore in January 2002 when they worked at the same company in Forest Hills, Olympia. After dating for about one year, they married in a civil ceremony on April 14, 2003. According to Connor, he and Moore then lived with her family until November 2003, when they moved into an apartment of their own. In January 2004, Connor left Olympia to take a temporary job in Alaska, where he spent five weeks. Connor stated that in May 2004, he confronted Moore with his suspicion that she was being unfaithful to him. After Moore suggested they divorce, the two separated in June 2004 and divorced on November 27, 2004, 19 months after their wedding.

U.S. Citizenship and Immigration Services (USCIS) had granted Connor conditional permanent resident status on September 15, 2004. On August 16, 2005, Connor filed a Petition to Remove Conditions on Residence with a request for waiver. *See* § 1186a(c)(4)(B).

Moore voluntarily submitted an affidavit concerning Connor's request for waiver. In that affidavit, Moore stated that "Connor never spent any time with [her] during the marriage, except when he needed money." They never socialized together during the marriage, and even when they resided together, Connor spent most of his time away from the residence. Moore expressed the opinion that Connor "never took the marriage seriously" and that "he only married [her] to become a citizen." Connor's petition was denied.

At Connor's hearing, the government presented no witnesses. Connor testified to the foregoing facts and provided documentary evidence, including a jointly filed tax return, an unsigned lease for an apartment dated November 2003, eight canceled checks from a joint account, telephone bills listing Connor and Moore as residing at the same address, an application for life insurance, and an application for vehicle title. There was no evidence that certain documents, such as the applications for life insurance and automobile title, had been filed. Connor also provided a letter from a nurse who had treated him over an extended period of time stating that his wife had accompanied him on most office visits, and letters that Moore had written to him during periods of separation.

Other evidence about Connor's life before and after his marriage to Moore raised questions as to his credibility, including evidence of his children by another woman prior to his marriage to Moore. Connor stated that Moore knew about his children but that he chose not to list them on the Petition for Conditional Status and also that the attorneys who filled out his I-751 petition omitted the children due to an error. Connor testified that he did not mention his children during his interview with the USCIS officer because he thought that they were not relevant to the immigration decision as they were not U.S. citizens.

In a written opinion, the immigration judge found that Connor was not a credible witness because of his failure to list his children on the USCIS forms or mention them during his interview and because of his demeanor during cross-examination. The immigration judge commented on Connor's departure for Alaska within eight months of his marriage to Moore, and on the lack of any corroborating testimony about the bona fides of the marriage by family or friends. The immigration judge concluded that the marriage had not been entered into in good faith and denied Connor the statutory waiver. The BIA affirmed.

Under the substantial evidence standard that governs our review of § 1186a(c)(4) waiver determinations, we must affirm the BIA's order when there is such relevant evidence as reasonable minds might accept as adequate to support it, even if it is possible to reach a contrary result on the basis of the evidence. We conclude that there was substantial evidence in the record to support the BIA's adverse credibility finding and its denial of the statutory waiver.

Adverse credibility determinations must be based on "specific, cogent reasons," which the BIA provided here. The immigration judge's adverse credibility finding was based on Connor's failure to inform USCIS about his children during his oral interview and on the pertinent USCIS forms. Failing to list his children from a prior relationship undercut Connor's claim that his marriage to Moore was in good faith. That important omission properly served as a basis for an adverse credibility determination.

Substantial evidence supports the determination that Connor did not meet his burden of proof by a preponderance of the evidence. To determine good faith, the proper inquiry is whether Connor and Moore intended to establish a life together at the time they were married. The immigration judge may look to the actions of the parties after the marriage to the extent that those actions bear on the subjective intent of the parties at the time they were married. Additional relevant evidence includes, but is not limited to, documentation such as lease agreements, insurance policies, income tax forms, and bank accounts, as well as testimony about the courtship and wedding. Neither the immigration judge nor the BIA may substitute personal conjecture or inference for reliable evidence.

In this case, inconsistencies in the documentary evidence and the lack of corroborating testimony further support the agency's decision. Connor provided only limited documentation of the short marriage. Unexplained inconsistencies existed in the documents, such as more addresses than residences. Connor provided no signed leases, nor any indication of any filed applications for life insurance or automobile title. No corroboration existed for Connor's version of events from family, friends, or others who knew Connor and Moore as a couple. Connor offered only a letter from a nurse, who knew him only as a patient.

Finally, Connor claims that Moore's affidavit was inadmissible hearsay, and that it amounted to unsupported opinion testimony on the ultimate issue. Connor misconstrues the relevant rules at these hearings. The Federal Rules of Evidence do not apply; evidence submitted at these hearings must only be probative and fundamentally fair. To be sure, Moore's affidavit does contain opinion testimony on Connor's intentions. However, the affidavit also contains relevant factual information drawn from firsthand observation. The immigration judge was entitled to rely on that information in reaching his conclusions.

It might be possible to reach a contrary conclusion on the basis of this record. However, under the substantial evidence standard, the evidence presented here does not compel a finding that Connor met his burden of proving that the marriage was entered into in good faith.

Affirmed.

In re Peterson Engineering Consultants

INSTRUCTIONS

1. You will be instructed when to begin and when to stop this test. Do not break the seal on this booklet until you are told to begin. This test is designed to evaluate your ability to handle a select number of legal authorities in the context of a factual problem involving a client.

2. The problem is set in the fictitious state of Franklin, in the fictitious Fifteenth Circuit of the United States. Columbia and Olympia are also fictitious states in the Fifteenth Circuit. In Franklin, the trial court of general jurisdiction is the District Court, the intermediate appellate court is the Court of Appeal, and the highest court is the Supreme Court.

3. You will have two kinds of materials with which to work: a File and a Library. The first document in the File is a memorandum containing the instructions for the task you are to complete. The other documents in the File contain factual information about your case and may include some facts that are not relevant.

4. The Library contains the legal authorities needed to complete the task and may also include some authorities that are not relevant. Any cases may be real, modified, or written solely for the purpose of this examination. If the cases appear familiar to you, do not assume that they are precisely the same as you have read before. Read them thoroughly, as if they all were new to you. You should assume that the cases were decided in the jurisdictions and on the dates shown. In citing cases from the Library, you may use abbreviations and omit page references.

5. Your response must be written in the answer book provided. If you are using a laptop computer to answer the questions, your jurisdiction will provide you with specific instructions. In answering this performance test, you should concentrate on the materials in the File and Library. What you have learned in law school and elsewhere provides the general background for analyzing the problem; the File and Library provide the specific materials with which you must work.

6. Although there are no restrictions on how you apportion your time, you should allocate approximately half your time to reading and digesting the materials and to organizing your answer before you begin writing it. You may make notes anywhere in the test materials; blank pages are provided at the end of the booklet. You may not tear pages from the question booklet.

7. This performance test will be graded on your responsiveness to the instructions regarding the task you are to complete, which are given to you in the first memorandum in the File, and on the content, thoroughness, and organization of your response.

IN RE PETERSON ENGINEERING CONSULTANTS

FILE

LIBRARY

FILE

In re Peterson Engineering Consultants

Lennon, Means, and Brown LLC
Attorneys at Law
249 S. Oak Street
Franklin City, Franklin 33409

TO: Examinee
FROM: Brenda Brown
DATE: February 25, 2014
RE: Peterson Engineering Consultants

Our client, Peterson Engineering Consultants (PEC), seeks our advice regarding issues related to its employees' use of technology. PEC is a privately owned, non-union engineering consulting firm. Most of its employees work outside the office for over half of each workday. Employees need to be able to communicate with one another, the home office, and clients while they are working outside the office, and to access various information, documents, and reports available on the Internet. PEC issues its employees Internet-connected computers and other devices (such as smartphones and tablets), all for business purposes and not for personal use.

After reading the results of a national survey about computer use in the workplace, the president of PEC became concerned regarding the risk of liability for misuse of company-owned technology and loss of productivity. While the president knows that, despite PEC's policies, its employees use the company's equipment for personal purposes, the survey alerted her to problems that she had not considered.

The president wants to know what revisions to the company's employee manual will provide the greatest possible protection for the company. After discussing the issue with the president, I understand that her goals in revising the manual are (1) to clarify ownership and monitoring of technology, (2) to ensure that the company's technology is used only for business purposes, and (3) to make the policies reflected in the manual effective and enforceable.

I attach relevant excerpts of PEC's current employee manual and a summary of the survey. I also attach three cases that raise significant legal issues about PEC's policies. Please prepare a memorandum addressing these issues that I can use when meeting with the president.

Your memorandum should do the following:

(1) Explain the legal bases under which PEC could be held liable for its employees' use or misuse of Internet-connected (or any similar) technology.

(2) Recommend changes and additions to the employee manual to minimize liability exposure. Base your recommendations on the attached materials and the president's stated goals. Explain the reasons for your recommendations but do not redraft the manual's language.

PETERSON ENGINEERING CONSULTANTS
EMPLOYEE MANUAL
Issued April 13, 2003

Phone Use

Whether in the office or out of the office, and whether using office phones or company-owned phones given to employees, employees are not to incur costs for incoming or outgoing calls unless these calls are for business purposes. Employees may make calls for incidental personal use as long as they do not incur costs.

Computer Use

PEC employees given equipment for use outside the office should understand that the equipment is the property of PEC and must be returned if the employee leaves the employ of PEC, whether voluntarily or involuntarily.

Employees may not use the Internet for any of the following:

- engaging in any conduct that is illegal
- revealing non-public information about PEC
- engaging in conduct that is obscene, sexually explicit, or pornographic in nature

PEC may review any employee's use of any company-owned equipment with access to the Internet.

Email Use

PEC views electronic communication systems as an efficient and effective means of communication with colleagues and clients. Therefore, PEC encourages the use of email for business purposes. PEC also permits incidental personal use of its email system.

*　　*　　*

NATIONAL PERSONNEL ASSOCIATION
RESULTS OF 2013 SURVEY CONCERNING COMPUTER USE AT WORK
Executive Summary of the Survey Findings

1. Ninety percent of employees spend at least 20 minutes of each workday using some form of social media (e.g., Facebook, Twitter, LinkedIn), personal email, and/or texting. Over 50 percent spend two or more of their working hours on social media every day.

2. Twenty-eight percent of employers have fired employees for email misuse, usually for violations of company policy, inappropriate or offensive language, or excessive personal use, as well as for misconduct aimed at coworkers or the public. Employees have challenged the firings based on various theories. The results of these challenges vary, depending on the specific facts of each case.

3. Over 50 percent of all employees surveyed reported that they spend some part of the workday on websites related to sports, shopping, adult entertainment, games, or other entertainment.

4. Employers are also concerned about lost productivity due to employee use of the Internet, chat rooms, personal email, blogs, and social networking sites. Employers have begun to block access to websites as a means of controlling lost productivity and risks of other losses.

5. More than half of all employers monitor content, keystrokes, time spent at the keyboard, email, electronic usage data, transcripts of phone and pager use, and other information.

While a number of employers have developed policies concerning ownership of computers and other technology, the use thereof during work time, and the monitoring of computer use, many employers fail to revise their policies regularly to stay abreast of technological developments. Few employers have policies about the ways employees communicate with one another electronically.

LIBRARY

In re Peterson Engineering Consultants

Hogan v. East Shore School

Franklin Court of Appeal (2013)

East Shore School, a private nonprofit entity, discharged Tucker Hogan, a teacher, for misuse of a computer provided to him by the school. Hogan sued, claiming that East Shore had invaded his privacy and that both the contents of the computer and any electronic records of its contents were private. The trial court granted summary judgment for East Shore on the ground that, as a matter of law, Hogan had no expectation of privacy in the computer. Hogan appeals. We affirm.

Hogan relies in great part on the United States Supreme Court opinion in *City of Ontario v. Quon*, 560 U.S. 746 (2010), which Hogan claims recognized a reasonable expectation of privacy in computer records.

We note with approval Justice Kennedy's observation in *Quon* that "rapid changes in the dynamics of communication and information transmission are evident not just in the technology itself but in what society accepts as proper behavior. As one *amici* brief notes, many employers expect or at least tolerate personal use of such equipment because it often increases worker efficiency." We also bear in mind Justice Kennedy's apt aside that "[t]he judiciary risk error by elaborating too fully on the . . . implications of emerging technology before its role in society has become clear." *Quon*.

The *Quon* case dealt with a government employer and a claim that arose under the Fourth Amendment. But the Fourth Amendment applies only to public employers. Here, the employer is a private entity, and Hogan's claim rests on the tort of invasion of privacy, not on the Fourth Amendment.

In this case, the school provided a computer to each teacher, including Hogan. A fellow teacher reported to the principal that he had entered Hogan's classroom after school hours when no children were present and had seen what he believed to be an online gambling site on Hogan's computer screen. He noticed that Hogan immediately closed the browser. The day following the teacher's report, the principal arranged for an outside computer forensic company to inspect the computer assigned to Hogan and determine whether Hogan had been visiting online gambling sites. The computer forensic company determined that someone using the computer and Hogan's password had visited such sites on at least six occasions in the past two weeks, but that those sites had been deleted from the computer's browser history. Based on this report, East Shore discharged Hogan.

Hogan claimed that East Shore invaded his privacy when it searched the computer and when it searched records of past computer use. The tort of invasion of privacy occurs when a party intentionally intrudes, physically or otherwise, upon the solitude or seclusion of another or his private affairs or concerns, if the intrusion would be highly offensive to a reasonable person.

East Shore argued that there can be no invasion of privacy unless the matter being intruded upon is private. East Shore argued that there is no expectation of privacy in the use of a computer when the computer is owned by East Shore and is issued to the employee for school use only. East Shore pointed to its policy in its employee handbook, one issued annually to all employees, that states:

East Shore School provides computers to teachers for use in the classroom for the purpose of enhancing the educational mission of the school. The computer, the computer software, and the computer account are the property of East Shore and are to be used solely for academic purposes. Teachers and other employees may not use the computer for personal purposes at any time, before, after, or during school hours. East Shore reserves the right to monitor the use of such equipment at any time.

Hogan did not dispute that the employee policy handbook contained this provision, but he argued that it was buried on page 37 of a 45-page handbook and that he had not read it. Further, he argued that the policy regarding computer monitoring was unclear because it failed to warn the employee that East Shore might search for information that had been deleted or might use an outside entity to conduct the monitoring. Next, he argued that because he was told to choose a password known only to him, he was led to believe that websites accessed by him using that password were private. Finally, he argued that because East Shore had not conducted any monitoring to date, it had waived its right to monitor computer use and had established a practice of respect for privacy. These facts, taken together, Hogan claimed, created an expectation of privacy.

Perhaps East Shore could have written a clearer policy or could have had employees sign a statement acknowledging their understanding of school policies related to technology, but the existing policy is clear. Hogan's failure to read the entire employee handbook does not lessen the clarity of the message. Perhaps East Shore could have defined what it meant by "monitoring" or could have warned employees that deleted computer files may be searched, but Hogan's failure to appreciate that the school might search deleted files is his own failure. East Shore drafted and published to its employees a policy that clearly stated that the computer, the computer software, and the computer account were the property of East Shore, and that East Shore reserved the right to monitor the use of the computer at any time.

Hogan should not have been surprised that East Shore searched for deleted files. While past practice might create a waiver of the right to monitor, there is no reason to believe that a waiver was created here, when the handbook was re-issued annually with the same warning that East Shore reserved the right to monitor use of the computer equipment. Finally, a reasonable person would not believe that the password would create a privacy interest, when the school's policy, read as a whole, offers no reason to believe that computer use is private.

In short, Hogan's claim for invasion of privacy fails because he had no reasonable expectation of privacy in the computer equipment belonging to his employer.

Affirmed.

Fines v. Heartland, Inc.

Franklin Court of Appeal (2011)

Ann Fines sued her fellow employee, John Parr, and her employer, Heartland, Inc., for defamation and sexual harassment. Each cause of action related to electronic mail messages (emails) that Parr sent to Fines while Parr, a Heartland sales representative, used Heartland's computers and email system. After the employer learned of these messages and investigated them, it discharged Parr. At trial, the jury found for Fines and against defendants Parr and Heartland and awarded damages to Fines. Heartland appeals.

In considering Heartland's appeal, we must first review the bases of Fines's successful claims against Parr.

In emails sent to Fines, Parr stated that he knew she was promiscuous. At trial Fines testified that after receiving the second such email from Parr, she confronted him, denied that she was promiscuous, told him she had been happily married for years, and told him to stop sending her emails. She introduced copies of the emails that Parr sent to coworkers after her confrontation with him, in which Parr repeated on three more occasions the statement that she was promiscuous. He also sent Fines emails of a sexual nature, not once but at least eight times, even after she confronted him and told him to stop, and Fines found those emails highly offensive. There was sufficient evidence for the jury to find that Parr both defamed and sexually harassed Fines.

We now turn to Heartland's arguments on appeal that it did not ratify Parr's actions and that it should not be held vicariously liable for his actions.

An employer may be liable for an employee's willful and malicious actions under the principle of ratification. An employee's actions may be ratified after the fact by the employer's voluntary election to adopt the employee's conduct by, in essence, treating the conduct as its own. The failure to discharge an employee after knowledge of his or her wrongful acts may be evidence supporting ratification. Fines claims that because Heartland delayed in discharging Parr after learning of his misconduct, Heartland in effect ratified Parr's behavior.

The facts as presented to the jury were that Fines did not complain to her supervisor or any Heartland representative until the end of the fifth day of Parr's offensive behavior, when Parr sent the emails to coworkers. When her supervisor learned of Fines's complaints, he confronted Parr. Parr denied the charges, saying that someone else must have sent the emails from his account. The supervisor reported the problem to a Heartland vice president, who consulted the company's information technology (IT) department. By day eight, the IT department confirmed that the emails had been sent from Parr's computer using the password assigned to Parr during the time Parr was in the office. Heartland fired Parr.

Such conduct by Heartland does not constitute ratification. Immediately upon learning of the complaint, a Heartland supervisor confronted the alleged sender of the emails, and when the employee denied the charges, the company investigated further, coming to a decision and taking action, all within four business days.

Next, Fines asserted that Heartland should be held liable for Parr's tortious conduct under the doctrine of respondeat superior. Under this doctrine, an employer is vicariously liable for its employee's torts committed within the scope of the employment. To hold an employer vicariously liable, the plaintiff must establish that the employee's acts were committed within the scope of the employment. An employer's vicarious liability may extend to willful and malicious torts. An employee's tortious act may be within the scope of employment even if it contravenes an express company rule.

But the scope of vicarious liability is not boundless. An employer will not be held vicariously liable for an employee's malicious or tortious conduct if the employee *substantially* deviates from the employment duties for personal purposes. Thus, if the employee "inflicts an injury out of personal malice, not engendered by the employment" or acts out of "personal malice unconnected with the employment," the employee is not acting within the scope of employment. *White v. Mascoutah Printing Co.* (Fr. Ct. App. 2010); RESTATEMENT (THIRD) OF AGENCY § 2.04.

Heartland relied at trial on statements in its employee handbook that office computers were to be used only for business and not for personal purposes. The Heartland handbook also stated that use of office equipment for personal purposes during office hours constituted misconduct for which the employee would be disciplined. Heartland thus argued that this provision put employees on notice that certain behavior was not only outside the scope of their employment but was an offense that could lead to being discharged, as happened here.

Parr's purpose in sending these emails was purely personal. Nothing in Parr's job description as a sales representative for Heartland would suggest that he should send such emails to coworkers. For whatever reason, Parr seemed determined to offend Fines. The mere fact that they were coworkers is insufficient to hold Heartland responsible for Parr's malicious conduct. Under either the doctrine of ratification or that of respondeat superior, we find no basis for the judgment against Heartland.

Reversed.

Lucas v. Sumner Group, Inc.

Franklin Court of Appeal (2012)

After Sumner Group, Inc., discharged Valerie Lucas for violating Sumner's policy on employee computer use, Lucas sued for wrongful termination. The trial court granted summary judgment in favor of Sumner Group. Lucas appeals. For the reasons stated below, we reverse and remand.

Sumner Group's computer-use policy stated:

Computers are a vital part of our business, and misuse of computers, the email systems, software, hardware, and all related technology can create disruptions in the work flow. All employees should know that telephones, email systems, computers, and all related technologies are company property and may be monitored 24 hours a day, 7 days a week, to ensure appropriate business use. The employee has no expectation of privacy at any time when using company property.

Unauthorized Use: Although employees have access to email and the Internet, these software applications should be viewed as company property. The employee has no expectation of privacy, meaning that these types of software should not be used to transmit, receive, or download any material or information of a personal, frivolous, sexual, or similar nature. Employees found to be in violation of this policy are subject to disciplinary action, up to and including termination, and may also be subject to civil and/or criminal penalties.

Sumner Group discovered that over a four-month period, Lucas used the company Internet connection to find stories of interest to her book club and, using the company computer, composed a monthly newsletter for the club, including summaries of the articles she had found on the Internet. She then used the company's email system to distribute the newsletter to the club members. Lucas engaged in some but not all of these activities during work time, the remainder during her lunch break. Lucas admitted engaging in these activities.

She first claimed a First Amendment right of freedom of speech to engage in these activities. The First Amendment prohibits Congress, and by extension, federal, state, and local governments, from restricting the speech of employees. However, Lucas has failed to demonstrate any way in which the Sumner Group is a public employer. This argument fails.

Lucas also argued that the Sumner Group had abandoned whatever policy it had posted because it was common practice at Sumner Group for employees to engage in personal use of email and the Internet. In previous employment matters, this court has stated that an employer may be assumed to have abandoned or changed even a clearly written company policy if it is not enforced or if, through custom and practice, it has been effectively changed to permit the conduct forbidden in writing but permitted in practice. Whether Sumner Group has effectively abandoned its written policy by custom and practice is a matter of fact to be determined at trial.

Lucas next argued that the company policy was ambiguous. She claimed that the language of the computer-use policy did not clearly prohibit personal use. The policy said that the activities "should not" be conducted, as opposed to "shall not."[1] Therefore, she argued that the policy did not ban personal use of the Internet and email; rather, it merely recommended that those activities not occur. She argued that "should" conveys a moral goal while "shall" refers to a legal obligation or mandate.

In *Catts v. Unemployment Compensation Board* (Fr. Ct. App. 2011), the court held unclear an employee policy that read: "Madison Company has issued employees working from home laptops and mobile phones that should be used for the business of Madison Company." Catts, who had been denied unemployment benefits because she was discharged for personal use of the company-issued computer, argued that the policy was ambiguous. She argued that the policy could mean that employees were to use only Madison Company–issued laptops and phones for Madison Company business, as easily as it could mean that the employees were to use the Madison Company equipment only for business reasons. She argued that the company could

---

[1] This court has previously viewed with approval the suggestion from PLAIN ENGLISH FOR LAWYERS that questions about the meanings of "should," "shall," and other words can be avoided by pure use of "must" to mean "is required" and "must not" to mean "is disallowed."

prefer that employees use company equipment, rather than personal equipment, for company business because the company equipment had anti-virus software and other protections against "hacking." The key to the *Catts* conclusion was not merely the use of the word "should" but rather the fact that the entire sentence was unclear.

Thus the question here is whether Sumner Group's policy was unclear. When employees are to be terminated for misconduct, employers must be as unambiguous as possible in stating what is prohibited. Nevertheless, employers are not expected to state their policies with the precision of criminal law. Because this matter will be remanded to the trial court, the trial court must further consider whether the employee policy was clear enough that Lucas should have known that her conduct was prohibited.

Finally, Lucas argued that even if she did violate the policy, she was entitled to progressive discipline because the policy stated, "Employees found to be in violation of this policy are subject to disciplinary action, up to and including termination . . . ." She argued that this language meant that she should be reprimanded or counseled or even suspended *before* being terminated. Lucas misread the policy. The policy was clear. It put the employee on notice that there would be penalties. It specified a variety of penalties, but there was no commitment or promise that there would be progressive discipline. The employer was free to determine the penalty.

Reversed and remanded for proceedings consistent with this opinion.

Afternoon Session

Essays

February 2014 Q001

Question 1

A city ordinance required each downtown business to install high-powered halogen floodlights that would illuminate the property owned by that business and the adjoining sidewalks. A study commissioned by the city estimated that installation of the floodlights would cost a typical business about $1,000, but that increased business traffic due to enhanced public safety, especially after dark, would likely offset this cost.

A downtown restaurant applied to the city for a building permit to construct an addition that would increase its seating capacity. In its permit application, the restaurant accurately noted that its current facility did not have sufficient seating to accommodate all potential customers during peak hours. The city approved the permit on the condition that the restaurant grant the city an easement over a narrow strip of the restaurant's property, to be used by the city to install video surveillance equipment that would cover nearby public streets and parking lots. The city based its permit decision entirely on findings that the increased patronage that would result from the increased capacity of the restaurant might also attract additional crime to the neighborhood, and that installing video surveillance equipment might alleviate that problem.

The restaurant has challenged both the ordinance requiring it to install floodlights and the easement condition imposed on approval of the building permit.

1. Under the Fifth Amendment as applied to the states through the Fourteenth Amendment, is the city ordinance requiring the restaurant to install floodlights an unconstitutional taking? Explain.

2. Under the Fifth Amendment as applied to the states through the Fourteenth Amendment, is the city's requirement that the restaurant grant the city an easement as a condition for obtaining the building permit an unconstitutional taking? Explain.

February 2014 Q002

Question 2

Ten years ago, a testator died, survived by his only children: a son, age 26, and a daughter, age 18.

A testamentary trust was created under the testator's duly probated will. The will specified that all trust income would be paid to the son during the son's lifetime and that upon the son's death, the trust would terminate and trust principal would be distributed to the testator's "grandchildren who shall survive" the son. The testator provided for his daughter in other sections of the will.

Five years ago, the trustee of the testamentary trust purchased an office building with $500,000 from the trust principal. Other than this building, the trust assets consist of publicly traded securities.

Last year, the trustee received $30,000 in rents from the office building. The trustee also received, with respect to the securities owned by the trust, cash dividends of $20,000 and a stock dividend of 400 shares of Acme Corp. common stock distributed to the trust by Acme Corp.

Eight months ago, the trustee sold the office building for $700,000.

Six months ago, the son delivered a letter to the trustee stating: "I hereby disclaim any interest I may have in the income interest of the trust." On the date the son delivered this letter to the trustee, the son had no living children; the daughter had one living minor child.

A statute in this jurisdiction provides that "a disclaimer of any interest created by will is valid only if made within nine months after the testator's death, and if an interest is validly disclaimed, the disclaiming party is deemed to have predeceased the testator."

1. How should the rents, sales proceeds, cash dividends, and stock dividends received prior to the trustee's receipt of the son's letter have been allocated between trust principal and income? Explain.

2. How, if at all, does the son's letter to the trustee affect the future distribution of trust income and principal? Explain.

February 2014 Q003

Question 3

On *March 1*, the owner of a manufacturing business entered into negotiations with a bank to obtain a loan of $100,000 for the business. The bank loan officer informed the business owner that the interest rate for a loan would be lower if the repayment obligation were secured by all the business's present and future equipment. The loan officer also informed the business owner that the bank could not commit to making the loan until its credit investigation was completed, but that funds could be advanced faster following loan approval if a financing statement with respect to the transaction were filed in advance. Accordingly, the business owner signed a form on behalf of the business authorizing the bank to file a financing statement with respect to the proposed transaction. The bank properly filed a financing statement the next day, correctly providing the name of the business as the debtor and indicating "equipment" as the collateral.

On *March 15*, the business owner had heard nothing from the bank about whether the loan had been approved, so the business owner approached a finance company for a loan. The finance company quickly agreed to lend $100,000 to the business, secured by all the business's present and future equipment. That same day, the finance company loaned to the business $100,000, and the business owner signed an agreement obligating the business to repay the loan and granting the finance company a security interest in all the business's "present and future equipment" to secure the repayment obligation. Also on that day, the finance company properly filed a financing statement correctly providing the business's name as the debtor and indicating "equipment" as the collateral.

On *March 21*, the bank loan officer contacted the business owner and indicated that the loan application had been approved. On the next day, March 22, the bank loaned the business $100,000. The loan agreement, signed by the owner on behalf of the business, granted the bank a security interest in all the business's "present and future equipment."

On *April 10*, the business sold an item of manufacturing equipment to a competitor for $20,000. This was the first time the business had ever sold any of its equipment. The competitor paid the purchase price in cash and took possession of the equipment that day. The competitor acted in good faith at all times and had no knowledge of the business's prior transactions with the bank and the finance company.

The business has defaulted on its obligations with respect to the loans from the bank and the finance company. Each of them has asserted a claim to all the business's equipment as well as to the item of equipment sold to the business's competitor.

Assume that the business owner had the authority to enter into all these transactions on behalf of the business.

1. *As between the bank and the finance company, which has a superior claim to the business's equipment? Explain.*

2. *Do the claims of the bank and the finance company to the business's equipment continue in the item of equipment sold to the competitor? Explain.*

Under sec 9. To have a superior claim there needs to be a "perfection" established/achieved by either Bank or the finance co. Over here although the Bank started its process on March 1 and FS was signed and properly filed but there was no possession of the money until March 22. So technical the Bank perfected its title on March 22 whereas the financing company perfected it [illegible] by March 15 when loan were handed over to the businessman and further perfected their title on March 15 on the same day when signed, filed & presented pro creation was on March 1 — Bank + Agreement sign So the financing co. has a superior and [illegible] perfect title to equipments.   X Bank b/c 3 party [illegible]

2. They would have continued if the competitor knew or had reasons to know absent this loan was attached to the equipments over here he had no knowledge of the attachment of liability hence no liability to pay. competitor will be a bonafide purchaser.

X not sold in the ordinary course of debtor's business

X first time sold

February 2014 Q004

Question 4

A builder constructed a vacation house for an out-of-state customer on the customer's land. The house was completed on June 1, at which point the customer still owed $200,000 of the $800,000 contract price, which was payable in full five days later.

On June 14, the basement of the house was flooded with two inches of water during a heavy rainfall. When the customer complained, the builder told the customer, "The flooding was caused by poorly designed landscaping. Our work is fine and fully up to code. Have an engineer look at the foundation. If there's a problem, we'll fix it."

The customer, pleased by the builder's cooperative attitude, immediately hired a structural engineer to examine the foundation of the house. On June 30, the engineer provided the customer with a written report on the condition of the foundation, which stated that the foundation was properly constructed.

Unhappy with the conclusions in the engineer's report, the customer then hired a home inspector to evaluate the house. The home inspector's report concluded that the foundation of the house had been poorly constructed and was inadequately waterproofed.

On July 10, the customer sent the builder the home inspector's report with a note that said, "Until you fix this problem, you won't get another penny from me." The builder immediately contacted an attorney and directed the attorney to prepare a draft complaint against the customer for nonpayment. Hoping to avoid litigation, the builder sent several more requests for payment to the customer. The customer ignored all these requests.

On September 10, the builder filed suit in federal district court, properly invoking the court's diversity jurisdiction and seeking $200,000 in damages for breach of contract. The customer's answer denied liability on the basis of alleged defective construction of the house's foundation.

Several months later, the case is nearly ready for trial. However, two discovery disputes have not yet been resolved.

First, despite a request from the builder, the customer has refused to provide a copy of the report prepared by the structural engineer who examined the foundation of the house. The customer claims that the report is "work product" and not discoverable because the customer does not intend to ask the engineer to testify at trial. The builder has asked the court to order the customer to turn over the engineer's report.

Second, the customer has asked the court to impose sanctions for the builder's failure to comply with the customer's demand for copies of all emails concerning construction of the foundation of the house. The builder has truthfully informed the customer that all such emails were destroyed on August 2. This destruction was pursuant to the builder's standard practice of permanently deleting all project-related emails from company records 60 days after construction of a project is complete. There is no relevant state records-retention law. x policy

work prod? vs at discovery?

1. Should the court order the customer to turn over the engineer's report? Explain. — introduced?

2. Should the court sanction the builder for the destruction of emails related to the case, and if so, what factors should the court consider in determining those sanctions? Explain. destruction ok? sanction ok?

① work product - For evidence is mostly considered as attorney client privileged work here work product which is this that its generally not shared with the opp party but where there is no other way of corroborating or getting evidence eg witness with a person who is dead and further cannot be cross examined that work must be given to the other party. If there is valid reason to believe that the information cannot be obtained any other way. while the builder has truthfully informed that the customer emails were destroyed on august 2, his standard pract. The customer should Not turn over as its his work product. customer does not want to testify the builder can testify / cross exam him.

② Yes Aug 2 he should not have because he intentional voluntarily destroyed the evidence. Although the work was completed the payment wasnt. & on Sep 10 the builder filed the suit himself. he was aware, intentio factors - voluntarily, punishment necessary by the court, intentionally, cause harm defect, fair trial

February 2014 Q005

Question 5

A defendant was charged under state law with felony theft (Class D) and felony residential burglary (Class C). The indictment alleged that the defendant entered his neighbors' home without their consent and stole a diamond ring worth at least $2,500.

Defense counsel filed a pretrial motion to dismiss the charges on the ground that prosecuting the defendant for both burglary and theft would constitute double jeopardy. The trial court denied the motion, and the defendant was prosecuted for both crimes. The only evidence of the ring's value offered at the defendant's jury trial was the owner's testimony that she had purchased the ring two years earlier for $3,000.

At trial, the judge issued the following jury instruction on the burglary charge prior to deliberations:

If, after consideration of all the evidence presented by the prosecution and defense, you find beyond a reasonable doubt that the defendant entered the dwelling without the owners' consent, you may presume that the defendant entered with the intent to commit a felony therein.

The jury found the defendant guilty of both offenses.

At the defendant's sentencing hearing, an expert witness called by the prosecutor testified that the diamond ring was worth between $7,000 and $8,000. Over defense objection, the judge concluded, by a preponderance of the evidence, that the value of the stolen ring exceeded $5,000. The judge sentenced the defendant to four years' incarceration on the theft conviction. On the burglary conviction, the defendant received a consecutive sentence of seven years' incarceration.

In this state, residential burglary is defined as "entry into the dwelling of another, without the consent of the lawful resident, with the intent to commit a felony therein." Residential burglary is a Class C felony for which the minimum sentence is five years and the maximum sentence is ten years of incarceration.

In this state, theft is defined as "taking and carrying away the property of another with the intent to permanently deprive the owner of possession." Theft is a Class D felony if the value of the item(s) taken is between $2,500 and $10,000. The sentence for a Class D felony theft is determined by the value of the items taken. If the value is between $2,500 and $5,000, the maximum

sentence is three years' incarceration. If the value of the items exceeds $5,000, the maximum sentence is five years' incarceration.

max 5yrs

This state affords a criminal defendant no greater rights than those mandated by the United States Constitution.

1. *Did the trial court err when it denied the defendant's pretrial motion to dismiss on double jeopardy grounds? Explain.*

2. *Did the trial court err in its instruction to the jury on the burglary charge? Explain.* did it violate Due process of law?

3. *Did the trial court err when it sentenced the defendant to an additional year of incarceration on the theft conviction based on the expert's testimony? Explain.*

① yes, here double jeopardy — same offense — tried by the same jurisd'n. no - if same offense but diff jurisd'n presuming its a diff jurisd'n & can be charged for both / one govern.

② yes, the jury did not come to a conclusion independently on its own. There was no need for the jury if the judge was going to instruct as he deemed fit.

③ yes err because owner's testimony from prior jury trial was for $3000. His issue has been tried and declared. hence plea judgement was violated plus trial sentence err. statute states it 3yrs b/w 2500 - 5000.
6th amen

February 2014 Q006

Question 6

Five years ago, Adam and Ben formed a general partnership, Empire Partnership (Empire), to buy and sell antique automobiles at a showroom in State A. Adam contributed $800,000 to Empire, and Ben contributed $200,000. Their written partnership agreement allocated 80% of profits, losses, and control to Adam and 20% to Ben. No filings of any type were made in connection with the formation of Empire.

Three years ago, a collector purchased one of Empire's antique cars for $3,400,000. The collector was willing to pay this price because of Ben's false representation (repeated in the sales contract) that a famous movie star had once owned the car. Without the movie-star connection, the car was worth only $100,000. One month later, when the collector discovered the truth, he sued Adam, Ben, and Empire for $3,300,000 in damages. The lawsuit is still pending.

Two years ago, Adam and Ben admitted a new partner, Diane, to Empire in return for her contribution of $250,000. The three agreed to allocate profits, losses, and control 75% to Adam, 10% to Ben, and 15% to Diane. Before joining the partnership, Diane learned of the collector's claim and stated her concern to Adam and Ben that she might become liable if the claim were reduced to a judgment.

Following Diane's admission to Empire, the three partners sought to convert Empire into a limited liability partnership (LLP). Adam's lawyer proposed to file with State A a "statement of qualification" making an LLP election and declaring the name of the partnership to be "Empire LLP." Ben's lawyer stated that this would not work and that a new LLP had to be formed, with the assets of the old partnership transferred to the new one. In the end, the conversion was done the way Adam's lawyer suggested with the approval of all three partners.

One year ago, a driver purchased a vintage car from Empire LLP, based on the representation that the car was "fully roadworthy and capable of touring at 70 mph all day." The driver took the car on the highway at 50 mph, whereupon the front suspension collapsed, resulting in a crash in which the car was destroyed and the driver killed. The driver's estate sued Adam, Ben, Diane, and Empire LLP for $10,000,000. The lawsuit is still pending.

Although profitable, Empire LLP does not have resources sufficient to pay the collector's claim or the claim of the driver's estate.

Assume that the Uniform Partnership Act (1997) applies.

1. *Before the filing of the statement of qualification,*

   a. *was Adam personally liable on the collector's claim? Explain.* no ✓

   b. *was Diane personally liable on the collector's claim? Explain.*

2. *After the filing of the statement of qualification, was Adam, Ben, or Diane personally liable as a partner on (a) the collector's claim or (b) the driver's estate's claim? Explain.*

general partner

limiting partner

① general partnership the profits and losses are shared as per the contributions made and similarly liabilities are based on the shares contribution by each. Further in event of losses the partners liability is not then in nature further the partners can be personally liable to the extent of the losses. Therefore their house / personal property can be held to pay off his debts and liability of the creditors. ∴ Adam will be personally liable 80% and Ben 20% for the collector claim. Further Adam will be liable for false representation in buying the car otherwise it would have not been purchased Empire will be liable as well

② Diane will not be liable for the collectors claim as she was not a part of the partnership when that transaction occurred. She was aware & she did not wanted to be a part of this deal & did not wanted to incur even liability.

✓② ⓐ Adam Ben still liable – because by
   ⓑ diners est claim – all 75% 10% 20% but if pierced corporate veil can be all personally liable again misrepresent / F.R. all free only LP is liable

Q1. __whether the city ordinance requiring to install floodlights__
__an unconsti taking, can an city pass such ordinance__
__is the ordinance valid__

Under the Commerce C. the state can regulate and pass
such laws regarding the values and ways to conduct
business in order to achieve necessary public health,
safety and welfare of the citizens of that state.
Congress has enumerated such CC and given the
power to the state to regulate its commerce for welfare.
Here, the city ordinance that required each downtown
business to install high powered halogen floodlights which
costing $1000 is not unconstitutional. Further it
would increase their profit and business. This
ordinance has been passed in view of public safety at
night in dark narrow sidewalks. Further the findings
show that this cost would offset as a result of more
incoming business. Further there is no taking over here.

__Issue:__ whether granting of easement over a narrow strip
of the rest'n prop. a valid taking. Further granting permit
based on such condition constitutional

Taking is where the govt regulates or undertakes ones
personal property for use of the public and no other
means of economic benefits are left is called takings.
Further, when taking occur, the govt has to provide
just compensation to the owner of the property. govt
using the property for a short period of time is
not called as takings. Over here, the city asking for
an easement on the property of the restaurant owner
by installing video surveillance camera is proper.
taking in futherance of public purpose. Placing of
camera and wires has held to be takings in a case
where setting up of cable box & wire was held taking.
It doesn't matter if the size of the taking is narrow
or wide. any physical instrusion would be considered
as taking. therefore from a condition for obtaining
permit is takings & therefore should be provided
with just compensation.

Q2. Under Trust. A valid trust is formed when a Trustee transfers his interest in any monetary form in a third person/ security interest party / establishment / agency for the benefit of a person - trustee.

A valid trust can be created by express / implied action over here the trustee created one by a duly probated will. prior to son's letter, the income disposal would have been the following? Rents, sale proceeds, cash + rents, stock dividends

during son's lifetime - It provided to 700k + public sale + 30k from the rents + 30k from cash + + stock of 400 shares during his lifetime & after trustee's death. If the son is dead their to Trustee's gc who shall survive the son. gc can be of Trustee's son or daughter. The gc should only survive the son thereby meaning after the death of the son the above mentioned income would be given to any of the gc surviving whether the son's children of daughter's or son, if both or whichever survive.

72 If the son's letter is valid and effectuated then the property distribution shall be as follows

(This jurisd" provides that a disclaimer would be valid if disclaimer After 9mths of the testators death, and if the interest is validly disclaimed, the disclaiming party is then deemed to have predeceased the testator. here the son's disclaimer is not valid as it was disclaimed. Byou the testator's death and not after the jurisd provides that it has to be declared w/in 9months after the death. hence this is not valid. so the means would go to the son and grand children as mentioned above.

Law of eminent Domain (Takings')

5th amend